Aging in an Aging Society

Aging in an Aging Society
Critical Reflections

Edited by
Iva Apostolova and Monique Lanoix

SHEFFIELD UK   BRISTOL CT

Published by Equinox Publishing Ltd.

UK: Office 415, The Workstation, 15 Paternoster Row, Sheffield, South Yorkshire S1 2BX
USA: ISD, 70 Enterprise Drive, Bristol, CT 06010

www.equinoxpub.com

First published 2019

© Iva Apostolova, Monique Lanoix and contributors, 2019

All rights reserved. No part of this publication may be reproduced or transmitted in any form or by any means, electronic or mechanical, including photocopying, recording or any information storage or retrieval system, without prior permission in writing from the publishers.

British Library Cataloguing-in-Publication Data
A catalogue record for this book is available from the British Library.

ISBN-13 978 1 78179 689 4 (hardback)
        978 1 78179 690 0 (paperback)
        978 1 78179 691 7 (ePDF)

Library of Congress Cataloging-in-Publication Data

Names: Apostolova, Iva, editor. | Lanoix, Monique, editor.
Title: Aging in an Aging Society : Critical Reflections / edited by Iva Apostolova and Monique Lanoix.
Description: Sheffield, UK ; Bristol, CT : Equinox Publishing Ltd, 2019. | Includes bibliographical references and index.
Identifiers: LCCN 2018035470 (print) | LCCN 2018037861 (ebook) | ISBN 9781781796917 (ePDF) | ISBN 9781781796894 (hb) | ISBN 9781781796900 (pb)
Subjects: LCSH: Aging--Social aspects. | Aging--Psychological aspects. | Older people--Social conditions.
Classification: LCC HQ1061 (ebook) | LCC HQ1061 .A4244147 2019 (print) | DDC 305.26--dc23
LC record available at https://lccn.loc.gov/2018035470

Typeset by S.J.I. Services, New Delhi, India

Contents

Acknowledgements   vii

A Note of Acknowledgment to Monique   viii

Introduction   1

Part 1: Hospitality and the Embodied Self

1. The Ethics of Hospitality: Reflections on Aging   15
   Sophie Cloutier

2. The Otherness within Us: Reframing, with Spinoza, the Self's Relationship to Disability and Aging   41
   Iva Apostolova and Élaina Gauthier-Mamaril

Part 2: Aging and the Loss of Presence

3. Aging and the Loss of Social Presence   65
   Christine Overall

4. LGBT Elders, Isolation, and Loneliness: An Existential Analysis   82
   Tim R. Johnston

5. Aging and Aesthetic Responsibility   99
   Elizabeth Lanphier

Part 3: Dependence and Independence in the Context of Care and Aging

6. Fostering a 'Community of Care': Supporting a Shared Experience of Aging in Co-housing   127
   Magdalene Goemans

7. Dependency and Vulnerability in the Twenty-First
   Century: The Swedish Case   148
   Hildur Kalman

8. Caring across Borders: Lessons from Transnational
   Families   168
   Marta Rodríguez-Galán

Part 4: Critical Perspectives on Aging

9. Missing Voices in Aging-Well Frameworks:
   A Postcolonial Analysis   185
   Lauren Brooks-Cleator and Audrey Giles

Index   203

Acknowledgements

There are many individuals who have contributed to the final stage of this multi-year project. Patricia Marsden-Dole and Lorraine Ste-Marie were tireless in getting community participants involved in a conversation on aging in an aging society. Thanks to their efforts and those of the many collaborators in the community, the conference "Building Hospitable Communities for Aging" was a success. We also wish to thank Saint Paul University for hosting the conference. We would like to acknowledge the help of all Saint Paul University students involved in it and wish to thank especially Elizabeth Marois, Emily York, Daphnée Orizier, and Charles Walsh for their enthusiasm and hard work. Special thanks to our copy-editor Colin Cordner for his patience with us. This book would not have been possible without the financial support of the Community Foundation of Ottawa and the Social Sciences and Humanities Research Council of Canada. Book projects take on a life of their own and, even if we were already aware of the importance of collaboration, this book made it a living reality. We are grateful for the community participation and encouragement that we received during this process.

A Note of Acknowledgment to Monique

I first got to know Monique when she graciously invited me to be a part of the "Building Hospitable Communities for Aging" team SSHRC Connection grant project back in 2015. In one of our subsequent post-grant meetings, Monique suggested that we collaborate on editing the current volume. And the rest is history, as the saying goes. I will never know what prompted her to want to collaborate with me, whom she knew very little at the time, but I am glad she took the leap. Editing a volume is a labor-intensive exercise in patience; any academic knows that. But it can be a bonding experience as well, which is what it turned out to be for us. I discovered that Monique is one of the most generous philosophers, academics, and human beings on the planet! The time we spent working on the volume proved to be a gestation period for a friendship that has gone well beyond the academic. Thank you for letting me hang out with you, Monique!

Iva Apostolova

Introduction

Iva Apostolova and Monique Lanoix

In the summer of 2015, according to the Canadian Broadcasting Corporation (CBC) the number of Canadians over the age of 65 surpassed the number of Canadians below the age of 15. This is the first time Canada has faced such a dramatic change. This notable change made headlines nationally and was interpreted not only as dire in terms of access to health care, but also as ominous for the future of the economy. The transformation is not unique to Canada as many countries are, or will soon be, facing a growing population of older individuals. The significance of this has to be analyzed, not only to prepare us for the needs of the changing demographics but also, and we believe this is a point of essence, to help us learn about the consequences of living in societies that are aging. Aging affects society on multiple levels: just as the personal dimension of aging cannot be ignored, the impact of aging on the communities we all live in must also be taken into account. Taking this as a unique opportunity, researchers from Saint Paul University and Dominican University College, along with community actors, all came together to organize a conference, "Building Hospitable Communities for Aging," which took place in September 2016. During the three days of the conference, we heard from various community groups, including religious groups, academics, and individuals, on the ways in which aging affected them personally, and how they, as members of the greater community, were to respond to the challenges aging posed. The conversations were rich and diverse which led us to the decision that the topic deserved further attention.

We believe that the topic of aging is more often than not given only superficial media attention. It is an undeniable fact that aging will change how taxes are collected and how governments structure retirement plans. It is also a fact that many families will be called upon to provide support for their aging loved ones. But is this all that aging has to teach us? Could it be that staring aging in the eye can teach us to be more human and to care for each other in better ways? The chapters in this collection strive to answer some of these questions. Any collection has its limitations in doing justice to a topic. Our volume, for example, does not engage with dementia, as we felt that this particular angle is already widely covered in the literature, and in addition, our initial desire was, rather, to emphasize various dimensions of aging within an aging society. In other words, our focus is on the impact of aging in a context where many other individuals are going through similar experiences. What is more, we wanted to explore the meaning of aging in a youth obsessed culture. Would such a culture try to deny the reality of aging or could it open the door to its acceptance? Although we fully realize the impossibility of the task of presenting a comprehensive analysis on the topic, we hope that the chapters featured in this volume offer an alternative interpretation, and will stir the readers' imagination in the direction of questioning the current discourses on aging.

The collection is divided into four parts, each designed to explore selected dimensions of aging. We thought it only fitting to start with philosophical perspectives on how aging changes the relationship one has to/with oneself. Aging has been the subject of extensive bioethical literature; however, the meaning of aging from a philosophical perspective is rarely the preferred topic of discussion. Even if philosophers have been notoriously silent about aging, their points of view can, nonetheless, be useful for understanding our relationship to/with our own aging. Part One makes use of modern and contemporary philosophers who examine how we can accept, without resignation, the transformations aging brings about. The personal take on aging affects the social aspect of it, and vice versa, and so we continue the discourse by shining light on how society perceives aging individuals. The popular perception of aging, coupled with deeply embedded biases concerning the process of aging, often leads to isolation, lack of representation, and even shunning of aging/aged individuals. We believe that, if we are to dispel the biases and counter these damaging effects, it is crucial to understand and expose the process of marginalization of aging/aged individuals. Part Two discusses the ways in which aging individuals and aging bodies are perceived and, more importantly, how they are hidden from view. Parts Three and Four highlight a more applied outlook. Part Three, for example, engages with the realities of aging and caregiving on the level of governments, individuals, or inter-generational actors, where the central question remains: what are the social responses to the growing frailty of the aged, as well as the increased need for assistance? Part Four also examines aging through the critical lens of non-dominant/non-Western paradigms of aging well: Western perspectives may be dominant, but they are certainly not the last word on the topic.

Part One, entitled *Hospitality and the Embodied Self*, examines the relationship we have with our own aging, as well as our embodied materiality as it evolves in time. Granted that we all begin to age as soon as we are born, aging has a greater impact, or turns into something to be avoided, especially as individuals reach a certain age, normally around 60 or 65. Even though there are many "how to" books on aging well, these guides are intended, at best, to help us avoid aging and, at least, to teach us how to manage it. But what does that imply about our relationship to our own aging bodies? The two chapters in Part One explore this precise relationship. If we seek advice and wisdom from traditional philosophers, we will find them mostly lacking in this department. It is not that philosophy has neglected the *how* and the *why* of human action and human relationships. Moral philosophy, for example, since ancient times, has occupied itself with the analysis of how humans should act towards one another; but this, we quickly realize, is of little use when we encounter our own aging process. Sophie Cloutier's chapter, "The Ethics of Hospitality: Reflections on Aging," proposes an exploration of the ethics of our relationship with other aging individuals. As Cloutier reminds us, hospitality is universal: it is present in every culture and religion, and it is the guide to welcoming the stranger at the door. It needs to be noted, however, that the chapter does not theorize hospitality as such: Jacques Derrida's insight, as Cloutier explains, is to understand how the arrival of a stranger can destabilize our expectations. The relationship of a host with her guest is not to be thought of as a form of reciprocation. The guest represents the unknown, the strange, the other. Yet, when confronted with this other individual who also happens to be in need, unconditional hospitality turns into a responsibility to act and to care for the person in need. Cloutier makes use of the concepts of stranger and openness, developed by Daniel Innerarity, who, following Derrida's analysis, further explores how we can actually welcome the unexpected stranger.

Cloutier makes the bold move of casting our own aging self as the stranger who shows up at the door. It is bold in the sense that it challenges the common assumption that we truly and completely know ourselves and that aging is just another process which we will become accustomed to. However, Cloutier recognizes, aging brings about surprises and unexpected transformations.

Nevertheless, following Innerarity, Cloutier posits that human beings are essentially relational beings who are receptive to learning how to welcome the unforeseen. Part of this process includes accepting that we are temporal beings: not only do we live in time, but we all experience time differently. This is a crucial point for Cloutier as it opens more fully the possibility for different generations to live with one another. This not only has implications for our social relationships, it fundamentally challenges our concepts of control and autonomy. Taking a broader stance, Cloutier proposes four conditions for making communities more hospitable to aging: recognizing the responsibility to care, acknowledging the fluidity of borders, realizing the importance of respecting various temporalities, and making the other feel at home. Using these four principles, Cloutier examines various actual places and practices of care for aging individuals.

The second chapter, "The Otherness within Us: Reframing, with Spinoza, the Self's Relationship to Disability and Aging," by Iva Apostolova and Élaina Gauthier-Mamaril, also adapts a philosopher's view – Baruch Spinoza in this case – to the question of aging. In the first part of the text, the authors explain both Spinoza's doctrine of the *conatus* and his theory of the affects. It is Spinoza's anti-dualist stance which proves particularly helpful for examining the embodied reality of the aging process. In addition, Spinoza makes clear that it is an illusion to think that we control our destinies. As was the case with Cloutier's chapter, a central insight here is the relinquishing of our quest for control over reality. This has theoretical implications, as becomes clear in the second part of the text. Having established their conceptual framework, Apostolova and Gauthier-Mamaril proceed to explain how relational ontology and care ethics can make use of Spinoza's philosophy. Spinoza's anti-dualist perspective is not only useful for thinking about embodiment, it also has implications for the way we conceptualize ourselves in relation with others. As the authors point out, it is a fact that each and every one of us is born into, and out of, a relationship. Misplacing the notion of autonomy into a framework of independence makes it harder to realize that we are relational beings, and it also prevents us from developing the skills that shape our responsibilities toward one another. As is the case with the first chapter, the authors expose the fact that one of the central notions that needs to be more fully acknowledged in the literature is our relationality. The authors do not miss the opportunity to point out certain pitfalls associated with the relational perspective, namely the criticisms that have been levied against care ethics, such as turning the cared-for into a passive and, ultimately, dependent object of care. Nevertheless, the authors put forward that the cultivation of compassion is a moral attitude that asks from each of us an effort to negotiate between our own interests and those of others. According to the authors, this is the best way for the relational self to "get real" — that is, to understand its own mortality without falling into despondent despair.

Part Two, entitled *Aging and the Loss of Presence*, focuses on various aspects of the social presence of aging understood as the process of aging, the aging person, and the aging body. Christine Overall's chapter, entitled "Aging and the Loss of Social Presence," aims at exposing what she considers to be a worrying tendency of enforced loss of social presence of old(er) persons. She opens with four examples of common individual-based, as well as institution-based, practices (physical presence is unperceived; one's cognitive and psychological abilities are ignored; one's moral worth is denied; one's needs are unacknowledged) indicating the loss of social presence of old(er) persons. The discussion is followed by a thorough criticism of the positions on aging maintained by the philosophers Leon Kass, Francis Fukuyama, Daniel Callahan, David Shapiro, and John Hardwig. To Kass's suggestion that there are benefits for the individual from withdrawing from professional and social life in old age, Overall counter-proposes a re-examination of the way the individual herself values her own aging and dying processes. She couples this with a sample of empirical evidence that withdrawal from social life is the cause of significant health decline among aging persons. She disagrees with Fukuyama's advocacy of a natural tendency for the older generation to get out of the way of the younger generation, which she considers to be nothing more than a demonstration of an enforced social pressure on old(er) persons to become socially invisible. Overall does not hesitate to call Callahan and Shapiro's positions an expression of the ableist, ageist, and sexist currents that plague our modern social life. She interprets Hardwig's advocacy of the duty to die as an extreme manifestation of the current pressures on aging persons aiming at depriving them of social presence, and consequently, of their identity.

Tim R. Johnston's chapter, "LGBT Elders, Isolation, and Loneliness: An Existentialist Analysis," examines evidence from geriatric specialists showing that isolation and loneliness have a profoundly negative impact on the individual's well-being. This is especially true for LGBT persons who have lost touch with their biological families as a result of them coming out or who are currently experiencing difficulties integrating in new, non-LGBT communities for fear of social stigma and ostracism. While Johnston examines loneliness and isolation as distinct phenomena, the claim he makes is that both isolation and loneliness in old age are harmful because they remove older adults from temporal rhythms, thus making it difficult for them to maintain a sense of self and precariously plunging them in the past, as opposed to allowing them to be involved in future-oriented projects. For LGBT older adults, the problem is even more acute since their temporal rhythms do not coincide with the mainstream temporal rhythm (of getting married or having children, for example) to begin with. Johnston uses the existentialist philosophies of Simone de Beauvoir and Jean-Paul Sartre to argue that isolation is a social problem and is best approached through a critique of neoliberal platforms of social justice, while loneliness is best examined through the existentialist concern for transcendence and action. Johnston concludes that existentialist philosophy can add nuance to new programs aiming at reducing loneliness and isolation among seniors.

Elizabeth Lanphier's text, entitled "Aging and Aesthetic Responsibility," looks at the process of aging from the point of view of the representation of the aging body, especially the aging female body, in mainstream visual arts. The question that Lanphier sets out to critically examine is the following: if Western philosophy privileges the visual landscape, and given that aging bodies are largely kept out of said visual landscape (especially in the context of American media and mainstream culture), then what sort of a challenge for an ethical responsibility toward older individuals does this present us with? The response that she seeks to establish is that there is, in fact, a particular type of ethical responsibility to visually represent aged bodies, in particular, and scenes of aging, in general. In developing her response, she begins with analysis of the relationship of philosophy to seeing, thus exposing Western philosophers' preoccupation with the faculty of sight as the dominant form of sensibility. Further, in using P. F. Strawson, David Shapiro, Gary Watson, and especially Susan Wolf's positions vis-à-vis moral responsibility, Lanphier argues in favor of a robust accountability on the part of the artist, which has undeniable ethical components. The robust accountability of the artist engages the moral imagination of the community and thus ensures that the aged persons are seen and valued by the community. While Lanphier acknowledges that artistic freedom needs to be respected, she insists that aging and aged persons have to be the focus of at least some art forms. That, in her view, is the only way to facilitate visibility of aging and to normalize the aged body within mainstream philosophy and culture.

Part Three, *Dependence and Independence in the Context of Care and Aging*, examines some of the practical concerns that aging brings forward, specifically in relation to caregiving. It focuses on three distinct aspects of caregiving: personal perspectives of having to provide care from a distance, a self-organized initiative of older persons who are making plans for their "aging in place," and Swedish policies on home care and aging. The reader will notice that dignity is a recurring theme, although it will be articulated in different ways in the three chapters.

Seniors can no longer rely on the traditional models of family caregiving. Families are often spread out in different cities, in different parts of one country, or even across the globe. Indeed, in North America, the already existing solutions, such as assisted living institutions or nursing homes, provide care which, however, can be rather costly. In addition, such institutional residences can be highly regulated, leaving little room for choice in how one receives care. Moreover, it is important to realize that older persons are not just passive recipients of care. The *Convivium Cohousing for Seniors* is an example of a self-organized group of persons over 55 whose goal is to establish a co-housing community. In "Fostering a 'Community of Care': Supporting a Shared Experience of Aging in Co-housing," Magdalene Goemans explains the history and hopes of this project. In the first part of her chapter, she reviews various models of "intentional communities". As the name implies, these are groups of individuals who seek alternatives to more traditional living arrangements. Goemans describes the model adopted by

Convivium as a "network of neighbors" with the goal of sharing services and helping each other. The co-housing model is a safeguard against social isolation, which is a very real risk for the aging. One of the important points brought forward by this initiative is the validation that seniors are individuals who remain engaged in their communities. Goemans discusses the complex evolution of such an initiative, which is still on-going. As she explains, *Convivium* puts together workshops which bring members together and serve as a place for discussion, and further education on co-housing. Making sure one's dignity is respected is a key concern for all human beings, and especially for older persons as they become more vulnerable. *Convivium* appears to be an adequate response to securing the dignity of its members. However, there are limitations to such an endeavor, and Goemans notes that a major challenge is finding an appropriate site—a site that is centrally located, near to services as well as public transit, and yet remains affordable. Well-situated sites may not be affordable and those that are more affordable may not be in locations that are accessible. In addition, co-housing risks segregating populations by age even further. Goemans recognizes that age segregation due to housing has been the subject of some of the literature which describes the negative impacts of loneliness and isolation.

In addition to individual efforts to put forward alternatives of institutional care, there has also been an emphasis by governments on developing public policies to support aging individuals in their homes. Many older persons prefer home care to nursing homes, and governments understand that it is a cheaper alternative to residential long-term care institutions. Therefore, many countries offer some home care support as part of their health care package. For example, in Canada, home care is not a part of the federally funded medical program; however, individual provinces offer some form of publicly funded home care support. The second chapter, entitled "Dependency and Vulnerability in the Twenty-First Century: The Swedish Case," by Hildur Kalman, illustrates the impact of regulations on the provision of care. Even if Sweden (as well as other Scandinavian countries) is perceived as having generous welfare policies and as offering some of the most comprehensive array of social advantages, Kalman explains that, over the last few decades, the Swedish state has changed the direction of its policies. Her chapter explores two main themes: intimate care, as it highlights more clearly the vulnerability of those receiving care, and the recent move toward marketization of care in Sweden.

The discourse of marketization of care frames the latter as a service that is "purchased" by those requiring it, even if this service is, in fact, provided by the state free of charge. The emphasis is on the possibility of choice, which casts the person requiring care as an autonomous individual, free to purchase the care package she finds to be the most adequate. However, as Kalman notes, this choice is more often than not illusory as the act of choosing requires capacities that are beyond those of many older persons. Frail older persons, for example, who do not have families to support them, are unable to adequately assess and compare the different care providers on offer. This means that the state shifts the responsibility of choosing a package of adequate care toward those who require it, yet it does not take into consideration the fact that such individuals may not be fully capable of making wise or appropriate choices. As a result, these person-centered policies place frail elders in a situation of greater danger.

The other side of the coin of care, as Kalman observes, is the care workers who provide at-home care for the elderly. Many care workers reported that the homes were not well adapted to the required care standards. For example, bathrooms and toilets were too narrow to facilitate or even support adequate intimate care. She concludes that the ideal of person-centered care as proclaimed by Swedish law and national guidelines is in opposition to what is happening in reality. From the illusion of choice to the realities of care provision, Kalman puts forward that the disconnect between abstract ideals and actual care practices indicates that such policies do not support those receiving care in their homes, nor do they facilitate the work of care providers. She concludes that more research is needed where the voices of older persons, the recipients of care, and those of the caregivers, are taken into consideration.

The final chapter in Part Three centers on a personal narrative that is used to explore the questions and concerns faced by immigrant children when their aging parents are in need of care. In "Caring across Borders: Lessons from Transnational Families," Marta Rodríguez-Galán shares the story of her mother's rapid decline due to an early onset of Alzheimer's. Confronted with the care needs of her mother and the caregiving that her father must now provide at home, she takes this opportunity to cast a wider net and review the policies that affect transnational families when it comes to caring for aging family members. As Rodríguez-Galán makes clear, this issue engages not only with the personal dimension, but also with various political considerations, such as immigration policies. Although fairly new, the question of caring from a distance has not been explored nearly enough in the scholarship. Weaving a review of literature with her own narrative, Rodríguez-Galán offers a unique blend of these two outlooks. Some of the questions that she engages with include the possibility of immigration for aging parents and government policies, as well as laws on home care for parents of transnational children. Albeit increasingly complex, the problem of care for aging parents of transnational children is becoming commonplace by the day. The question of caring from a distance does not only engage the feelings of being far away and, thus, of being unable to do some of the actual caregiving; it also brings about the need for preserving the relationships within the family and safeguarding the dignity of all of its members.

Part Four is dedicated to *Critical Perspectives on Aging* such as the post-colonial criticism of the neoliberal take on aging well. The only contribution in this final part is entitled "Missing Voices in Aging-Well Frameworks: A Postcolonial Analysis," by Lauren Brooks-Cleator and Audrey Giles. The focus of this chapter is twofold: a critical discussion of dominant aging-well frameworks combined with policies from the point of view of both postcolonial theory and Indigenous perspective. The text opens with a claim that the Indigenous population in Canada has not only remained the most neglected social class, but is also rapidly aging. However, there is a staggering lack of research on the multitude of health-related and social inflictions on the Canadian Indigenous population resulting from such colonial acts as the residential schools and the Sixties Scoop that have led many Indigenous peoples to suffer from systemic abuse, poor housing, food insecurity, or outmigration of young Indigenous adults. In order to remedy the current scholarly lacuna on Indigenously informed aging-well frameworks and policies, the authors propose the use of postcolonial theory which not only exposes the role of colonialism in Canada but also enables us to see the unequal power relations that exist between the Indigenous and non-Indigenous population. Admittedly, mainstream aging-well frameworks focus on successful and active aging, promoting the need for self-discipline, self-sufficiency, and individual responsibility. This outlook, however, ignores historical, social, and cultural structures which either contribute to or prevent the general population—and the Indigenous population in particular—from aging well. For example, the dominant Western/Eurocentric aging-well frameworks follow a scientific model of aging well which interprets successful aging as disease-free aging to be secured by both the "experts" on aging as well as the individual herself. In contrast, Indigenous communities perceive the role of the "expert" differently. The "experts" for an Indigenous community are the elders who are elected by the community for their resilience, wisdom, and strength. Particularly important is the role of the Indigenous grandmothers. As a result, Indigenous communities define aging well in a multi-dimensional way, where physical, mental, emotional, and spiritual health are not only defined differently than in the dominant framework, but are also intimately inter-connected. Brooks-Cleator and Giles plead for the construction of new, inclusive, and culturally safe aging-well frameworks and policies.

Our hope in this volume has been to do at least partial justice to the very complex topic of aging in the current demographic context. Our goal here has been twofold: on the one hand, to adequately reflect what transpired during the three-day 2016 "Building Hospitable Communities for Aging" conference, and on the other hand, to open up new avenues of research. We believe that, as the conference itself demonstrated, the topic of aging not only deserves but, in fact, demands an inter-disciplinary approach. Our desire was to balance theoretical approaches with practical accounts of the process of aging, the care for the aging self, and the social presence of aging persons (and the perception of their bodies). We also sought to combine philosophical, ethical, aesthetical, and sociological perspectives that shed light on the multi-faceted phenomenon of aging. Some of the contributions in the volume have chosen a critical stance, while others a more descriptive approach, and yet others are on an exploratory path toward clarity and understanding. But one thing remains consistent throughout: all the pieces in this volume are in dialogue with one another, while offering new and little-explored sides of aging. We sincerely hope that there is something for every type of reader here!

About the authors

Iva Apostolova is Associate Professor at Dominican University College. Her main areas of research interest are analytic philosophy, epistemology, philosophy of mind with emphasis on memory, feminist thought, and ethics of care. She has published in *Russell: The Journal of Bertrand Russell Studies*, *Feminist Philosophy Quarterly*, and has a monograph on critical thinking.

Monique Lanoix is Associate Professor in the Faculty of Philosophy and the School of Ethics, Social Justice and Public Service, and co-director of the Research Centre in Public Ethics and Governance at Saint Paul University. She has published on care work in *Hypatia* and the *International Journal of Feminist Approaches to Bioethics*. She has also written on disability and her chapter on dance and Parkinson's disease is forthcoming in the book *The Aging/Disability Nexus* in 2020 (UBC Press).

Part One

Hospitality and the Embodied Self

Chapter One

The Ethics of Hospitality: Reflections on Aging

Sophie Cloutier

Abstract

"The Ethics of Hospitality: Reflections on Aging" by **Sophie Cloutier** proposes an exploration of the ethics of our relationship with other aging individuals. Hospitality is universal: it is present in every culture and religion, and it is the guide to welcoming the stranger at the door. Cloutier proposes that we, humans, are relational beings who are receptive to learning how to welcome the unforeseen.

Introduction

In recent years, there has been a renewed interest in hospitality as a subject matter in philosophy, ethics, and the social sciences, thus expressing a common concern for the responsibility that we owe to others and, more specifically, to strangers. The ethics of hospitality has indeed gained much interest in multicultural studies, migration studies, and refugee studies. While it is still not an ethical framework commonly used in bioethics or in gerontology, it could nonetheless prove to be fruitful, for elders and people with dementia are often pushed to the margins and estranged from what is considered to be active or productive society. I will thus argue that the research on hospitality undertaken in philosophy and in the social sciences holds insights for ethical reflection on aging. Readers familiar with the ethics of care will find some affinities with the ethics of hospitality, namely regarding vulnerability, interdependency, and receptivity. Indeed, both forms of ethics call into question the modern ideal of autonomy. Although a dialogue between the ethics of care and the ethics of hospitality[1] would be interesting, I will focus mainly

---

1 For a deeper account of the affinities between care and hospitality, see Bourgault (2015).

on hospitality in order to show the fruitfulness of this framework for reflecting on how to build hospitable communities for aging populations. Nonetheless, as I move forward, I will point out some affinities and distinctions between care and hospitality in order to show the compatibility between both and, above all, to show the specific contributions that hospitality can make towards improving conditions for older people, particularly with respect to welcoming strangers and strangeness. In our modern society, so obsessed with youth, aging seems to have become a curse or a 'strange state,' something that we would like to eradicate rather than welcome. I will suggest that the ethics of hospitality can help us in welcoming this state of life and guide us in developing better ways to care for the elderly.

I will begin by recalling the historical and usual sense of hospitality, understood as a practice, because the theoretical reflections of Jacques Derrida and Daniel Innerarity remain connected to these practical roots and historicity. As will be evident throughout this chapter, the ethics of hospitality can be formulated and understood as a practice, as a virtue, and as a philosophical anthropology. In the second section, I will explain, following Derrida (1997), how hospitality can take two different expressions: recognition and hostility. These two facets will lead our investigation into the fundamental ethical dimension of hospitality, which will be analyzed in the third section; that analysis will be mainly based upon the thoughts of Derrida (1997) and Innerarity (2009). In the fourth section, I will explore the relationship between hospitality and health care in order to show how the spirit and principles of hospitality seem to pervade the practice of care, the foundation of hospitals in the Middle Ages, and the modern hospice movement—even though that spirit seems to have vanished from modern hospitals. Based on these theoretical considerations on the ethics of hospitality, I will make a few remarks on hospitality and aging, and I put forward four conditions that could guide and inspire the development of hospitable communities for aging populations. I will conclude with some examples to illustrate these conditions.

The Practice of Hospitality

Historically, hospitality is a practice present in every culture and religion which guides us in how we should welcome strangers. It is like a golden rule common to all civilizations. For instance, hospitality is present in the Bible wherever God evaluates the character and the goodness of believers by sending angels disguised as beggars to ask for hospitality. Those answering the needs of the strangers are rewarded and saved by God. Hospitality was also at the center of Ancient Greek traditions. Indeed, Ancient Greeks regarded hospitality as a sacred duty and as a tribute to Zeus. They had to welcome anyone knocking on their door and provide for them as best as they could. Hospitality had the sacred character of the receptivity that we owe to strangers by virtue of our human vulnerability. Indeed, the practice of hospitality reminds us that we are embodied subjects, that is, beings with physical needs, who hunger, thirst, and tire. Without the ancient practice of hospitality, people would not have survived. For example, if a person walking through a barren land cannot find a place to rest, to eat, and the friendship of a host, she is condemned to death. In this sense, hospitality is a response to the hostility of the world and to the necessary solidarity between human beings: we need to help each other, and we need to practice generosity and welcome the traveler whomever she is. Following this, Patrick Verspieren (2006) argues that the ethics of hospitality is fundamentally a form of bioethics, understood in its etymological sense of an ethics of life (*bios*), because it is concerned with our perishable and fragile bodies; it is concerned with the care for the life and well-being of the other, and recognizes the fundamental vulnerability of human beings (2006, 35–36).

As the linguist Emile Benveniste (1969) explains in his chapter on the etymology of 'hospitality' in his famous work *Le vocabulaire des institutions indo-européennes*, the Romans pursued and extended the Greek tradition by instituting hospitality as a pact. In so doing they gave it a more formal and legal meaning that established the duties, obligations, and rights of both the guest and the host. They translated the Greek word *xenos* as the Latin *hostis*. The term *xenos* incorporated both the host and the guest, and the same word thus designated both terms in the relationship of hospitality, thereby emphasizing the sense of reciprocity embedded in this relationship wherein both had duties and rights. The pact of hospitality established how the host should treat his guest and what the guest should give in return for being welcomed, and what compensation should be offered.

With the changes in the Roman Empire, the Latin word *hostis* came to refer to the enemy and the Romans used the word *hospes* to designate the master of the house, who provides hospitality. The term *hostis* came to refer to the hostile stranger who cannot be included in Roman law—the enemy who opposed the Roman Empire.[2] We see that etymology bears witness to the hostility that can be attached to the stranger and the fear caused by strangeness, by that which is not like us. We can find many examples in literature in which the stranger is a threatening figure who wants to usurp the power and appropriate the house of the host and to expropriate the host's very home. This hostile figure of the stranger is sometimes sadly invoked in the debate on immigration when immigrants are accused of coming to our country to steal our jobs and to threaten our identity. The immigrant is then reduced to the guest living on borrowed time, living at the mercy of his host who can request that she leave at any moment.

We can expand on the meaning of hostility, as this feeling can take different forms. Indeed, hostility can be linked to the burden felt by the host, who will have to meet the needs of the stranger. In her pioneering work *Caring* (1984), the feminist care ethicist Nel Noddings points out how hospitality involves a work of care that can be difficult for the host. As she aptly expresses: "the stranger has an enormous claim on me, because I do not know where he fits, what request he has a formal right to make, or what personal needs he will pass on me. I can meet him only in a state of wary anticipation and rusty grace, for my original innocent grace is gone and, aware of my finiteness, I fear a request I cannot meet without hardship" (1984, 47). This is especially true for women who usually do the concrete tasks involved in the practice of hospitality (cooking, cleaning, etc.) on top of their daily tasks.[3] Noddings's concerns come from the point of view of the one caring, but the ethics of hospitality has ways to alleviate the burden—and we may find here a distinction between the ethics of care and the ethics of hospitality. As mentioned previously, the Romans instituted hospitality as a pact defining not only the duties and obligations of the host

---

2   For the full explanation of the etymology of the word 'hospitality' and the link with 'hostility', see Benveniste (1969, 87–101).

3   Tracy McNulty (2007) is one of the rare theorists of hospitality to analyze the role of women in the economy of hospitality.

but also of the guest. In this sense, the host is not the servant of their guest, and they can negotiate together the hospitality arrangements. Moreover, hospitality involves an exchange of roles. Indeed, Derrida (1997) conceives of hospitality as a chain, in which the host will become the guest, or, to use the terms of care, in which the one caring will become the one cared-for. The expectation of mutuality can thus help in alleviating the feeling of self-sacrifice.

The hostile stranger can also take the form of the hostile patient who is being difficult with nurses or the incurable patient whose sickness is hostile to medicine. As we will see in the fourth section, people with chronic illnesses or dementia, or seniors with special needs, have become types of hostile strangers to contemporary health care systems. They do not fit into the modern paradigm of acute care which relies on producing cures. Martha Holstein, Jennifer Parks, and Mark Waymack (2011) are thus analyzing the limit of this paradigm from a feminist ethics perspective in order to promote a 'critical turn'. As they point out:

> [O]ur health care system focuses on acute care, given the possibilities in acute medical treatment for saving lives, curing illnesses, and maintaining the false illusion of control that is so important in our culture. The main goal of medicine thus comes to be, as it is in wider society, to control the body. This is not often possible in chronic care situations, and it is worse in palliative care where the goal is to ease individuals into death. (2011, 13)

The false illusion of control of the body that the authors mention here supports the conception of the body as an object, a sophisticated machine that can be repaired if broken, and as we know, a machine is not subjected to death. Therefore, this illusion of control has an impact on our attitude toward death, as it reinforces the desire to escape the human condition of mortality. This desire is not modern per se; we can find traces of it in the ancient wish for immortality, in the myth of the Fountain of Youth, or in *Faust*, to name only a few examples. Perhaps what is new is the modern technological means deployed to achieve this goal, which results in an even greater hostility toward death. Ciro Augusto Floriani and Fermin Roland Schramm (2010) thus talk about a 'double stranger' that the hospice movement seeks to welcome:

> The proposal of the modern hospice movement represents a central challenge to the health care professionals involved in this know-how,

characterized by the ability to accept those which one can call a 'double stranger': persons who are dying—who are strangers due to their distinct identity from the subject who receives them—and death, a stranger by its own unknown nature to those who are alive. (2010, 215)

I will come back to the modern hospice movement and the roots of the hospital (*hospitalis*) and its link to hospitality in the fourth section. We will see that the hospice can be viewed as an example of hospitality, a welcoming space, and an ultimate refuge. In the next sections I will delve further into the ethics of hospitality to highlight how it rejects the idea of control and instead teaches acceptance of the unforeseen.

Two Facets of Hospitality: Recognition and Hostility

More fundamentally, hospitality refers to the relationship between two persons or groups of persons, and is best exemplified by the dialectic between the guest and the host, or between 'us' and 'them'. This relationship can take two different forms. The first demonstrates feelings of recognition and respect between the host and the guest. The host recognizes the guest as someone who deserves care and the guest recognizes the host as someone who deserves gratitude, thereby both establish together the relation of reciprocity. Hospitality is, in this form, a two-way experience. The second form involves feelings of anxiety, rivalry, and hostility. This form arises when the power of the host on the guest is perceived as threatening or, on the opposite side, when power exerted by the guest reveals a desire to take the position of the host, i.e., the desire to steal the host's home. We can now understand how the word 'hostage' also derives semantically from the word 'host'.[4] The hostage relationship transforms hospitality into a one-way experience and impedes reciprocity.

The tension and confusion between these two forms is at the heart of hospitality because hospitality supposes the possibility of

---

4 Jacques Derrida uses the Greek word *xenos*, which refers to the host and the guest, to explain that the host and the guest are exchanging roles. The guest will become the host of his host and the host will become the guest of his guest. He adds that those substitutions make each one of us the hostage of the other and those are the laws of hospitality. As he writes: "Ces substitutions font de tous et de chacun l'otage de l'autre. Telles sont les lois de l'hospitalité" (Derrida 1997, 111).

an exchange of roles between the host and the guest. Such reciprocity presupposes that the guest will play the role of host in return if the host ever comes to knock at his door. But the exchange of roles could also happen in the house of the host when the hostile guest threatens to expropriate the host's household. The relation of reciprocity presupposes that the other gives in return, but this relationship could always go awry. There are many examples in Western literature of this menacing situation of hostility between the host and the guest. Odysseus, for instance, returns home to find his wife and his house under siege by usurping guests who threaten to appropriate his kingdom and who deny him the sacred right of hospitality in his own house.

However, hospitality, understood as the self in relation to others, teaches us that if we want to generously welcome the other, we have to forget any notion of mastery over our identity, i.e., the idea that we can control our identity. Any host who wishes to stay in control is not well equipped to perform hospitality because hospitality requires that one faces and accepts uncertainties. In the practice of hospitality, we experience the unknown and the contingency of the world. For this reason, hospitality cannot be regulated by universal norms, but can only be guided by general principles. Indeed, if hospitality is a universal practice in the sense that it is present in every culture, it is also always at the same time a particular practice that depends on the specific host and guest,[5] like friendship. It also requires one to be ready to enter into the chain of hospitality in which roles will be exchanged. In other words, to practice hospitality necessitates that we be ready to risk both losing what is ours and transforming our identity. Indeed, encounters with a stranger will inevitably transform us, for better or worse. Welcoming others implies that we open our home and open our own identity to what is unfamiliar, to what is strange. In a very interesting manner, Innerarity (2009) expands the realm of hospitality to include all that is uncontrollable in our life. He even argues that our identity is not under our control, and that we cannot master it. In a certain way, we remain strangers to ourselves because our identities are constructed through a communicative process with others and through

---

5   The ethics of care shares a similar conception as there are general principles of care, but the practice of care is always particular, as it has to meet the specific needs of a concrete individual. See, for instance, Tronto (1993).

inter-subjective recognition (2009, 69). In that sense, the subject is not autonomous; one is always indebted to others, as ethics of care also argues (Tronto 1993).

It thus seems to me that opening to the other and the acceptance of the transformation involved in the relationship with a stranger can be transposed to aging. Aging is a process in which we might feel estranged from what we used to be: our physical and mental abilities inevitably change over time, and we are confronted with the fact that we cannot do all the things that we used to do or, at least, not at the same pace. Before this natural process, we can feel disempowered and frustrated, or we can accept the changes. It seems to me wiser to accept the inevitable changes, an option that provides greater opportunity to find happiness as opposed to feeling nostalgic and frustrated. The ethics of hospitality can therefore be considered as a way to learn to accept transformations in ourselves and in others who are aging.

Hospitality and Ethics

In recent years, there has been a revival of interest in the theme of hospitality in the humanities and social sciences which reflects a shared concern with issues of belonging and identity (Dikeç, Clark, and Barnett 2009, 4). The work of the French philosopher Jacques Derrida has contributed to this resurgence of interest. "His later writings focus on a set of attentive, generous, and responsive ways of relating to others" (Dikeç, Clark, and Barnett 2009, 3). Derrida explores the idea of receptiveness to the arrival of a stranger. His thought thus indicates that hospitality denotes something essential in ethics because the latter is primarily concerned with the relationship with the other. When we open our home to a stranger, we open the question of ethics itself. We begin a relationship with someone else, which raises questions. How will I treat this person? What is right and wrong to do to this person? How should I expect this person to act? What should I expect in return? If we consider hospitality from the ethical point of view, then we understand that the goal of hospitality is to open up to others and risk the transformation of ourselves. As Tracy McNulty explains:

> *ethics is the opening of what is familiar to man to the unfamiliar.* On the basis of this definition, one might argue—as Jacques Derrida has— that hospitality is not merely one ethics among others, but the ethics

par excellence. In the gesture of the host opening his home to the stranger, what is familiar to man is at the same time made to open itself to what is unfamiliar. (2007, xvi–xvii, italics by the author)

In addition, the stranger also has a crucial ethical function as she enables us to become more conscious of our customs and habits. When surrounded only by people who think and act like us, we are unaware of our behavior and cultural habits. The stranger disrupts the normal course of things and opens up the possibility to call into question our behavior and customs. By inspiring us to ask how and why, the stranger moves us to evaluate the morality of our practices. Through exchange with others, we can learn new ways of doing things and improve old ways. It is in this sense that hospitality transforms us. The practice of hospitality generates not only knowledge of others, but also knowledge of ourselves.

Derrida analyzes the transformative aspect of hospitality and explains that the arrival of a stranger breaks through any prior assignment of roles, duties, and conventions. He conceives of hospitality as a relationship that cannot be contained in the strict form of reciprocation, in which one could ever give back exactly what he or she received. Thus, he introduces the idea of unconditional hospitality which takes the form of a moral imperative (Derrida 1997, 75–77). He uses this notion of unconditional hospitality, understood as an ideal practice of exposure to the demands of the other, to criticize the politics of territorial inclusions and exclusions wherein some will be denied hospitality. Unconditional hospitality thus supports a political and ethical project that would have those in positions of privilege take greater responsibility for others "whose life chances are being adversely affected by our own action or inaction" (Dikeç, Clark, and Barnett 2009, 3). Derrida respects the original nature of hospitality as a practice, and it is for this reason that his notion of unconditional hospitality takes the form of a responsibility to act and to care for anybody in need.

Following Derrida, the Spanish philosopher Innerarity (2009) argues that hospitality is an attitude placed halfway between two extreme positions. The first is one of pure improvisation wherein we let events determine our reactions. The second is the desire to control everything, the desire to anticipate and plan all things. Hospitality allows us the space to welcome the contingency of the world while also remaining aware that we cannot entirely control the future. The future is by definition unknown and is therefore that which is uncontrollable. In contrast with improvisation, in which we are more passive when faced with events, hospitality involves an active attitude wherein we seize opportunities (Innerarity 2009, 14). Thus, it requires attention and receptivity, such that we be attentive to what surrounds us in order to see opportunities to respond.

Innerarity regards hospitality as an anthropological category that shows that human beings are fundamentally receptive and relational beings. Receptivity is a robust readiness to be surprised and moved, a vigorous intention to be awake to everything we cannot control. Innerarity thinks that because we are always confronted by the unforeseen and by the strangeness of life, we need to cultivate receptivity and openness. We need to be attentive to what is different, and we need to be able to hear and see the enticements of the world. An attitude which welcomes the unexpected and such strangeness keeps us from shutting ourselves away from the world. As we are fundamentally social or relational beings, our contact with others and interactions with the world are constitutive of our selves. We can even add to that that all living organisms need to interact with their environment, whereas the lack thereof causes death.

Moreover, Innerarity thinks that the receptive existential structure of human beings shows that what concerns us more is not what we do, but what happens to us. And what happens to us is more important than what we do voluntarily. It is more important in the first sense that there are more unexpected events in our life than things that we plan. And secondly, it is in the course of unexpected events that we can reveal our moral character (Innerarity 2009, 13). Innerarity argues that ethics is not so much about universal principles as it is about concrete practices: it is one thing to know universal principles and another to act morally. For instance, in a romantic relationship, we will come to know our partners better when we are confronted with unexpected incidents. Or, we could say that it is only when faced with danger that we can know if we are courageous or not.

Furthermore, life is not made up only of our voluntary actions, but also and mostly of the unforeseen. With the ethics of hospitality, Innerarity proposes an ethics of contrariety, i.e., an ethics that guides us in dealing with what upsets and disturbs us. As an example, Innerarity uses the figure of the unexpected guest: the midnight visitor symbolizes all that is unexpected in life, like falling in love or getting sick. Indeed, no one adds to their calendar a future sickness or an accident; sickness is the midnight visitor who disturbs our daily life.

Innerarity also incorporates the question of temporality into his understanding of hospitality (2009, 167–82). Hospitality has mostly been thought of with regards to its spatial implications, and through questions such as 'who can cross the borders?' or 'how do we make space for newcomers?'. But Innerarity emphasizes the idea that welcoming the other necessitates time and that we need to make time for unexpected incidents. To cohabit with other people implies the need to adjust our temporality with someone else's and to respect it. In addition, our fast-paced society with its ceaseless production of new technologies and innovations of all sorts—all propelled swiftly by information networks—challenges our capacity to adapt. Now more than ever we are confronted by the strangeness of the world in the form of such new technologies, and thereby ever more confronted with feelings of insecurity. We can try to protect ourselves from strangeness, but that would probably require withdrawing from modern society. Or, we can practice hospitality and learn to welcome strangeness. Xenophobia, the fear of the stranger, is not an essential characteristic of human beings; we are not by nature afraid of otherness. We can become curious and generous, and open to the unknown (Innerarity 2009, 136).

In summary, the ethics of hospitality starts with the fact that life is short, that time determines our actions, and that the essential in our lives escapes our predictions. Hospitality teaches us to be attentive to the needs of others and to be attentive to the excluded, to those who are left behind. It teaches us to take their point of view into account and include them in our political and health care institutions. Being receptive to others also means being open to different temporalities, because we do not all experience time in the same way. Our parents and grandparents always seem to be living on different time than we do, and for this reason they feel more like strangers than those friends living in the same 'time zone' as us. In this sense, it is important to welcome the other while being respectful of their own temporality. As human beings, as temporary beings, we will be confronted with different temporalities. The temporality at work is not the same as at home; the time spent waiting at the hospital does not correspond to the time spent on the internet. Our life is filled with 'meanwhile' and 'waiting time'. To be a temporal being also means that we are affected by the passage of time, that we are vulnerable and mortal beings. In old age, the feeling of vulnerability will become stronger as the passage of time imprints its marks on the body. Thus, a community wishing to be hospitable to aging needs to adapt to this situation and provide the necessary care, while also respecting the specific temporality of old age. In the next section, I will look at how hospitality has guided and can still guide the practice of health care—a practice that focuses on the humanization of care and stands in contrast with the modern acute care model.

Hospitality and Health Care

Even if the ethics of hospitality is not an ethical framework commonly used in bioethics circles, its spirit and principles seem to pervade the practice of care and hospitals in general. Indeed, at the end of the fourth century, and under the influence of Christianity, the Roman conception of the *hospitalis domus*, the house where guests are welcome, engendered the creation of the first hospitals. They then served as a refuge for travelers and indigent patients. In this sense, it is worth noting that there is a link between the duty of hospitality and the institution of a specific space for health care. The Hospitaller Order of the Brothers of Saint John of God played a key role in defining a model of care inspired by hospitality. The early history of the Hospitaller is linked to the creation by Pope Gregory I in 603 of a hospital in Jerusalem to treat and care for Christian pilgrims to the Holy Land. González-Serna et al. have proposed that this order inspired the nursing model:

> The nursing model based on the tradition that comes from the figure of Saint John of God goes beyond the understanding that other authors have had about receptivity or hospitality in the health sphere. This model emphasizes hospitality as a receptivity paradigm, which encompasses a set of sub-values necessary for a humanized patient care: respect, responsibility, quality and spirituality. The humanistic and anthropological philosophy of the Hospitaller Order of the Brothers of Saint John of God (OHSJD acronym in Spanish) has a key role in the value hospitality [sic], because for them this term means alterity or humanization of the personal relationships of professionals

and patients, as well as the social collectivity, i.e., the mutual concern for the each other [sic.]. For the OHSJD, hospitality means receptivity, effective physical, moral, psychological and social support, valuing the multiple aspects of human needs. (2017, 2)

The authors mobilize this tradition of the Hospitaller to develop what they call the 'Hospitality Axiological Scale' which serves to "evaluate nursing attitudes in relation to hospitality for the humanization of nursing care" (2017, 1). The scale takes into account such ethical values as receptivity, empathy, proximity, justice, altruism, and compassion. This sort of scale, which focuses on the principles of hospitality, could prove useful in improving the quality of care in hospitals and nursing homes. The authors conclude that the practice of hospitality is now a challenge for health services. This challenge does not lie so much in the understanding of nursing professionals regarding the way reception should happen, but instead in the lack of recognition by the institution of the importance of the humanization of care. In other words, the modern hospital does not take full account of the importance of the relationship involved in the care practices and the necessary attitude of receptivity. In contrast,

> Hospitality generates attitudes based on professional values, as it is capable of promoting the relational bond between professionals and users, allowing to stimulate personal care, improve understanding of the disease and promote co-responsibility during treatment. It also enhances universal access, strengthens multidisciplinary and intersectional work, qualifies care, humanizes practices and encourages actions aiming to combat injurious [sic.]. (González-Serna et al. 2017, 7)

Alan Bleakley (2006) identifies a similar problem in the functioning of teamwork in the operating theatre. He also thinks that the paradigm of hospitality could provide a different model for teamwork. His study shows that many problems and accidents arise when health professionals are working in a 'monological' climate or under an individualistic model. According to him, this climate is rooted in "a legacy of a strongly hierarchical, self-regulating medical culture that values technical expertise above non-technical expertise as a basis to professionalism" (2006, 310). Bleakley argues that hospitality can become a principle that can transform health practices into 'patient-centered' practices or what he called an 'ecological' conception, as opposed to an 'egological' conception, that promotes a "wider imperative of 'education of attention,' or witnessing, as sensitivity to environmental conditions" (2006, 306). He recommends a change in culture to improve the collaborative nature of care, in which the patient is involved in care, and interprofessionalism is encouraged. For Verspieren (2006) and Basile Ngono (2014), the key questions are also how to make the modern hospital more hospitable, and how to make the modern practice of health care a practice of receptivity. The issue is that the professional model of modern hospitals, segmented according to specialities, serves research and the production of care, but leaves behind the elderly and the incurable. Chronically ill persons are treated like a burden by the modern hospital because it is constructed for the primary purpose of curing people as fast and as effectively as possible (Verspieren 2006, 49).

Indeed, the acute care model has been criticized for its insufficiency in answering the needs of an aging population and its promotion of an ideal of autonomy (Holstein, Parks, and Waymack 2011). The development of palliative care and end-of-life care facilities has been aimed at answering the needs of those left behind by the acute care model. For instance, Floriani and Schramm (2010) consider the modern hospice movement as an example of the paradigm of hospitality and argue that this model should inspire different health care provisions and institutions. Dame Cicely Saunders was the inspiration for the modern hospice. She started to work as a volunteer nurse in 1948 and then pursued her training as a doctor. She was particularly concerned by issues surrounding the care of the dying and pain reduction techniques. She inaugurated the first voluntary hospice in the United Kingdom in 1967 to provide palliative care, enabling people whose illness was no longer curable to achieve the best possible quality of life. She named it after St Christopher, patron saint of travelers, which shows how unconditional acceptance of the difference of the stranger was at the heart of the mission of the hospice. She wanted to give patients the feeling of inclusion and belonging. As Floriani and Schramm relate:

> Saunders explores the idea of the importance of welcoming people, whoever they may be, in a spirit of complete and unconditional receptivity: "Come just as you are—you are welcome" (Saunders 1977, p. 163). She was particularly sensitive to the delicate state of rejection and humiliation in which terminally ill patients lived, especially as regards their suffering from the inadequate treatment for the pain. In reaction to this, she promoted an ideal of receptivity which should permeate

all actions: "Those who welcome each patient to St. Christopher's do so with the conviction that he or she is an important person and that hospitality to a stranger is a prime necessity" (Saunders 1977, p. 163). (2010, 216)

Saunders exemplified and embodied the unconditional hospitality that Derrida was promoting. She was attentive to the particular needs of each person arriving to the hospice and she created a space to welcome the ultimate stranger: death itself.

With more and more people aging alone and living longer, Western industrialized societies face the need to invent new structures and new forms of hospitality for those left behind by the modern hospital and its acute care model. And with an aging population, our societies also face an increase in cases of dementia. To quote the Annual Report 2014–2015 of the Alzheimer Society of Canada:

> It was not surprising when the World Health Organization declared dementia as a global health priority now affecting 46.8 million people worldwide. For 30 years at the Alzheimer Society of Canada, we have seen the numbers rise at an alarming rate. Right now, 747,000 Canadians are living with Alzheimer's disease and other dementias and it's predicted by 2031 that figure will grow to 1.4 million.[6]

One of our challenges will be to build hospitable communities and dementia-friendly environments for this growing number of people. This will also imply a need to review, and perhaps abandon, our modern conception of autonomy in order to adopt a model of interdependency or relational autonomy. As Holstein, Parks, and Waymack explain:

> When understood as 'relational', autonomy is divested of both a voluntarist model of human exchange conducted among equals, and the concept of self as detached and self-interested. Instead, human beings are viewed as beings-in-relationship — as being *necessarily* and not only contingently ensconced in relationships of care — and human relationships are understood according to vulnerability rather than a voluntaristic model. (2011, 23–24)

For Holstein, Parks, and Waymack, the conception of relational autonomy means that we have to pay attention to the "external conditions that support or impede" the exercise of autonomy (2011, xii).

---

6   To consult the full report, see: http://www.alzheimer.ca/sites/default/files/files/national/financial/financial_annualreport_2015_e.pdf (accessed December 2017).

We find a similar conception in the ethics of hospitality, and also the idea that the practice of hospitality will be negotiated by the host and the guest together. As I explained previously with respect to Derrida and Innerarity, hospitality is a space in which we experience this relational autonomy and our fundamental vulnerability. Thus, the ethics of hospitality and the ethics of care promote a change in our modern conception of autonomy, which also means abandoning the idea that we can control our bodies and our identities. The understanding of autonomy as a form of relational autonomy seems to be a crucial aspect to take into consideration in order to review our understanding of health care and medicine. Indeed, with an aging population, we will have to rethink medicine because it should not be reduced to a product and patients should not be seen as sole consumers of technology. The first duty of medicine should be hospitality, understood as a non-indifference to humans in need of care (Ngono 2014, 27). A hospitable hospital or nursing-home should be a welcoming space, and, for some, an ultimate refuge, where solicitude is manifested toward the stranger and where the stranger is accepted and befriended — whomever he or she is.

Four Conditions to Build Hospitable Communities for Aging

In our contemporary era, aging is not usually regarded as a blessing, but rather as a curse. Our modern industrialized societies invest a lot of money in pushing back the effects of time, and cosmetics have become a very lucrative business. There are examples of research into aging being carried out whose main concern is stopping or reversing the process of aging of cells. British biologist Aubrey de Grey argues that aging should be considered a disease because its symptoms have a solution.[7] It seems to me that we live in a society that is trying to estrange aging and run away from our human condition. We have even coined the word 'ageism' to name the sort of prejudice or discrimination which is directed against particular age-groups — most especially, the elderly. The paradox is that science, technology, and medicine are all being aimed at extending

---

7   See https://futurism.com/more-scientists-are-pushing-to-have-aging-classified-as-a-disease/ (accessed December 2017). Transhumanism is a movement which also seeks to develop technologies to eliminate aging and enhance human capabilities.

human life, but the prospect of growing old is seen as almost horrifying. Or, I should rather say that what is horrifying is the prospect of becoming vulnerable, of becoming a burden for our loved ones, and of depending on others. We also fear the solitude that we see the elderly suffering from. We are obsessed with the idea of aging healthily and with trying to remain the same, and with staying in control of our bodies and identities. Of course, we live in a society that promotes the ideal of autonomy. In opposition to this modern ideal, hospitality reveals that we are fundamentally receptive and vulnerable beings, always indebted to others.

Based on the principles of the ethics of hospitality, I propose four characteristics or conditions that could guide and inspire the development of hospitable communities for aging. The first condition is the responsibility to care. By nature, human beings need care: we need care from birth through childhood and so we live in communities because it makes it easier to survive. In this sense, we are vulnerable beings and it is for this reason that hospitality was a sacred duty for the Ancient Greeks. The responsibility to care for children and the elderly is present in all cultures. Unfortunately, more and more people are aging alone, either without family to take care of them or without family that has time to do so. Thus, we could think of a social responsibility to care for the elderly as unconditional hospitality. In this way, we find that convergence arises between the ethics of hospitality and the ethics of care, as both champion the responsibility to care for others.

The second condition is the fluidity of borders and boundaries. Hospitality involves the possibility of the exchange of roles, wherein the guest can also play the role of host. The relationship of care should also involve this exchange of roles or the establishment of a relation of reciprocity. To paraphrase Verspieren (2006, 47), if there is only a gift from the caregiver, then the care receiver is reduced to a pure recipient. Sally Stewart and Lorraine Farrelly also note: "The 'total care' philosophy—which the elderly themselves often vehemently reject—is one that creates a burden because it is disabling by its very function. The elderly are rarely seen as a resource in their own lives, and almost never as a resource in their own community" (2014, 87). The research of Janine Wiles (2011) also shows that older people are making great contributions as caregivers as they support each other, their families, and communities through financial means and voluntary work. Wiles criticizes the ageist views, which label older people "as passive, dependent, frail, and 'at-risk' or vulnerable objects of care" (2011, 576), and challenges "apocalyptic demographies" by emphasizing the contributions of older people as caregivers. The elderly should not be objectified as 'care receivers' because it does not represent the reality. On this point, we have to mention the specific contribution of the ethics of care which brings our attention to the issue of the invisibility of care and, to quote Julie White and Joan Tronto, how "more powerful people can fob the work of care on to others: men to women, upper to lower class, free men to slaves" (2004, 443). The feminist theorists of care have shown the intersections of gender, race, and class regarding the question 'who does the dirty work of care?' (Tronto 2015, 19). Thus, we have to recognize that receiving care now depends on having money and that care work is not equally distributed among all. We need to take into account that some 'unprivileged' people may have a heavy care work-load without also having the necessary resources to meet their own needs.

In a different way, the fluidity of borders can refer to contact between generations, which has positive consequences. Younger people can learn to welcome their own aging through contact with the elderly. They can learn to tame what is now being regarded as a strange state of life; the unknown could be befriended. In return, the frail elderly can be empowered by the idea that they can give something in return for care, that they can still be a host in their own way. Retired people, especially men who devoted their life to supporting a family, can suffer from the sense of having no further purpose in life, of having no recognized function in active society. The possibility of the exchange of roles needs to stay open—no one should be confined in a specific role as a sort of hostage. Existing research also points us in the direction of reciprocity: "Paid home helpers also felt they received a lot from the elderly people receiving care, stating that they felt appreciated and welcome and that the work they were doing was valued, as well as seeing potential role models for their own old age" (Wiles 2011, 577–78). That being the case, while caregivers can feel appreciation and reciprocation from care receivers, we have to recognize that care work is not highly regarded in society in general, as the difficult working conditions and low salary of care work reveal. Indeed, the invisibility of care has become a central issue for ethics of care and this is an issue that has to be addressed because it affects the quality of care.

The third condition is realizing the importance of respecting other temporalities. Time has become an important question in the literature on nursing and care for the elderly. Research shows that in senior home care, nurses complain that they don't have enough time to respond to the needs of residents.[8] They have to rush them through pre-established tasks, such as the pre-set amount of time dedicated to bathing and eating. This situation highlights the clash between the temporality of life and the temporality of work. Residents are dispossessed from their own temporality and forced into the time imposed by the institution and the work-schedule of caregivers. Aggarwal et al. (2003) have observed that care has become very task oriented, leaving almost no room for the social, emotional, and spiritual needs of the elderly. As they write:

> Convenience or speed may be an issue, i.e. it was simply quicker to make decisions and to do things for people with dementia, than allow the person time to do it for themselves. The characteristics of institutions, such as care homes, could be compared to the regimes discussed by Goffman (1961) — the focus being on organization and order, rather than on promoting choice and independence amongst residents. In contemporary terms, such homes could fail to empower residents. (2003, 195)

They analyze this situation with regards to societal attitudes which perceive "people with disabilities to be incompetent, incapable of making their own decisions and choices, and as dependent on others" (2003, 195). The problem is that people with disabilities may internalize those societal attitudes, which then become a self-fulfilling prophecy. It is thus important to give elders and people with disabilities the time they need to do the tasks that they want to do instead of doing everything for them in order to save time. Otherwise, it may aggravate feelings of incompetency and worthlessness.

The fourth and final condition is a feeling of being at home: the highest quality of hospitality that a host can demonstrate is to make us feel at home. It is often the slogan hotels use: 'Your home away

---

8   At the beginning of 2018, Quebec nurses mobilized to speak out about their difficult working conditions, namely that the mandatory overtime, the lack of resources, and the higher number of patients jeopardize the care that they give to patients. The situation was highly publicized in Quebec's media (Radio-Canada, CBC, *Le Devoir*, *La Presse*), but structural changes have yet to be made.

from home.' Or, a good host may say: 'Make yourself at home.' Of course, there are always implicit limits. However, those limits can be negotiated together by both sides. We must not forget that hospitality also implies a pact between the host and the guest, which is not the same as a contract imposed by one party on the other. The form of hospitality varies depending on the persons involved, as we can see from the various practices of hospitality throughout history and across cultures. Hospitality is a dynamic practice guided only by general principles and common sense, hence the importance of receptivity, attention, and openness. The generous host must be attentive to the needs of his guest and the attentive guest must understand when he is exceeding the patience of his host. Stewart and Farrelly also mention that "The home is inevitably the place where we assert the most influence and control, and when this is not possible we can feel disempowered and alienated" (2014, 83). Thus, it is crucial to provide people with dementia with a feeling of being at home, without which they might feel even more disorientated.

Hospitable Communities for Aging

To conclude, I want to provide some examples that illustrate how we can build more hospitable communities for aging. The first example is Humanitas, an independent senior living facility in which university students can live for free if they spend thirty hours per month socializing with their senior housemates. The project aims at warding off the negative effects of aging. Students can do a variety of activities with senior residents, such as watching sports, celebrating birthdays, and offering company when residents fall ill. The students thus help to diminish the feelings of disconnectedness of senior residents; research has shown that social isolation and loneliness are factors associated with increased mortality. Students bring the outside world in. Humanitas has been the object of much attention world-wide, and many documentaries have been filmed in which students testify to the deep relationships and friendships which they developed with their senior housemates. And through those relationships, students learned both that death is approaching but that it is also a part of life.

This example shows how some young students feel the responsibility to care. Of course, the act is not totally disinterested because they receive free accommodation in exchange. But the pact of hospitality seems to be advantageous and beneficial for both parties. It also shows the fluidity of the borders between generations. Young students can learn about the process of aging and may, by making it less foreign, become more welcoming towards their own aging processes. In return, the elderly can feel that they can still contribute to society — that they can still have a feeling of purpose by listening to and advising young students. But mostly the elderly can feel their humanity and dignity by developing new friendships. The human connections they develop with their younger housemates can make them feel more at home in the world. By contrast, traditional nursing homes in which residents are almost only ever in contact with employees, and restricted visiting hours are commonly imposed, can make residents feel estranged from the rest of the world — like hostages of a place where people are left to die. The intergenerational living arrangement, on the other hand, can teach young people how to live with differences and different temporalities. They can learn that it is not everybody who is following the fast-pace of society at large, and that they need to respect the fact that some people may need more time to do things. They might even learn that it feels good to slow down and take time to create human connections, to develop friendship in the real world, and not just in the virtual one. Although similar intergenerational programs exist in France, the United States, Spain, and Canada,[9] they are still marginal.

Of course, it could be argued that the intergenerational model is not new but traditional in many respects. However, if the norm used to be that children should take care of their aging parents, things have changed dramatically in recent years for many different reasons. More could definitely be done in order to collectively support families who take care of, or wish to take care of, elders — as well as, in a more general sense, of people with special needs. Nonetheless, as more people are aging alone, we still have to create a welcoming space — and time — for them. In his reflections on the

---

9 In Trois-Rivières (Canada), the retirement home Les Maronniers announced in September 2017 a project similar to Humanitas. The retirement home wants to welcome two students with free accommodation in exchange for forty hours of volunteer work per month. The director of the home thought that this project could answer the need for volunteer work while bringing dynamism into the life of senior residents. See http://ici.radio-canada.ca/nouvelle/1058472/loyer-residence-personnes-agees-etudiant-concours-uqtr (accessed December 2017).

ethics of hospitality, Innerarity reminds us of our responsibility to pay attention to those relegated to the margins, to those who are left behind. Humanitas's project is thus a way to maintain the tradition of intergenerational living and its advantages.

Another example is the Netherlands dementia village, Hogeweyk, where all residents suffer from severe dementia and Alzheimer's. Hogeweyk seeks to provide care for people who require significant support, while trying to preserve a sense of continuity with a familiar environment. Indeed, in this self-contained, village-like facility, the residents can have the care that they need while maintaining a sense of independence. Their website explains that the monthly cost is similar to other nursing homes, but that the lifestyle is not. The village is divided into building blocks with a total of 23 apartments divided into six different 'varieties' of lifestyle: Christian, Artisan, Indonesian, Cultural, Homey, and Upper Class. The apartment gives residents a familiar living environment. "The interior design and dining preferences as well as the experiences and interests of the residents are taken into account when they are placed into a building block. Residents live in groups of six to eight, with at least two trained caregivers who assist them throughout the day" (Sampson 2014). To quote the website of Hogeweyk:

> The residents manage their own households together with a constant team of staff members. Washing, cooking and so on is done every day in all of the houses. Daily groceries are done in the Hogeweyk supermarket. Hogeweyk offers its dementia-suffering inhabitants maximum privacy and autonomy. The village has streets, squares, gardens and a park where the residents can safely roam free. Just like any other village Hogeweyk offers a selection of facilities, like a restaurant, a bar and a theatre. These facilities can be used by Hogeweyk residents AND residents of the surrounding neighbourhoods. Everybody is welcome to come in![10]

The village offers a sense of openness in which residents can go out and engage in activities. There are also clubs in which residents can do all sorts of activities, such as baking or making music. In fact, music plays an important role in this village, as the caregivers think that it is a good way to communicate with some residents with severe dementia.

---

10 https://hogeweyk.dementiavillage.com/en/ (accessed December 2017).

Hogeweyk also has a particular view on care, founded on the idea that even people with severe dementia still have a valid opinion on their day-to-day life and surroundings. The self-contained village provides a safe environment in which residents can move freely both inside and outside of the house. As Stewart and Farrelly indicate: "Although De Hogeweyk has been criticized for the apparent artificiality of the environment it provides, the situation is no more synthetic than any medium-sized housing development. De Hogeweyk may be seen as a highly articulated, even unique, response to housing for those requiring significant support" (2014, 87). Indeed, residents at Hogeweyk can enjoy life and feel that they are welcome on this earth. The social contact and the stimulating activities and visits from family and friends have a positive impact on their health. The feeling of still being human and the opportunity to still be a person leads to better health, and residents consequently need less medication and physical restraint. Hogeweyk exemplifies the importance of feeling at home in promoting the well-being of residents.

The last example, Carpe Diem, is an Alzheimer's resource center in Quebec that offers a diversity of services: housing for people with Alzheimer's or other kinds of dementia, short-term housing, and home care support. It also organizes sensitization activities to promote and defend the rights and interests of people living with dementia, and those of their relatives. It offers prevention, help, and support services adapted to the specific needs of persons living with dementia and those of their relatives. The center also provides training to care workers from Quebec and abroad, and both encourages and supports research that contributes to the improvement in the living conditions of people with dementia. It thus aims at making accessible an innovation model of accompaniment, care, and housing.

Carpe Diem has developed a philosophy of care[11] that resonates with the ethics of hospitality. Its main goal is to modify the way society regards people living with Alzheimer's or dementia, to fight prejudices surrounding the disease, and, thus, to support a positive change in practices intended for people experiencing a loss in

---

11 For a full account of Carpe Diem's philosophy and mission, see their website: http://alzheimercarpediem.com/lapproche-carpe-diem/lapproche-carpe-diem/ (accessed April 2018).

their cognitive autonomy. The website of the center provides a list of principles that guides its philosophy. The first principle is that the person should be considered before the disease. Second, support should be designed around the resources and the capabilities of the person and not around her deficits. Third, structure and services should be adjusted to fit the specific needs of the person, and not the other way around. This is the reason why Carpe Diem has developed a large range of services. Carpe Diem also believes that labels are invalidating and it thus aims at expelling labels by continually questioning its own practices and its responsibility when faced with difficult behavior. Carpe Diem's approach follows the principle of the unconditional acceptance of the person, and promotes an empathic understanding of both the person and her relatives. The center's schedule is flexible and thus allows the person to choose her activities and time schedule. Furthermore, she can also feel helpful by participating in everyday activities that contribute to the center according to her interests and tastes. In brief, we could say that Carpe Diem exemplifies the ethics of hospitality by its openness and receptivity to the person. It respects the specific temporality of each person.

Of course, we could give many other examples of good practices and a variety of living arrangements around the world — and also many counterexamples of bad practices and abuse of elders. Yet, these examples show that it is possible, with some creativity and generous attention, to build hospitable communities for aging populations. They also demonstrate a paradigm shift away from the acute care model, in which the patient needs to be cured and needs to leave as soon as possible, to a relational model that welcomes the person as she is, for as long as she wants,[12] in a hospitable space. Humanitas is a simple initiative built around the traditional intergenerational living that has been lost in our modern society, whereas Hogeweyk offers a new way of looking at modern nursing homes in which the points of view of residents with severe dementia are taken into consideration. Carpe Diem has developed an innovative, multifaceted approach that provides home care support services as well as housing. It also has a strong sense of mission, for

---

12 Of course, this statement is made from an ideal perspective, for we know that nursing homes are expensive and thus not accessible to all. Thus, the question of the accessibility of services has to be thought through from a perspective of social justice. The question of the accessibility of services is at the center of ethics of care.

it also intends to educate, to fight prejudices, to defend the rights and interests of people living with dementia, and offers training. These are only some examples of how the ethics of hospitality can be applied to care for the elderly, but the principles of hospitality could inspire many other different forms of living arrangements. However, one thing seems crucial: we have to bring some humanity back into the care for aging individuals.

References

Aggarwal, N., A. A. Vass, H. A. Minardi, R. Ward, C. Garfield, and B. Cybyk. 2003. "People with Dementia and their Relatives: Personal Experiences of Alzheimer's and of the Provision of Care." *Journal of Psychiatric and Mental Health Nursing* 10: 187–97.

Benveniste, Émile. 1969. *Le vocabulaire des institutions indo-européennes*. Paris: Éditions de Minuit.

Bleakley, Alan. 2006. "A Common Body of Care: The Ethics and Politics of Teamwork in the Operating Theater are Inseparable." *Journal of Medicine and Philosophy* 31: 305–22.

Bourgault, Sophie. 2015. "Sollicitude, attention et réceptivité. L'éthique de l'hospitalité comme éthique du care." In *Le temps de l'hospitalité. Réception de l'œuvre de Daniel Innerarity*, edited by L. Vigneault, B. Navarro Pardiñas, S. Cloutier, and D. Desroches, 37–57. Québec: Presses de l'Université Laval.

Derrida, Jacques. 1997. *De l'hospitalité. Anne Dufourmantelle invite Jacques Derrida à répondre*. Paris: Calmann-Lévy.

Dikeç, Mustafa, Nigel Clark, and Clive Barnett. 2009. "Extending Hospitality: Giving Space, Taking Time." *Paragraph: A Journal of Modern Critical Theory* 32 (1): 1–14.

Floriani, Augusto Ciro, and Fermin Roland Schramm. 2010. "How might Levinas' Concept of the Other's Priority and Derrida's Unconditional Hospitality Contribute to the Philosophy of the Modern Hospice Movement?" *Palliative and Supportive Care* 8: 215–20.

González-Serna, Galán José María, Soledad Ferreras-Mencia, and Juan Manuel Arribas-Marín. 2017. "Development and Validation of the Hospitality Axiological Scale for Humanization of Nursing Care." *Revista Latino-Americana de Enfermagem* 25: 1–9.

Holstein, Martha B., Jennifer A. Parks, and Mark H. Waymack. 2011. *Ethics, Aging, and Society: The Critical Turn*. New York: Springer.

Innerarity, Daniel. 2009. *Éthique de l'hopitalité*. Translated by Blanca Navarro Pardiñas and Luc Vigneault. Québec: Presses de l'Université Laval.

McNulty, Tracy. 2007. *The Hostess: Hospitality, Femininity, and the Expropriation of Identity*. Minneapolis: University of Minnesota Press.

Ngono, Basile. 2014. "Hôpital et hospitalité: aux fondements d'un lien indissoluble." *Journal International de Bioéthique* 25 (4): 17–28.

Noddings, Nel. 1984. *Caring: A Feminine Approach to Ethics & Moral Education*. Berkeley: University of California Press.

Sampson, Trinica. 2014. "Holland's Dementia Village Revolutionizes Alzheimer's Caregiving." Accessed December 2017. http://www.utne.com/community/holland-dementia-village-revolutionizes-alzehimer-caregiving.aspx
Stewart, Sally, and Lorraine Farrelly. 2014. "Redesigning Domesticity: Creating Homes for the Elderly." *Architectural Design* 84 (2): 80–87.
Tronto, Joan. 1993. *Moral Boundaries: A Political Argument for an Ethic of Care*. New York: Routledge.
___. 2015. *Who Cares? How to Reshape a Democratic Politics*. Ithaca: Cornell University Press.
Verspieren, Patrick. 2006. "L'hospitalité au cœur de l'éthique du soin." *Laennec* 54: 33–49.
Vigneault, Luc, Blanca Navarro Pardiñas, Sophie Cloutier, and Dominic Desroches (ed.). 2015. *Le temps de l'hospitalité. Réception de l'œuvre de Daniel Innerarity*. Québec: Presses de l'Université Laval.
White, Julie A., and Joan Tronto. 2004. "Political Practices of Care: Needs and Rights." *Ratio Juris* 17 (4): 415–53.
Wiles, Janine. 2011. "Reflections on being a Recipient of Care: Vexing the Concept of Vulnerability." *Social and Cultural Geography* 12 (6): 573–88.

About the author

Sophie Cloutier is Associate Professor in the Faculty of Philosophy and the School of Ethics, Social Justice and Public Service, and co-director of the Research Centre in Public Ethics and Governance at Saint Paul University. Her main area of research is political philosophy and public ethics. She has published several articles on Hannah Arendt's thought, multiculturalism, hospitality, and ethics of care. She has also edited and contributed to *Le temps de l'hospitalité: Réception de l'oeuvre de Daniel Innerarity* (Presses de l'Université Laval, 2015).

Chapter Two

The Otherness within Us: Reframing, with Spinoza, the Self's Relationship to Disability and Aging

Iva Apostolova and Élaina Gauthier-Mamaril

Abstract

"**The Otherness within Us: Reframing, with Spinoza, the Self's Relationship to Disability and Aging**" by **Iva Apostolova** and **Élaina Gauthier-Mamaril** adapts the philosopher Baruch Spinoza's anti-dualist theory of the *conatus* to the question of aging. The authors argue that since we always conceptualize ourselves in relation with others, the cultivation of compassion is a moral attitude that asks from each of us an effort to negotiate between our own interests and those of others.

Introduction

In this chapter, we seek to address the complex and difficult topic of aging into disability, namely, the relationship of the self with its aging body and, more specifically, with the "natural" disability that occurs as we lose possession and exercise of our former mental and physical capacities when we grow older. In order to circumscribe this very specific take on disability, we will be using the ontological and anthropological frameworks of the seventeenth-century Dutch philosopher Baruch Spinoza. It is our claim that the key to fruitfully approaching the disabilities that come with age lies in relational ontology and care ethics. By having contemporary concepts such as "participatory epistemology" and "moral remainders" engage with a Spinozist framework, we aim to showcase a different possible take on the existential experience of aging and to place it within the context of community.

It might not be immediately apparent how a detour to a seventeenth-century philosopher would be appropriate for this endeavor. However, though it will neither be necessary nor pertinent to discuss every aspect of Spinoza's philosophy here, his doctrine of the *conatus* and his subsequent theories of affects are central to the elaboration of our conceptual framework (1996, Part III, Proposition 9). This is what sections one through three of this chapter will address. The experience of disability that comes with our inevitable passage through time is captured in Spinoza's radical rejection of the mind/body separation and his understanding of agency through what 'augments' and what 'diminishes' our 'power'. Spinoza's is a philosophy of life, of life that is affirmed in the transition to greater agency and that is repressed in the transition to passivity. But the passivity that comes with aging is inevitable, and Spinoza also recognizes this in his deterministic view of nature.

We did not choose Spinoza's philosophy as a framework because it deals explicitly with aging, or with disability for that matter. We do not claim to make a special reading of his corpus that would make these themes into a central concern for the philosopher. Rather, in these short pages, we would like to explore a path where ontological, epistemic, and affective theories can inform a contemporary relational ontology and lead to a critical outlook on how the self copes with its diminishing power to act. In order to do this, it is important to first highlight Spinoza's anthropological presupposition that humans (and indeed all things) have a *conatus* — a life drive or desire that is constitutive to their very existence. All of the experiences of an individual are impacted by how and how much their *conatus* is helped or hindered. Understanding the role of active and passive affects in Spinoza's framework will allow us to consider the aging process through an affective lens. This will lead us to our second consideration, which is Spinoza's conception of the mind and body unit(y). Our experience of aging and disability is (em)bodied and Spinoza's anti-dualistic stance is a supremely important element in his *conatus* theory. Finally, we will extend the terrain of the reflexive self to challenge our stubborn infatuation with autonomy by considering the role of community in the process of becoming disabled with age. Precisely because Spinoza's philosophy is very de-anthropocentric, it opens up a myriad of possibilities for a relational ontology, as well as the examination of the role of relationships for the life of the self.

The second part of this chapter (sections four and five) will be devoted to explaining how relational ontology and care ethics can use Spinoza as a springboard to inform participatory epistemology, which may lead to the discovery of new ways of addressing the complexities of disability that come with aging. Grounding ourselves in a relational ontology matrix, in our view, leads to a more realistic appraisal of the human condition. Facing reality includes embracing grieving as an individually customizable process (much like the customizable notion of the good) that resonates with every other human. Grieving represents the dynamic way in which we engage with mortality, and, as such, respecting it as a concept rebukes the temptation of comforting ourselves with an aesthetic nihilism or a form of neo-stoicism. We are firmly convinced that the way we experience aging and disability in ourselves and in others cannot be resolved by the use of broad, will-powered strokes; we are left with an ethics of "moral remainders". Thus, sections four and five of this chapter will lay out what it means for communities to deal with these moral remainders as they face their own mortality.

Critique of Autonomy as a Goal: Agency, Power, and Desire

"Desire is the essence itself of man in so far as it is conceived as determined to any action by any one of its modifications" (Spinoza 1996, Part III, Definition of the Affects 1). In this passage, Spinoza explains that, although the impulses or desires of an individual would continue to exist whether that individual is conscious of them or not, he did find it important to include the idea of consciousness in his definition of the "essence itself of man". Every single thing in the universe is affected or modified by its environment, but humans have the capacity to reflect on their affective "modifications". In *Ethics*, Spinoza is very clear that we must start by forgoing the following illusions: a) that the universe was made with us and our goals in mind, and b) that we are in control of our destinies (1996, Part I, Appendix). There will always be bigger fish in the pond and we will never be able to have everything that we want by exerting the sheer force of our will. In this cosmoanthropological perspective, Spinoza recognizes our need for control; at the same time, he states the futility and ultimately harmful quality of this desire because it is based on an inadequate assessment of the world. What we strive for, according to Spinoza, is to augment our power to be active, to promote the part of us that causes effect. It is very important to understand that we will never cease to be passive and affected by others and the world while we exist as (em)bodied things. However, we do our utmost to place ourselves in situations in which the environment and our encounters affect us positively, therefore contributing to the strength of our being-desire, to the flourishing of our *conatus*. This framework allows us to easily perceive how the loss of mobility, which is, for example, brought on by age, can be painful and distressing. On the one hand, we never cease to desire or to persevere in our being, and yet, on the other hand, we are being 'thwarted' by the failings of our body.

In the Spinozist affective regime, it is in the passage from a lesser degree of activity to a greater one that we experience positive affects such as joy and love; conversely, it is the transition from an active stance to a more overwhelming passivity that we experience as sadness or hatred. Spinoza, therefore, does not sugar-coat the disabling process: our entire being takes a hit when our body ceases to enjoy its former relative abilities. Yet, ability, and the ensuing autonomy, is not the right term. Autonomy per se, does not fit into Spinoza's deterministic landscape, and perhaps, given the purposes of this chapter, it is for the best. If becoming unable to exercise our power in the way we were accustomed to is frustrating and possibly distressing, seeking an elusive former autonomy is not the path that Spinoza proposes to counter the negative affects brought on by disability. Very simply, and yet harshly, he affirms that "By reality and perfection I understand the same thing" (1996, Part II, Definition 6). Cultivating our desire to persevere is not to be understood as a doomed fight against our inevitable deterioration. We should not deny what is real, because the act of denying harms us even more by diverting our energy to fight a senseless battle. In a sense, Spinoza is advocating for Stoicism and a placid outlook on life, come hell or high water. But more importantly, he is highlighting the absurdity of upholding untethered autonomy as a goal.

This might seem like a contradiction within his *conatus* theory, but it is, in fact, a logical consequence of his relational ontology. It is never rational, in the prime of our youth, to believe that we can stand alone, defiant will, hubris, and all, against the course of the world; neither is it an adequate belief to hold as we age. The way to benefit our *conatus* lies in our strategic and rational association with others so that our affects may be as active as our encompassing situation can allow. We will come back to this relational posture in the third part of this section, but first, we feel it is necessary to expand on a significant presupposition of our argument, namely Spinoza's claim that our mind and body are not two distinct parts in need of uniting but that each are the other side of the same coin that is our *(em)bodied existence*.

A Philosophy of Life and/or of Resignation: Dealing with the Necessary Repression Caused by Aging and Disability

We have deliberately avoided the use of references to mental or physical disabilities thus far. Instead, we have favored a more global, albeit broader, terminological approach to the loss of ability that comes with aging, necessitated by the Spinozist framework. Indeed, Spinoza does not support the notion that our mind and body are two separate substances or forces that oppose each other in warring terms. For Spinoza, what we call 'mind' is the way we see and understand ourselves through the attribute of Thought and our body is seen through the attribute of Extension. As (em)bodied beings, we inevitably experience ourselves as a whole that can be viewed from different perspectives. Spinoza (1996, Book III, Definition 6) explains that "when [he] said above that the mind's power of thinking is increased or diminished, [he] meant nothing but that the mind has formed of its body (or of some part of it) an idea which expresses more or less reality than it had affirmed of the body." What this means, in our context, is that our mind's or our will's power cannot be augmented or lessened without our experiencing a passage in our body. And this passage should not be interpreted as a consequence of the will but as a simultaneous occurrence. Our experience of the world is always (em)bodied; it cannot be otherwise. Therefore, we must keep this at the forefront of our minds when we consider how to pursue our being-desire in a state of ongoing disability. While the importance of motivation and healthy habits is by no means negated, Spinoza bluntly points out that no amount of strength of the will can reverse the irreversible. We must find a way to reflect on the never-ending quest for increased activity in a different paradigm than that of autonomy.

The Key to Self-Coping: The Role of Community

Spinoza's radical anti-dualistic position has a pivotal influence on how he perceives human sociability and politics. By postulating that the mind and the body are not opposing factions that need to be held together, but are rather two attributes through which all human experience and knowledge comes to be, Spinoza asserts that there can be no other rationality but (em)bodied rationality. This is important to keep in mind as we consider the issue of disability that comes with aging. As we have seen above, Spinoza does not place *autonomy-autarky* as the ultimate life-giving goal, but rather holds that the core of what it is to be human lies with desire. This does not stop when we start (and continue) to lose the ability to exercise our bodies and our minds the way we were accustomed to. In Spinoza's terms, we never cease to strive to persevere in our beings. As we grow older, we tend to become more aware of the relational quality of our self because we must face our growing and complex dependence on others. Relational ontology (which will be fully defined later in this chapter) may not be the most striking characteristic of Spinoza's system at first glance, but it is where his seemingly self-centered affective theory is heading. The full expression of rationality is when we realize that we are better off the more rational and stable our surrounding community is.

This is the moment of realization that Spinoza's outlook offers something other than bare resignation to our determined situation. Certainly, understanding that we are an infinitesimal part of the universe which is in no way concerned with our happiness is an important step towards realizing that there is very little we can do to rationally 'fight' adverse situations, because we are simply outnumbered or overpowered. However, Spinoza does not preach a gospel of despair, nor would it be accurate to say that he is merely proposing a reiteration of Stoic resignation. The adequate understanding of our human, (em)bodied situation is the understanding that it is not only futile but damagingly frustrating to live with the belief that we can 'face the world' on our own. First and foremost, we are a part of the world; we are not standing alone opposite it. Second, our own individual strength, though its health very much affects us, is ultimately powerless to sustain us. As we age, we are increasingly faced with the naked reality of our diminished control over ourselves; we become acutely aware of the reality that exists for all humans in this world: that we all depend on our communities and on our relationships to subsist and continue to act. In a Spinozist perspective, it is inadequate and ultimately harmful to entertain the thought that our loss of ability and activity is a good thing. As an ongoing repression on the *conatus*, disability is experienced as negative affection that forces us into passivity. However, if an acceptance of our situation is the only rational way to go ("By reality and perfection, I mean the same thing" [Book III, Definition 6]), this acceptance takes in its stride both our decrepitude and our deep-rooted relationality.

The Tri-Vector of Relational Ontology, Ethics of Care, and Participatory Epistemology

As discussed above, we believe that the context of relational ontology, whose roots we found in Spinoza's philosophy of life, and ethics of care, combined, provide the most fertile ground for a healthy ethical attitude toward disability resulting from aging. Relational ontology presupposes a relational self. The relational self recognizes not only that we are in various relationships with other selves, but also that the relationship with others is necessary for the very existence of the self. Put in Spinozist terms, it is damaging to ourselves to think that we are capable of facing the world alone. The constitutive role of relationships and the inherent social nature of humans does not, however, deny individuality or agency to the self. This further complicates the analysis of the self. As Lorraine Code aptly notes, the relational nature of the self under relational ontology requires a remarkable "balancing act" between the interdependence of the self and the other, while acknowledging the individuality and independence of the self within the relationship with the other (1991, 82). Christine Koggel explains further: a "relational conception of the self suggests that we come to know ourselves and others only in a network of interactive relationships and that this shapes and is necessary for exercising self-determining capacities" (1998, 128). The relational ontological framework suggests that complete independence of the self is not only impossible but also undesirable.

Relational ontology calls for a type of inclusivity which, as Leslie Francis and Anita Silvers aptly note, traditional (liberal) models of justice have ignored (2010, 237). The inclusivity in question is incorporating differences in capacity to conceptualize the good.

Trusteeship

"Humans differ in regard to their good, both in conception and in the process from which notions about the good emerge" (2010, 238). The alleged liberal devotion to pluralism should, logically, lead to personalized, customized accounts of the good and, yet, there are a significant number of "outliers" who do not fit into a traditional/liberal framework. Take, for example, John Rawls's account of justice which, for all intents and purposes, is a liberal account of justice. Although Rawls's view is emphatically anti-foundationalist by design, it is still based on "reasonable" principles of the good, supposedly followed by everyone. In other words, under a Rawlsian view, participants in the system of justice have to be capable of self-validation, that is, they have to be capable of justifying their principles. "But," Francis and Silvers ask, "what of individuals who for reasons of biological or psychological limitation seem incapable of self-validation?" (2010, 243). We believe, together with Francis and Silvers, that if a system of justice, which presupposes a specific conception of the self and its autonomy, cannot answer this question, then it should be replaced with a different system. In an attempt to improve Martha Nussbaum's capabilities approach toward rights and duties, Francis and Silvers introduce the "theory of trusteeship," where anyone, whether able-bodied or disabled, can be a trustee, that is, a reasoner and communicator who is capable of executing parts or all of someone else's thinking process without changing the subject's original notions of the good (2010, 247). The analogy with prosthetic limbs allows us to better understand the motivation behind the trusteeship theory: anyone, even a severely cognitively impaired individual, can be the executioner of her own, customized notion of the good via a trustee. In this sense, the trustee plays the role of a conceptual midwife of sorts (2010, 249). This safeguards the notion of the good against a too-demanding requirement of reciprocity. Although we will come back to the idea of reciprocity at the end of the chapter, it is worth mentioning here that, if the condition of reciprocity in the context of either a social contract theory of justice or a structure of care is too demanding, many individuals will fail to meet the requirement. In other words, if the interdependence of individuals is primarily based on the reciprocity of the cooperative effort to care for one another, some individuals (with severe cognitive impairments, for example) will not enjoy the benefits of care on account of their failure to offer comparable reciprocal care.

The moral to take away from the theory of trusteeship and the condition of reciprocity is that a commitment to a relational ontology needs to spell out the degrees of relationality of the self's interdependence with other selves. Our claim here is that if we are as committed to a full-blown relationality as we would like to think that we are, a cooperative environment where reciprocity is the benchmark of relationality simply will not do. What we claim, inspired by Francis and Silvers, is that a relational self is a self which *always* forms its customizable notion of the good in a cooperative, assistive manner. This way, the emphasis is on the process of engaging other selves to participate in the formation of the notion of the good, and not on the end result of who will get what. In this sense, autonomy or self-determination, or self-origination, is always understood through the lens of one's responses to the other. Without this notion of responsiveness, autonomy turns into a myth which, apart from being convenient for a capitalist economy which views care as little more than a high cost, is rather damaging to our own customizable notion of the good. What is more, if we insist on viewing autonomy as independence in the sense of freedom from all dependence, we are essentially claiming that human agents can single-handedly create the preconditions for their own actions which is, of course, impossible, and would eventually render the social contract superfluous.¹ To put it in the words of Sandra Harding (1991, 150), we need to allow "the Other to gaze back 'shamelessly' at the self who had reserved for himself the right to gaze autonomously at whomsoever he chooses."

What is more, the undeniable reality is that we are all born into and out of relationships. Displacing the notion of autonomy and misplacing it within the framework of independence threatens to prevent us from noticing and developing the skills that will ultimately shape our responsibilities toward each other. In this sense, autonomy is also a skill that requires continuous practice and revision. This inter-dependence of the self, and the ubiquitous context of care within which the self exists, *is* its reality. It is not something constructed in the sense of depending on the current theoretical framework. Denying the reality of inter-dependence is denying the self its (*sense of*) *reality*. The same applies to the rationality of the self. To define the self exclusively by its rationality is to abstract

---

1   The point is originally expressed by Holmes and Sunstein (1999, 204).

from reality, which turns the self into a fictitious rather than a full-bodied entity. As Spinoza would put it, albeit never in these terms, our rationality is (em)bodied rationality. Thought and Extension are two attributes/perspectives of the same self. In other words, making relationships the bedrock of ethical analysis, as well as ethical praxis, allows us not only to see the nuances in the fabric of the agency of the self, but also to realize the important role affect plays in moral conduct.

If we accept that autonomy of the self, understood as self-reliance and independence, is not a given, existing in a social vacuum, then a viable alternative can be offered. Autonomy is a set of skills/capabilities/responsibilities which are not given to us once and for all but, on the contrary, require learning, experience, and practice, as Susan Sherwin (2012), quoting Diana Meyer's seminal work,[2] suggests. The skills involved in autonomous decision-making processes call not only for a 'know-how' on acting but also on *being* in the world. It will be, indeed, rather foolish to assume that anyone can assert their autonomy at any point of time, disregarding personal and social circumstances (e.g., being in an abusive relationship, being forced to work multiple jobs to support oneself or one's family, or living in a country with a totalitarian political regime are all forms of oppression that curtail autonomy). In addition, making the 'right' decisions is neither simple nor straightforward. It triggers various skills developed over time, as well as multi-layered ethical analysis of the current as well as past similar or dissimilar situations. This, in turn, requires an inventory of one's past and current responsibilities, as well as planning and anticipation of some newly arisen responsibilities. Thinking about responsibilities entails the use of (practical) judgment. Judgment, in turn, as Hannah Arendt has aptly observed, entails the use of common sense as well as an "enlarged thought" (1982, 42). Both the enlarged thought and common sense raise the question of the role of affect. Does thinking from the point of view of someone else require putting oneself in someone else's shoes? But putting oneself in someone else's shoes does call for an empathetic reaction; are we to distinguish between empathy and sympathy, then? And if we do, on what grounds? It is clear from the outset that empathy and sympathy do not engage the

---

2   Sherwin refers to Diana Tietjens Meyers's work *Self, Society, and Personal Choice* (New York: Columbia University Press, 1989).

same skills. To clarify the matter but without going into great detail, we think it will be helpful to emphasize the difference between emotion and feeling.

Empathy, sympathy, and compassion can easily be grouped under affect. We believe, however, that there are important distinctions to be made here, distinctions which will lead us to a new type of epistemology, namely "participatory epistemology," where the agent does not passively absorb information about the world, but on the contrary, actively participates in the process of knowing.[3] Under participatory epistemology, empathy is an emotional response towards the environment.[4] We agree with Antonio Damasio (2010) that while emotions, albeit complex, are predominantly automated responses that have to do with the evolutionary development of the species, feelings are reflected responses. The feelings of sympathy and compassion, unlike empathy, allow one to put oneself in someone else's shoes, but without necessarily engaging in feeling someone else's pain and suffering. In other words, compassion involves, to peruse Nussbaum's (1985, 521) reflection on moral imagination, a highly lucid perception of reality, the type of perception that requires responsiveness (and not just passive absorption of events). It is a move away from universal moral principles, which cause moral obtuseness, and into the light of the fine details that make up the fabric of human social interaction which turns us into the type of people "on whom nothing is lost" (1985, 526). This heightened moral attention is what compassion is made of. Although Spinoza would not have approved of the use of compassion as a positive affect, we believe that he would have agreed whole-heartedly with the need for a reflected response to one's environment. The reflected response also entails a reflection upon one's current emotional state, a decision whether to engage with an empathetic reaction, as well as a set-up for (explicit or tacit) negotiation with individuals or groups (1985, 516).

To belabor the point further, for Spinoza, as already mentioned, we are (em)bodied minds. We are driven by our desires to love, be loved, prosper, or simply be. Thus, our compassionate/sympathetic attitude toward others is (em)bodied compassion. 'Getting

---

3 We echo Josephine Donovan's application of the notion of participatory epistemology as defined by Christian de Quincey (Donovan 2014; Quincey 2002).

4 For a more detailed discussion on empathy and the mirror neurons associated with it, see Thomas Metzinger (2009).

real' is not about resigning to our fate, but about living fully which, in our context, and in accordance with Spinoza, means accepting one's limitations. We think it is important to emphasize here that our limitations are not only cognitive, but also conative. Our desires and attachments are often dictated by, or, at least, co-dependent on, our relationship with bodies (our own as well as other bodies), and all the changes which this relationship undergoes as we age.

This understanding of one's limitations is the premise behind participatory epistemology, wherein the subject and the object of inquiry are not artificially separated but, on the contrary, define each other. Participatory epistemology calls for a certain amount of humility or what Eva Kittay calls "epistemic modesty" — that is, knowing what one does not know (2010, 404). In describing what it takes to care for a disabled child, Kittay concludes that, "The close attentive eye needed to care for the dependent individual gives rise to perceptual capabilities that are not shared by those who have at best a glancing acquaintance" (2010, 406). Developing a variety of perceptual sensitivities, in turn, requires expanding the subjectivity into inter-subjectivity in more than one way, and handling all the cognitive and moral dissonances that one might encounter in the process. For example, inquiring about aging and its repercussions on the self should lead us, at the end of the day, to an acceptance of dying. But this acceptance does not come easy; it takes effort and practice which eventually turn into a skill. One such skill is the skill of grieving. It is through grieving, as Lori Gruen (2014) points out, that we come face to face with, and learn how to cope with, our mortality.

We feel it is important to point out, beyond Gruen's analysis, that we see grieving as an inevitable but yet customizable and unique process. It is through grieving that we are able to understand that aging and dying are also inevitable yet customizable and unique processes. This, we hope, along with Spinoza, will take away some of the catastrophizing about aging that is so prevalent in Western cultures. Speaking in practical terms, it will allow us, for example, to consider the possibility of dying at home as opposed to dying in an institutional environment (e.g., a hospital). But on the other hand, it will prevent us from going into neo-Stoic/quietist resolve or surrendering to the inevitability of death. Human life is fragile and, to use Spinoza's intuition again, life does not succumb to the human will. However, and more importantly, it is precisely the recognition of the fragility of life that allows us to recognize the importance of attachment/relationship.

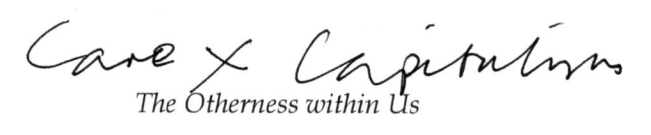

And so, accepting the fact of loss and death does not mean that we should retreat into moral shells, or create moral bubbles. It only means that we should infuse our worldview with enough humility to allow us to either live our lives the best we can, or, and often at the same time, heal and move on. This 'moving on' is particularly valuable if one intends to use ethics of care as one's moral platform. Ethics of care, which we will turn to in the next section, has a strong tendency to focus on the very process of caring, as opposed to regulations and procedures of care. The process of care can take the shape of solving concrete moral problems, or simply of recognizing the limitations of one's moral intentions. This will bring us to what Karen Emmerman, referring to Margaret Urban Walker (1995), calls "moral remainders" which are part and parcel of ethics of care as well as relational ontology (2014, 162).

The Pitfalls of Care. Moral Remainders

Relational ontology, as already noted, presupposes a self-with-others. This balancing between interdependence and independence of the self creates tension which is at the heart of the practice of care. Care, we insist along with Nel Noddings (1984), is preceding rights-based, or principle-based, notions of justice. We do not consider justice and care to be at odds with one another, but we do believe that care is, from an ethical standpoint, a more fundamental attitude toward the world. When we approach the world with care, our sense of compassion does not simply rely on already existing rules (including legal rights). We are conditioned to be both carers and cared-for. Natural care, out of which we are all born, transforms soon enough into ethical care through practice and engagement. The practice of care, however, especially from an ethical point of view, is not without problems. As Joan Tronto (2013) suggests, in an overarching capitalist framework, care, as a moral attitude as well as a practice, will always be seen as epiphenomenal and subordinate to the attitude of domination. What is more, Tronto (together with Julie White), quoting Deborah Stone, affirms that we are confronted with a "care crisis" (White and Tronto 2004, 425). The crisis referred to here is the fact that care still dominates only in the private sphere, failing to govern institutional and public relations and, thus, failing

Empathy defined

to ensure a fair allocation of care. If fairness and justice are not linked to care, Tronto and White contend, we risk further exploitation of care workers (2004, 427). Moreover, failure to see that justice, in fact, needs care leads to failure to understand that justice requires empathy and compassion (toward the other) in order to deliver its principles successfully (2004, 427). On a basic level, empathy, taken to mean a "relationship between two actual agents with distinct self-histories who manifest emotional understanding across their distinctness," combined with our earlier analysis of compassion, can and has, in fact, successfully replaced the traditional requirement of impartiality in a system of justice (2004, 430). Impartiality places on us the demand to think from the point of view of everybody, where this 'everybody' is an abstracted entity. This demand, however, falls short in both treating the individual as (em)bodied and accounting for the richness of social interactions that the individual engages in.

Tronto and White, along with many other care ethicists and relationalists, see the transition from care as a private good into care as a public good through the lens of the rhetoric of needs. Needs are juxtaposed to rights, where the latter is viewed as an abstract, unstable, and indeterminate category which fails to account for the complex social networks that we are all entangled in. It has to be made clear, however, that Tronto and White do not propose to simply substitute rights with needs; on the contrary, the suggestion is to consider needs as the basis for rights (2004, 433). This eliminates the unnecessary and harmful contrast between "the needy" and "the capable"/"autonomous" individuals. What is more, the rhetoric of needs affirms that "ultimately, all selves are needy" in the sense that all selves require care; to require care is to have a need (2004, 433). With the realization that we all need (various degrees and types of) care, the easy but very dangerous slip into the division between vulnerability and authority is avoided. Under this slip, the vulnerable are seen as the needy, who are relying on the support of the non-needy, capable members of society. However, needing the help and support of others, as Tronto and White astutely observe, is more often than not interpreted as needing the authority of others too, which, in turn, creates the false division between dependent and independent individuals (2004, 440).

To continue, along with Tronto's social criticism of care ethics, disability scholars such as Sunaura Taylor (2014) and Christine Kelly (2013) argue that there is an intrinsic tension imbedded in care itself which needs to be looked at more closely. Care, writes Kelly, is the "unstable tension among emotions, actions, and values, simultaneously pulled toward empowerment and coercion" (2013, 790). The instability of care comes from the fact that the relationship between the cared-for and the carer does not presuppose symmetry. In the model of ethics based on justice and inalienable human rights, care is interpreted along the lines of a social contract: both parties benefit from the care offered and received. In other words, I take care of my child so that she can take care of me when I am old. But if we want to change the paradigm where care itself, and not contract, is primary, then care, much like justice, can no longer be interpreted against the backdrop of cost and benefit. I should not demand that my child take care of me out of a contractual obligation of sorts as this will undermine the attitudes of love, compassion, and empathy which are the bedrock of care.

This is particularly alarming when we put care in the context of disability and aging. While we share appreciation for Noddings's safeguards of receptive attention, motivational displacement, recognition, and at least a degree of reciprocity, we believe Kelly's and Taylor's approach to be more appropriate for our purposes (Taylor 2014, note 19). Theirs is specifically geared toward care in the context of disability, and thus, it aims at disarming a potentially ableist interpretation of care where the cared-for is left in a permanently vulnerable position. We believe that the latter is in unison with Spinoza's views on *conatus* and the role of the affect in moral decisions. For Kelly and Taylor, the only way to avoid an ableist view of care where asymmetry is perceived as common, but, nonetheless outside the normal symmetrical relationship between cared-for and carer, is to view disability, along with vulnerability and dependence, as the actual norm with respect to which there are differences in degree, but not in kind.

To put this, once again, in the context of needs (versus rights), everyone has different needs which have to be met on their own terms. Some sets of needs can be met by the market while others cannot. Needs are also unstable and can be undetermined, which is why there cannot be one universal mechanism of meeting those needs. On the contrary, needs have to be brought out in the open, examined, and re-examined, allowing us to negotiate their terms of fulfillment. This is what Tronto and White call "a duty to public care" (2004, 448). The duty to public care, based on the aforementioned assumptions of universal need of care, is the only way, according to Martha Holstein, to disarm the current "deplorable system of long term care" which rests on such false cultural beliefs as the belief of the independent, autonomous, and personally responsible individual who single-handedly carves up her fate (2013, 11). Holstein, who often quotes Tronto and White, remarks that such myths are socially convenient for sustaining the status-quo of the current system of care in which care is a privilege and a luxury to be afforded by the able-bodied, wealthy members of society. The myth of personal responsibility has not only forced women to remain the primary-caregivers under the pretense of choice (when, in reality, there are hardly any viable alternatives), but it has also supported the commodification of care which can be acquired for a price instead of being done out of public duty. For Holstein, the best way to assume collective responsibility to provide care is to think of long-term care which often accompanies aging and various forms of disability. "We might start by arguing," Holstein writes, "that a justifiable moral foundation for long-term care policy starts from the position that our need for others is neither pathological, nor avoidable, nor the result of human failings but is universal and an inevitable part of human development" (2013, 24). If we are to be involved in the process of negotiating the needs of those who require long-term care, for example, we must start not by giving abstract definitions or establishing "one-size-fits-all" procedures of distribution of care services, but by asking those involved in the care relationships themselves (2013, 28).

To appeal once more to Spinoza's moral intuition, because we are (em)bodied existence, changes in the body affect the way we perceive and interact with the world. Putting things into perspective by considering the fact that we are beings in time (i.e., finite and mortal) brings to the forefront the fact of disability accompanying aging. We are all to become disabled as we age—that is, less able-bodied—due to the weakening or loss of our bodily functions. Under this paradigm, disability and dependence are not to be categorized as flaws or disadvantages. It is our belief that the experience of loss of advantage associated with old age can be re-shaped only via radical overhaul of our ethical outlook, inspired by Spinoza's de-anthropocentric world-view, and not via the introduction of new rules.

To paraphrase Margaret Urban Walker (1995, 145), if we are to see moral life as a tissue rather than a (rigid) system of rules, we are

Moral remainder

to relinquish the control we (delusionally) think we have over our moral conduct (as individuals). This will allow us to take the moral principles not only as nothing other than guidelines, but, more importantly, as moral understandings which configure, respond to, and reconfigure relations as they go. In this sense, we will witness and should anticipate moral residues and carry-overs; many moral claims will be left unfulfilled, and most moral responses will be nothing short of imperfect. So, Walker pronounces, moral remainder is the norm, not the exception (1995, 145). Thus, if we take moral remainder to be the norm(al) ethical response, we are to realize that fear of aging and the accompanying disability is not to be suppressed or repressed but to be allayed, without being eliminated; there are important lessons to be learnt from the fact of mortality.

In other words, fear of loss of ability does not have to generate only passive and, thus, purely negative affects such as sadness or even hatred (of one's own body). The realization that disability is ubiquitous is the first step towards allowing ourselves to access such social loci where the positive affects of joy, love, sympathy, compassion, etc., are at least possible, if not always pervasive. This means at least two things. First, all members of the community need to have access to this realization. We do not mean that all members have to be on the exact same page as far as disability and dependence goes. We only mean that all members of the community need to at least have access to the view we have exposed here. How, when, and to what degree they process the view is a different matter. But if a sizeable portion of the community (say, half or two thirds) operates under a false, systematically enforced pretense that autonomy is independence and stand-aloneness, this will burden the rest of the community with the responsibility of dispelling the illusion or having to deal with the consequences of the actions taken under this pretense.

And second, all members of the community have to at least entertain the possibility of non-standard, qualitatively different contributions to the community by some members. In this sense, an already severely disabled member of the community due to age and possible health complications may not be able to contribute to the life of the community in the classical/standard sense (e.g., by putting x amount of physical and mental effort into it) but this does not mean that the value of her contribution is lessened; an aging and bedridden grandfather may not be capable of bringing the grandchildren to school, or making their lunches, as is often expected of grandparents, but he can tell them stories, teach them how to behave in certain situations, or simply show them how to *be*. Favoring acting and respectively achieving above being is a moral bias, and not a closely examined one at that. As Kittay, in the transcript from the exchange between her, Peter Singer, and Jeff McMahan at the 2008 Stony Brook conference, notes, "Because what it is to be human is not a bundle of capacities. It's a way that you are, a way you are in the world, a way you are with one another" (2010, 408). In her account of caring for her disabled daughter, Sesha, Kittay emphasizes that a child, disabled or not, is never the sole responsibility of the parent; a parent cannot do her job as a parent unless others have acknowledged the worth of the child that deserves care. We believe that the same line of thinking applies to any relationship, really.

Conclusion

What we hope to have achieved in this chapter is a recommendation for an approach toward disability as a result of aging which is inspired by Spinoza's de-anthropocentric system and informed by relational ontology and care ethics. We have anchored our research in Spinoza's key ideas of *conatus* and (em)bodied mind. Following the logic of his philosophy, we have reached the conviction that autonomy interpreted as independence is a (dangerously) illusive notion, one that has the potential of causing significant damage to the moral community. We have argued that as we age and lose the power to be active, as per Spinoza's understanding of *conatus*, we become increasingly aware of the relational element of our selves. This awareness brings to the forefront the realization that our dependence upon the care of others is universal, the difference being only in degree, and not in kind.

We are convinced that accepting relationality as constitutive for the self not only better explains human interaction, but also prevents us from falling into the traps of ableist accounts of care, where the carer overpowers or uses the cared-for for personal gain. When interpreted as relational, the autonomy of the self is seen as a balancing act between the independence and inter-dependence of each individual self within the community. We believe that Spinoza's philosophy provides a fairly comprehensive account of a realistic/practical attitude toward the world, as opposed to a merely abstract and overly theoretical attitude. Thus, instead of searching for the perfect definition of care, we have aimed to describe (at least one version of) the praxis of care as the most fundamental moral attitude. The emphasis on the praxis of care allows us, in turn, along with Spinoza, to draw our attention to the nature of affect (as opposed to the rule- and principled-based approach of classical ethics) and moral need.

Using various relationalists, ethicists of care, and disability scholars, we have been able to draw important distinctions between what we consider to be the most fundamental moral attitudes—namely, empathy, sympathy, and compassion. We have argued that compassion, unlike empathy, is a moral attitude which calls for a continuous negotiation between one's own interests and the interests of others. This process of continuous negotiation, we have argued, allows the relational self to 'get real'—that is, to face the reality of one's mortality without catastrophizing the loss of ability or death. We believe that the sense of reality is intimately linked to the sense of being in the world, a sense so different and, sometimes, even opposed to the sense of achieving. The above-mentioned sense of reality/presence in the world of the self which is always a self-with-others, requires an acute awareness (i.e., moral imagination) of one's cognitive and conative limitations. The awareness and acceptance of our limitations is the groundwork for participatory epistemology, an attitude of inquiry which calls for compassionate involvement with the world, an involvement which, at the same time, avoids the pitfalls of a quietist and dispassionate resolve to one's (tragic) end as a mortal being. In this sense, we have concluded that we have no (moral or other) grounds to view disability as a result of aging as a disadvantage, leading to a presumed imminent loss of dignity. We do not dispute the fact that under the current social and economic conditions, we do experience aging as a disadvantage. However, we do believe that a more radical Spinoza-inspired and relationalist overhaul of our moral intuitions will lead us to appreciate disability as a natural state of being which, in turn, will inspire an appropriate adjustment of our goals, needs, and desires.

References

Arendt, Hannah. 1982. *Lectures on Kant's Political Philosophy*. Chicago: University of Chicago Press.

Code, Lorraine. 1991. *What Can She Know? Feminist Theory and the Construction of Knowledge*. Ithaca, NY: Cornell University Press.

Damasio, Antonio R. 2010. *Self Comes to Mind: Constructing the Conscious Brain*. New York: Pantheon.

Donovan, Josephine. 2014. "Participatory Epistemology, Sympathy, and Animal Ethics." In *Ecofeminism: Feminist Intersections with Other Animals and the Earth*, edited by Carol J. Adams and Lori Gruen, 75–90. New York: Bloomsbury.

Emmerman, Karen. 2014. "A Contextualized Ecofeminist Approach in Action." In *Ecofeminism: Feminist Intersections with Other Animals and the Earth*, edited by Carol J. Adams and Lori Gruen, 159–74. New York: Bloomsbury.

Francis, Leslie P., and Anita Silvers. 2010. "Thinking about the Good: Reconfiguring Liberal Metaphysics (or not) for People with Cognitive Disabilities." In *Cognitive Disability and Its Challenge to Moral Philosophy*, edited by Eva Feder Kittay and Licia Carlson, 237–59. New York: Wiley.

Gruen, Lori. 2013. "Entangled Empathy: An Alternate Approach to Animal Ethics." In *The Politics of Species: Reshaping Our Relationships with Other Animals*, edited by Raymond Corbey and Annette Lanjouw, 223–31. New York: Oxford University Press.

———. 2014. "Facing Death and Practicing Grief." In *Ecofeminism: Feminist Intersections with Other Animals and the Earth*, edited by Carol J. Adams and Lori Gruen, 127–42. New York: Bloomsbury.

Harding, Sandra. 1991. *Whose Science? Whose Knowledge? Thinking from Women's Lives*. Ithaca: Cornell University Press.

Holmes, Stephen, and Cass Sunstein. 1999. *The Cost of Rights: Why Liberty Depends on Taxes*. New York: Norton.

Holstein, Martha. 2013. "A Looming Dystopia: Feminism, Aging, and Community-Based Long-Term Care." *International Journal of Feminist Approaches to Bioethics* 6 (2): 6–35.

Kelly, Christine. 2013. "Building Bridges with Accessible Care: Disability Studies, Feminist Care, Scholarship, and Beyond." *Hypatia* 28 (4): 784–800.

Kittay, Eva Feder. 2010. "The Personal is Philosophical is Political: A Philosopher and Mother of Cognitively Disabled Person Sends Notes from the Battlefield." In *Cognitive Disability and Its Challenge to Moral Philosophy*, edited by Eva Feder Kittay and Licia Carlson, 393–413. New York: Wiley.

Koggel, Christine M. 1998. *Perspectives on Equality: Constructing a Relational Theory*. New York: Rowman and Littlefield.

Metzinger, Thomas. 2009. *The Ego Tunnel: The Science of the Mind and the Myth of the Self*. New York: Basic Books.

Noddings, Nel. 1984. *Caring: A Feminine Approach to Ethics and Moral Education*. Berkeley: University of California Press.

Nussbaum, Martha. 1985. "'Finely Aware and Richly Responsible': Moral Attention and the Moral Task of Literature." *The Journal of Philosophy* 82 (10): 516–29.

Quincey, Christian de. 2002. *Radical Nature: Rediscovering the Soul of Matter*. Montpelier, VT: Invisible Cities.

Sherwin, Susan. 2012. "Relational Autonomy and Global Threats." In *Being Relational: Reflections on Relational Theory and Health Law*, edited by Jennifer

J. Llewellyn and Jocelyn Downie, 13–34. Vancouver: University of British Columbia Press.
Spinoza, Benedict de. 1996. *Ethics*. Translated by E. M. Curley. London: Penguin Classics.
Taylor, Sunaura. 2014. "Interdependent Animals: A Feminist Disability Ethics-Of-Care." In *Ecofeminism: Feminist Intersections with Other Animals and the Earth*, edited by Carol J. Adams and Lori Gruen, 109–26. New York: Bloomsbury.
Tronto, Joan. 2013. *Caring Democracy: Markets, Equality, and Justice*. New York: New York University Press.
Walker, Margaret Urban. 1995. "Moral Understandings: Alternative 'Epistemology' for a Feminist Ethics." In *Justice and Care: Essential Readings in Feminist Ethics*, edited by Virginia Held, 139–52. Boulder, CO: Westview.
White, Julie A., and Joan C. Tronto. 2004. "Political Practices of Care." *Ratio Juris* 17 (4): 425–53.

About the authors

Iva Apostolova is Associate Professor at Dominican University College. Her main areas of research interest are analytic philosophy, epistemology, philosophy of mind with emphasis on memory, feminist thought, and ethics of care. She has published in *Russell: The Journal of Bertrand Russell Studies*, *Feminist Philosophy Quarterly*, and has a monograph on critical thinking.

Élaina Gauthier-Mamaril is a PhD candidate at the School of Divinity, History, and Philosophy at the University of Aberdeen. Her main research focus is on Baruch Spinoza's philosophy, with emphasis on his political thought.

Part Two

Aging and the Loss of Presence

Chapter Three

Aging and the Loss of Social Presence

Christine Overall

Abstract

"Aging and the Loss of Social Presence" by **Christine Overall** aims at exposing the worrying tendency of enforced loss of social presence of old(er) persons. To the suggestion touted by some philosophers that there are benefits for the individual from withdrawing from professional and social life in old age, Overall counter-proposes a re-examination of the way the individual herself values her own aging and dying process.

Introduction

I define social presence simply as being seen, heard, recognized, respected, and responded to within formal and informal contexts of social interaction.[1] Obviously, then, social presence is a matter of degree. One may be granted more or less attention in different contexts. Sometimes, for example when one is a member of an audience at a talk, one neither seeks nor expects a high degree of social presence (unless, perhaps, one asks a question at the end). At other times, for example when attending parties, visiting friends, or browsing in a store, one is ordinarily entitled to at least as much social presence as any other person in attendance. On occasion, one may expect, and may have earned, more social presence than others—such as when a birthday party is thrown in one's honor, or during an event recognizing one's achievements. In other words, it would be unreasonable to expect a high degree of social presence within every social interaction. But, by the same token, it would be

---

1 I thank Monique Lanoix for her comments on an earlier version of this chapter.

reasonable to expect that one would not be ignored, snubbed, overlooked, or shunned in most, if not all, of the exchanges which one has with other human beings.

As people age, they gradually lose their social presence. The degree of this loss may vary depending on an individual's gender, race, socio-economic status, and ability. But describing the situation in this way may be misleading: it is not that people somehow (carelessly, inexplicably) *lose* social presence; they are, in fact, more often *deprived* of it, intentionally or unintentionally. As Carlos Prado puts it, "In our society, the older one grows, the less seriously one is taken by younger persons. ... Growing old is losing social presence in the sense that one's social being is eroded by attitudinal shifts" (pers. comm.).

In other words, people are not always free to choose whether or not they have social presence, or how much social presence they have. While what we do can in fact influence our social presence, our behavior cannot fully determine it because our social presence is a function of others' choices, responses, and actions. In a culture where the loss of social presence is often imposed, primarily through informal social mechanisms of ignoring, redirection of attention, or even outright rejection, it is implausible to suppose that individuals can simply choose how much they are seen, heard, recognized, respected, and responded to. Some loss of social presence may be chosen, as when, for example, a person freely decides to make herself less visible in a social environment, to decline new professional commitments, to resign from organizations and committees, or to withdraw from a particular social group. But it is unlikely that anyone chooses to be rejected or shunned. A person can choose to quit work or retire, but he or she does not necessarily choose to be underestimated or overlooked.

The loss of social presence is very often something that is done *to* old(er) people—at least as much as, or even more than, it is chosen. Moreover, the expectation and enforcement of this loss may well vary across different socially defined identities. Given that we live in a society that is sexist, heterosexist, racist, ableist, and classist, some groups of people—women, those who are LGBTQ, people of color, persons with disabilities, and working class and poor people—face the imposition of loss of their social presence to a greater degree than, for example, wealthy, heterosexual, white men. Because ageism interacts with other forms of oppression, they are expected—and often urged or even coerced—to disappear more quickly.

Here are some cases illustrating some informal ways in which old(er) people (including myself, a member of the Baby Boom generation) experience the loss of social presence.

> I am standing, alone, on a street corner in the late afternoon, waiting for the light to change so that I can cross. Suddenly, a woman running along the street I am standing on crashes directly into me. I almost lose my balance, dropping my bag, but fortunately do not fall. She says "sorry" in a perfunctory way, and keeps running. (Apparently, I, an "old" woman, am invisible.) My ninety-three-year-old mother experiences the same phenomenon frequently. One time, for example, a young man briskly walked straight into her, she started to fall, and he (fortunately) grabbed her, set her on her feet, and kept going.

> A young man remarks, about his seventy-five-year-old grandmother: "Don't mind her; she's all but dead." In another situation, a younger person says, somewhat more kindly, of a much older one, "There's no need to explain to him; at his age he won't really understand." (Prado, pers. comm.)

An institutionalized form of loss of social presence is manifested in the expectation—whatever the laws may say to the contrary—that older people will withdraw from their jobs, give up leadership, become less visible, defer to younger people, get out of the way professionally, and eventually just fade away into the sunset. At age forty-four, James Shapiro, for example, boasts about asking a senior, distinguished colleague "whether it wasn't time to step aside so that a young scholar might have a chance" (2000). What Shapiro wants most is for senior academics to give up their tenure. Such people should also give up endowed chairs, stop applying for academic fellowships, stop running institutes, stop editing book series, and even cease serving on editorial boards. Failing that, he recommends that such people refuse to serve on tenure-review committees or thesis defense committees if the candidate is "two generations removed" from their own.

Despite this kind of attitude toward old(er) people who are still doing paid work, retirement is sometimes seen as akin to social death from the point of view of those who are still working. Kathleen W. Jones describes the attitudes she encountered when preparing for retirement as "condescension, a benign but emotionally painful discrimination that marginalizes faculty of a certain age." She points out that "retiree" is used as "an all-encompassing identifier," and that retirement is often conflated with "the infirmity that often accompanies 'old age'" (2016, A12).

As these examples illustrate, the loss of social presence occurs when one's physical presence is literally unperceived, when one's cognitive and psychological abilities are ignored, when one's moral worth is denied, and when one's needs are unacknowledged. Thus, it encompasses a broad range of ways in which an individual may fail to be recognized. Enforced loss of social presence is not, of course, confined to those who are aging; it may well be inflicted on young people, particularly those who are the "wrong" gender, race, or socio-economic class. But the focus of this chapter will be the enforced loss of social presence imposed upon older or elderly persons.

The philosophical question I wish to raise is, can the enforced loss of social presence be justified? What reasons might be given to defend the enforced loss of social presence of aging people? I shall present and evaluate two possible justifications, both of them well-represented in the philosophical and popular literature by bioethicists, cultural commentators, and supposed experts on aging. The first concerns the alleged benefits of loss of social presence to the individual him/herself. The second concerns the alleged benefits of individuals' loss of social presence for the broader society, but particularly for young(er) people. Both of these justifications, I shall argue, are deeply inadequate.

The Loss of Social Presence Benefits the Individual

According to some, the process of aging includes a gradual withdrawal and disappearance of the individual from the human community — in other words, the gradual loss of social presence. This process is claimed to be both normal and valuable, because it serves the individual who experiences it as a good preparation for death. To make this point, bioethicist Leon Kass quotes approvingly from the essays of the sixteenth-century philosopher Michel de Montaigne:

> I notice that in proportion as I sink into sickness, I naturally enter into a certain disdain for life. I find that I have much more trouble digesting this resolution when I am in health than when I have a fever. Inasmuch as I no longer cling so hard to the good things of life when I begin to lose the use and pleasure of them, I come to view death with

much less frightened eyes. This makes me hope that the farther I get from life and the nearer to death, the more easily I shall accept the exchange. ... If we fell into such a change [decrepitude] suddenly, I don't think we could endure it. But when we are led by Nature's hand down a gentle and virtually imperceptible slope, bit by bit, one step at a time, she rolls us into this wretched state and makes us familiar with it; so that we find no shock when youth dies within us, which in essence and in truth is a harder death than the complete death of a languishing life or the death of old age; inasmuch as the leap is not so cruel from a painful life as from a sweet and flourishing life to a grievous and painful one. (Montaigne quoted in Kass 2003, 26)

The idea expressed in this passage is that physical and mental decline and the loss of social presence serve important psychological functions in an individual's life: as the pleasures and practices of ordinary life gradually wither away, one becomes accustomed to the miseries of aging and ready for the complete loss that is death.

Arguably, Montaigne had in mind the kinds of changes that were, in his time, the almost inevitable fallout of declining health. Kass, however, is ready to argue that the loss of social presence is so important in our lives that societies should take steps to reinforce it and ensure that it continues. He extolls the idea that "we are born, age, replace ourselves, decline, and die—and know it" (2003, 27), and he holds that the "decline" stage is so valuable that it must be preserved.

Like Montaigne, Kass believes that if elderly people remained fully immersed and involved in life, they would not be ready to die:

> Would it be good if each and all of us lived like light bulbs, burning as brightly from beginning to end, then popping off without warning, leaving those around us suddenly in the dark? Or is it perhaps better that there be a shape to life, everything in its due season, the shape also written, as it were, into the wrinkles of our bodies that live it? (2003, 25)

These questions are not rhetorical. Kass clearly believes that "burning brightly" until the end of life is a bad thing. Instead of burning out, it is better to dwindle away to nothing. Ultimately, Kass's claim is not only that our bodies must slow down and decline in order to prepare us for death, but also that there should be a gradual slowing down, a fading out, a disengagement of our minds and personalities, and a surrendering of our relationships and connections to the world of activity. Furthermore, his claim entails the belief that we should value fading out as part of the narrative arc of the human life, which dictates that old(er) people should withdraw from involvement in the social world. It is this withdrawal, he holds, that will help people to resign themselves to and accept their ultimate withdrawal—death.

For these reasons, Kass worries that medical advances that enable people to "avoid senility, crippling arthritis, the need for hearing aids and dentures, and the degrading dependencies of old age" will make people "even more disinclined to exit" their lives. He warns that the prevention of the diseases and impairments commonly associated with old age would increase "the fear and loathing of death," and make it "even more of an affront" (2001). A period of suffering and disability in old age, on the other hand, encourages acquiescence to the inevitability of death. Kass is thus literally saying that being healthy and able-bodied, competent and autonomous, up until one's death would be bad for human beings. According to this account, the loss of social presence in old age is in the interests of aging individuals themselves.

However, there are many flaws in this perspective. It is impossible to see why being wholly engaged with and immersed in life right up until death is such a bad thing for individuals. First, the continuing and deepening withdrawal from life that Kass advocates bears little or no connection to most people's desires for their old age. Most people do not value "decline". Most people think that an old age spent in dementia, unable to recognize one's family and friends, unable to recall one's past life, unable to participate in one's typical activities, interactions, and communications, and entirely dependent on the mercies of others, is wholly unattractive. Most people do not aspire to losing their sight and hearing, and spending their last years immobilized and in pain. Moreover, it seems highly improbable that the friends, families, and caregivers of old people wish to see them in a state of disengagement and incompetence. The kind of withdrawal advocated by Kass, then, is actually contrary to the hopes of most people.

Furthermore, there is empirical evidence indicating that having strong social ties promotes good health. In industrialized nations,

> studies consistently show that individuals with the lowest level of involvement in social relationships are more likely to die than those with greater involvement. ... Moreover, this finding held even when socioeconomic status, health behaviors, and other variables that might

influence mortality, were taken into account. Social ties also reduce mortality risk among adults with documented medical conditions. ... Several recent review articles provide consistent and compelling evidence linking a low quantity or quality of social ties with a host of conditions, including development and progression of cardiovascular disease, recurrent myocardial infarction, atherosclerosis, autonomic dysregulation, high blood pressure, cancer and delayed cancer recovery, and slower wound healing. (Umberson and Montez 2010, S55)

Thus, because maintaining social presence promotes good physical health, there are sound health-related reasons for people not to want to lose their social presence as they age. By contrast, Kass's argument about the supposed need for decline and disengagement as preparation for death has a very shocking implication: that what aging individuals should do is allow or even encourage their health to degenerate and their minds to deteriorate as a preparation for death, and that social and health care policies should in fact facilitate people's degeneration and deterioration in old age. In other words, Kass's argument is a prescription for both personal self-destruction, and the social neglect of elderly people. I know of no doctors, therapists, teachers, or spiritual leaders who would recommend such an approach to old age, whether taken individually or collectively. The absurdity of Kass's advocacy for the "degrading dependencies of old age" (2001) is evident.

In addition, we need to interrogate what exactly this much-vaunted decline is supposed to prepare us for. Death itself is simply the terminus of life, the line between existence and non-existence. Ceasing to exist is not something for which one could possibly prepare, because it is not the kind of thing for which one *can* prepare. But perhaps decline and disengagement are supposed to be preparation for what supposedly comes *after* death. Even if there is some sort of after-death existence for us, it is hard to believe that a period of increasing pain, incapacity, and isolation can be a good preparation for it. The kinds of things that earn one passage to an afterlife, according to most religious and spiritual teachings, are good works, devoted prayer, contemplation of scriptures, and love for other beings. These are not the sorts of activities that can be engaged in very well from an attenuated physical and psychological condition, and one's diminished social presence would only make them even more difficult to engage in.

Maybe Kass's intended meaning is that a period of decline and loss of social presence is preparation for the *process* of dying. But what Kass is advocating sounds like the *prolongation of dying*. How can more time spent dying prepare one for the process of dying? Or maybe Kass's idea is that decline and loss of social presence prepare us for the fact that life simply ends. But if we assume (because we have no evidence to the contrary) that there is no further existence after we die, then there is nothing to prepare for. By definition one cannot experience non-existence. Moreover, if death is non-existence, then there is no way in which one can somehow look back, from the perspective of being dead, and compare one's pre-death existence to one's post-death existence. Unless one smuggles in religious assumptions about an afterlife, there is nothing about the termination of life that requires that we prepare ourselves. It is not a journey for which one has to pack, and it is not a transition to another form of life for which one must be educated. It is merely non-existence.

To the contrary, I suggest that the end of life is like the end of anything else we might value. We don't usually hope that worthwhile experiences will decline and deteriorate in order to prepare us for their cessation. For example, if we go away on an interesting and enjoyable trip, we don't usually want it to become a miserable experience toward the conclusion of the trip so that we are prepared for it to end. Rather, we want to enjoy the occasion right up until the moment that the trip is over. Similarly, it seems reasonable to want to live—and to take steps to live—as well as possible, in as healthy and engaged and socially present a manner as is achievable, for as close to the end of one's life as is possible. And it is entirely reasonable to advocate and vote for a health care system and a social safety network that support and enable individuals to live healthy, autonomous, active, and connected lives for as long as possible in old age.

True, if one is hale and hearty and deeply involved in life until just before death, one may not be happy to die and may even dread the end of one's life—just as people are seldom happy to foresee the end of any good experience. But, people for whom this dread is a serious psychological problem could deal with it by cultivating peace of mind, seeing a therapist who specializes in dealing with fears of the end of life, learning how to meditate, or even (!) studying philosophy. But it is impossible to see why spending months or years in a state of incompetence, withdrawal, and impairment is better than being aware and engaged and actively dealing with one's own impending mortality. Kass wants to say that if one remains engaged and immersed in social life in extreme old age, one will fear death more. But if one is truly engaged and immersed in life, then it is less likely that one will be spending a lot of time fearing death. Indeed, if—as he advocates—one's health were declining and one were withdrawing from social life, one might be *more* likely to spend time worrying about and fearing death, because one would have more time to do so, fewer alternate activities to engage in, and a greater number of reasons to feel unhappy. Kass's recommendation, then, is a prescription for making the anticipation of death worse, not better.

Finally, if one's time on earth is becoming more and more limited (as of course everyone's is), why not enjoy that time and celebrate one's life? Why not savor our connections to each other, remaining involved in social life to whatever extent we can manage? Being a long-functioning lightbulb is a good thing! I endorse Hunter S. Thompson's widely quoted and paraphrased comment: "Life should not be a journey to the grave with the intention of arriving safely in a pretty and well-preserved body, but rather to skid in broadside in a cloud of smoke, thoroughly used up, totally worn out, and loudly proclaiming 'Wow! What a Ride!'."² I'm not necessarily advocating uncontrolled profligacy, unrestrained hedonism, and licentiousness, but I am saying there are no advantages, vis-à-vis one's death, in withdrawing from life and deliberately losing or being required to give up social presence.

The Loss of Social Presence Benefits Other People

The second reason that is commonly given to justify the loss of social presence by old people is that it benefits others—*not* older people themselves, but rather those who are young or middle-aged.

---

2 See, for example, http://www.goodreads.com/quotes/47188-life-should-not-be-a-journey-to-the-grave-with. There are various versions of this quotation. For example: "Life should NOT be a journey to the grave with the intention of arriving safely in an attractive and well preserved body, but rather to skid in sideways, chocolate in one hand, champagne in the other, body thoroughly used up, totally worn out and screaming 'WOO HOO what a ride!'" (https://eflorence.wordpress.com/2007/01/03/%E2%80%9Csliding-homewoo-hoo-what-a-ride%E2%80%9D/). See also: https://answers.yahoo.com/question/index?qid=20081214093617AA273kw. All weblinks accessed May 2017.

The gradual loss of social presence is enforced through an ideology that attempts to naturalize the process, making it seem not only normal but also desirable, commendable, and inevitable. Thus, for example, Francis Fukuyama speaks of "[t]he *natural* tendency of one generation to get out of the way of the up-and-coming one" (2002, 65, my emphasis). He refers to this process with the sunny label "generational succession" (66), but it's evident that what he means is the voluntary, or, if necessary, enforced loss of social presence on the part of older people.

He apparently sees no need to explain what makes this change supposedly "natural". Nonetheless, even by his account, its origins seem to be at least partly *social*. The reason for the need for "generational succession," he says, is that people's life views and preferences are shaped by specific generational life events, and "it is very difficult to get them to change broad outlooks" (66). He provides no empirical evidence for this claim, but instead gives two invented examples. First, "[a] black person who grew up in the old South has a hard time seeing a white cop as anything but an untrustworthy agent of an oppressive system of racial segregation, regardless of whether this makes sense given the realities of life in a northern city" (66). Second, "Those who lived through the Great Depression cannot help feeling uneasy at the lavish spending habits of their grandchildren" (66).

According to Fukuyama, the person of color's distrust and the elderly person's uneasiness cannot rest on good, objective reasons. But in both cases, we can easily see that the individuals who sustain such beliefs from earlier in their lives may well have good evidence for doing so. His very own examples tell against themselves: there may be plenty of good reasons for members of racialized minorities and older people to hold on to viewpoints forged early in life. People's beliefs are indeed shaped by "generational life events," and that is not necessarily a bad thing, since broad social forces are slow to change. Younger generations could learn a lot from older people's perceptions of racism and their experiences of living frugally. Far from being outlooks to be abandoned, they should be valued and passed on. Fukuyama's very examples show that if "generational succession" is taken to mean not learning from the life experience of one's elders, then "generational succession" is a mistake.

Kass, not surprisingly, agrees with Fukuyama about the supposed need for "generational succession": "What would the relations between the generations be like if there never came a point at which a son surpassed his father in strength or vigor? What incentive would there be for the old to make way for the young, if the old slowed down little and had no reason to think of retiring …? One cannot think of enhancing the vitality of the old without retarding the maturation of the young" (Kass 2003). Similarly, Daniel Callahan (2013), though still publishing ageist screeds well into his eighties,[3] worries that "[a] society where the aged stay in place for many more years would surely throw [the] fruitful passing of the generations into chaos." And according to Shapiro, the man, quoted earlier, who boasts about asking a senior colleague to retire,

> Intellectual progress depends on a complicated intergenerational exchange. It is predicated on the assumption that those who control the mechanisms by which scholarship is made possible—tenure, endowed chairs, service on editorial boards, fellowship and tenure-review committees, directorships of patronage-dispensing institutes —will turn them over to the next generation after an appropriate time, even as their mentors did for them. (2000)

Like Fukuyama, Kass, Callahan, and Shapiro are making claims about the supposed cultural need for the decline and disappearance of elderly people's social presence. According to all of them, the flourishing, well-being, and indeed the very presence of old people somehow compromise the flourishing, well-being, and presence of the young. Thus, relationships between old and young are understood as a zero-sum game; the young cannot thrive unless the old wither.

But even in a context of limited resources, this seems false. It is hard to imagine any other social group being told that it must decline and withdraw in order to enhance the well-being of an up-and-coming group. It is also condescending in the extreme to suggest that younger generations will remain forever immature if

---

3 It is truly ironic that pundits like Callahan continue to advance doctrines that are likely to be harmful to people in their own age cohort. Unlike their peers, they still get noticed and, presumably, respected in many ways. It must be assumed that they are rendered somewhat immune to the effects of enforced loss of social presence because of other forms of privilege they retain, based on their gender, race, socioeconomic class, and the (sometimes puzzling) esteem in which they are held. But in addition, of course, they are advancing views that enable younger people to feel not only justified but even virtuous for behavior that, if directed at persons in any other social group, would be recognized for what it is: morally odious.

older ones remain vital, since that implies significant psychological weakness in young people. And if some individuals' flourishing is dependent on others' decline, that flourishing is, surely, immoral.

Moreover, these claims overlook the fact that the young are related and connected to the old. Old people are the parents, grandparents, and great-grandparents of the young. Old people teach, mentor, guide, and advise younger ones. They often take care of some young ones and employ others. Being old is the future of everyone who manages not to die. It is more likely that the young cannot thrive *unless* the old do—and vice versa.

There is tremendous handwringing in the press, in social media, and on television about the supposed "burden" that older people generate for younger ones.[4] How, then, can it be in the interests of young people for older people to decline and withdraw? If older people remain as active as possible, engaged in the world, working to the extent they can or otherwise interacting with the community, they are surely contributing to the broader well-being of the whole of society and thereby reducing the so-called "burden" on younger generations.

Fukuyama himself admits that there are many contexts—in politics and business, for example—where people are reluctant to "get out of the way" and do not do so. He therefore prescribes what can only be labelled as an enforced loss of social presence in order to rid society of people with the temerity to hang on to beliefs derived from their own experiences of their society. In the interests of adjusting rapidly to political, social, and intellectual change, societies will, he says, have to "establish rules mandating *constant retraining and downward social mobility* at later stages in life" (2002, 66, my emphasis). In other words, let's take those old people, subject them to propaganda, manipulate their minds, and forcibly withdraw them from their current social connections and positions.

If society chooses not to do so, or if older people refuse to be brainwashed and to step aside, or down, from the positions they have achieved, Fukuyama predicts a societal apocalypse: "Generational warfare," he says, "will join class and ethnic conflict as a major dividing line in society. Getting older people out of the way of

---

4   As Linda Marsa (2016) notes, "The fear is that, as baby boomers ... march lockstep into 'retirement age' ... there will be fewer young workers to support us old folk, which will curb spending, strain the healthcare system, and drain Social Security and Medicare benefits."

younger ones will become a significant struggle, and societies may have to resort to impersonal, institutionalized forms of ageism in a future of expanded life expectancies" (2002, 67). In the struggle for finite resources, the old must give way to the young.

If these predictions seem extravagant, there are more of them from other philosophers who are committed to the enforced loss of social presence of aging people. Philosopher John Hardwig is well-known for his advocacy of the existence of a "duty to die": the moral responsibility not just to get out of the way, not just to retire and withdraw from society, but to deliberately *end one's life* if and when one becomes a psychological, medical, financial, or social "burden" to one's family — or even *before* becoming a burden to them:

> [T]here is a duty to refuse life-prolonging medical treatment and also a duty to complete advance directives refusing life-prolonging treatment. But a duty to die can go well beyond that. There can be a duty to die before one's illnesses would cause death, even if treated only with palliative measures. In fact, there may be a fairly common responsibility to end one's life in the absence of any terminal illness at all. Finally, there can be a duty to die when one would prefer to live. (2000, 121)

I suggest that belief in and support for an alleged duty to die are simply extreme manifestations of the pressures actually and presently aimed at depriving aging people of social presence. Hardwig is clear about what he regards as the diminishing social value of older people, arguing that "there is more duty to die as you grow older" (2000, 90) because at that point, regardless of how good or bad your life is, you have less to lose in terms of years of life and life plans (2000, 129). As Marilyn Bennett, who supports the notion of a duty to die, accurately notes,

> [T]he assertion of a duty [to die] sounds more like an insult — 'Why can't they just stop breathing?' or 'Drop dead' — than a reasoned moral position. It seems to imply that people can become so tiresome, expensive, or otherwise burdensome that they ought to take steps to eliminate themselves from our presence. Too bad, the idea would go, the rest of us are not in a position to eliminate you, but surely you must see how wrong it is of you to go on requiring our attention, using up our resources, and generally making a nuisance for the rest of us. (2000, 43–44)

Even in cultures where there is provision for a social safety net, says Hardwig, the duty to die will sooner or later prevail, and elderly people are the obvious individuals on whom to place that duty: "Medical progress will almost certainly overwhelm our social will—perhaps even our social ability—to pay for all needed medical treatments for everyone and also for care needed by all debilitated, demented, or chronically ill citizens. A finite world with finite resources seems to preclude indefinitely increasing socially provided payment for health care" (2000, 180).[5]

Critics of Hardwig's duty to die have rightly foreseen the consequences it could have for those who fail to fall in line: "I am horrified by the thought that some such duty would become a part of health policy, complete with reimbursement schemes based on whether people fulfill this responsibility and penalties for those who are 'irresponsible' and refuse to die in a timely and efficient fashion" (Churchill in Hardwig 2000, 155). Bennett, in support of a duty to die, speculates that individuals who refuse to act on their (supposed) duty to die might lose their "right to continue using health care resources" (2000, 48). But even barring any formal institutionalization of a duty to die, the informal social consequences could also be serious: "[O]ctogenarians who are not ready to die [may] be publicly shamed as the moral community shuns them" (Hentoff in Hardwig 2000, 138). Bennett's conception of the scope of the duty to die, for example, goes beyond persons who are simply a "burden" on their family, and includes elderly people whose money their young heirs could make good use of (2000, 45).

I suggest that arguments about the alleged benefits of older persons' loss of social presence reflect, in part, an assumption that old people have "had their day," "lived long enough," and should be willing to quietly disappear, not only from public view and public support, but even from private relationships. For his part, Hardwig endorses what he says is one old woman's advice to other "seniors": "'Don't ever, *ever* say to your children, "Promise me you won't ever put me in a nursing home." And if you've already said that, go to your children, take it back, and apologize for having said that'" (anonymous woman quoted in Hardwig 2000, 171, Hardwig's emphasis; see also 198). Similarly, bioethicist Ezekiel Emmanuel claims to want to die by seventy-five, a point by which he figures

---

5   Similarly, Callahan (2013), who has a history of critiquing life extension, asks whether "we can afford" to live longer—even though he acknowledges that he himself has had a "seven-hour emergency heart operation to save [his] life" and is on oxygen at night for emphysema.

he will no longer be creative and vital, because old age "transforms how people experience us, relate to us, and, most important, remember us. We are no longer remembered as vibrant and engaged but as feeble, ineffectual, even pathetic" (2014).

This latter comment (inadvertently) reveals the real force behind the advocacy of elderly people's loss of social presence: the negative, ageist views that younger people have of those who are old. In the words of anti-ageist writer Ashton Applewhite, the hallmark of ageism "is the irrational insistence that older people are Other, not Us—not even future us—and [people] go to great lengths to distance [themselves] from that future state" (2016, 18). It is ironic that in a culture now so focused on identities of many kinds, the repression and erasure of the identities of aging people is seen as desirable and somehow socially progressive.

Conclusion

My topic in this chapter has been the loss of social presence that is enforced by others, not the loss of social presence that is genuinely chosen by an individual. Samuel Scheffler points out that people sometimes choose to withdraw from relationships, and he argues that such a withdrawal can in some cases be reasonable:

> If people genuinely and appropriately value their important relationships, it strikes me as unreasonable to expect of them—as the years go by and as more and more of those relationships become archived [ended by the death of the other person]—that they should seek to develop new relationships. It is not unreasonable for them to feel instead that their lives as social creatures are primarily defined by their existing interpersonal histories and slowly to withdraw from active engagement with the ongoing social world. Doing this can be a reasonable way of responding to the cumulative normative significance of their archived relationships, the cumulative normative significance of what they have lost. (2016, 515–16)

Of course, even the latter kinds of cases should sometimes be an occasion for concern. An individual who chooses to withdraw from the world out of depression or despair, or because s/he has come to feel that social engagement is unrewarding or difficult, is deserving of support and assistance, not passive acquiescence in her/his withdrawal. Bertrand Russell likewise advocated a kind of withdrawal, in old age, from the bustle and rush of activities and interactions that characterize the first parts of life. He wrote:

> An individual human existence should be like a river: small at first, narrowly contained within its banks, and rushing passionately past rocks and over waterfalls. Gradually the river grows wider, the banks recede, the waters flow more quietly, and in the end, without any visible break, they become merged in the sea, and painlessly lose their individual being. The man who, in old age, can see his life in this way, will not suffer from the fear of death, since the things he cares for will continue. And if, with the decay of vitality, weariness increases, the thought of rest will not be unwelcome. (1956, 52–53)

Nonetheless, Russell was not advocating a complete withdrawal. He cautioned against "undue absorption in the past. It does not do to live in memories, in regrets for the good old days, or in sadness about friends who are dead. One's thoughts must be directed to the future, and to things about which there is something to be done" (1956, 51). He added: "I should wish to die *while still at work*, knowing that others will carry on what I can no longer do and content in the thought that what was possible has been done" (1956, 53, my emphasis). In other words, Russell advocated continued engagement with the world in old age, and he would surely have been horrified by the notion that older people must be forced to withdraw from it.

In this chapter I have shown that the enforced loss of social presence by old(er) people is justified neither by benefits to old(er) people themselves nor by benefits to other people. Furthermore, I have shown that it is implausible to suppose that the loss of social presence by elderly persons is somehow valuable for its own sake. I therefore conclude that, in the absence of other discernible justifications, the enforced loss of social presence on the part of aging individuals cannot legitimately be defended or supported. Older people are as much entitled to be engaged and involved in our social world as younger ones are. Indeed, humanity needs them to be.

References

Applewhite, Ashton. 2016. *This Chair Rocks: A Manifesto against Ageism*. N.p.: Networked Books.

Bennett, Marilyn. 2000. "Do We Have a Duty to Die?" In *Is There a Duty To Die?*, edited by James M. Humber and Robert F. Almeder, 43–59. Totowa, NJ: Humana Press.

Callahan, Daniel. 2013. "On Dying After Your Time." *The New York Times*. November 30.
http://www.nytimes.com/2013/12/01/opinion/sunday/on-dying-after-your-time.html

Emanuel, Ezekiel. 2014. "Why I Hope to Die at 75." *The Atlantic*. October. https://www.theatlantic.com/magazine/archive/2014/10/why-i-hope-to-die-at-75/379329/

Fukuyama, Francis. 2002. *Our Posthuman Future: Consequences of the Biotechnology Revolution*. New York: Picador.

Hardwig, John, with Nat Hentoff, Dan Callahan, Larry Churchill, Felicia Cohn, and Joanne Lynn. 2000. *Is There a Duty to Die? And Other Essays in Medical Ethics*. New York: Routledge.

Jones, Kathleen W. 2016. "Finding the Path to Retirement." *The Chronicle of Higher Education*. November 27: A12. http://www.chronicle.com/article/Finding-the-Path-to-Retirement/238497

Kass, Leon R. 2001. "L'Chaim and Its Limits: Why Not Immortality?" *First Things*. May. The Institute on Religion and Public Life. https://www.firstthings.com/article/2001/05/lchaim-and-its-limits-why-not-immortality

___. 2003. "Ageless Bodies, Happy Souls: Biotechnology and the Pursuit of Perfection." *The New Atlantis: A Journal of Theology and Science* (Spring): 9–28. http://www.thenewatlantis.com/publications/ageless-bodies-happy-souls

Marsa, Linda. 2016. "Retiring Retirement." *Nautilus*. May 26. http://nautil.us/issue/36/aging/retiring-retirement

Russell, Bertrand. 1956. "How to Grow Old." In *Portraits from Memory and Other Essays*, 52–53. New York: Simon and Schuster.

Scheffler, Samuel. 2016. "Aging as a Normative Phenomenon." *Journal of the American Philosophical Association* 21: 505–22. https://doi.org/10.1017/apa.2017.4

Shapiro, James. 2000. "Please Place This in an Appropriate Colleague's Mailbox." *The Chronicle of Higher Education*. April 14: A88. http://www.chronicle.com/article/Please-Place-This-in-an/30515

Umberson, Debra, and Jennifer Karas Montez. 2010. "Social Relationships and Health: A Flashpoint for Health Policy." *Journal of Health and Social Behavior* 51: S54–S66.

About the author

Christine Overall is Professor Emerita of Philosophy at Queen's University, Kingston, Ontario, where she holds a University Research Chair. Her main areas of research and publication are feminist philosophy and applied ethics. Her book, *Aging, Death, and Human Longevity: A Philosophical Inquiry* (University of California Press, 2003) won the Canadian Philosophical Association's 2005 book prize and the Royal Society of Canada's Abbyann D. Lynch Medal in Bioethics in 2006. Her most recent books are *Why Have Children? The Ethical Debate* (MIT Press, 2012), and the edited volume, *Pets and People: The Ethics of Our Relationships with Companion Animals* (Oxford University Press, 2017).

Chapter Four

LGBT Elders, Isolation, and Loneliness:
An Existentialist Analysis

Tim R. Johnston

Abstract

"LGBT Elders, Isolation, and Loneliness: An Existential Analysis" by **Tim R. Johnston** examines evidence showing that isolation and loneliness have a profoundly negative impact on the individual's well-being because they remove, especially from older LGBT adults, temporal rhythms, thus making it difficult for them to maintain a sense of self and precariously plunging them into the past, as opposed to allowing them to be involved in future-oriented projects.

Introduction

As human beings, we need to find ourselves located within a shared social sense of time. On the most basic level, this involves understanding ourselves to be living in the same point in history, and using various tools and cultural norms to coordinate our behaviors and expectations. We have watches, time zones, schedules, calendars, school years, seasonal events, award shows, and elections — all of which create a shared temporal world and help us to coordinate and mark the passage of time as we move from childhood, into our adult years, and on to old age.

Many older adults are isolated and/or feeling lonely. Lesbian, Gay, Bisexual, and Transgender (LGBT[1]) older adults report particularly high rates of loneliness and isolation. As people age, family provides a multigenerational social and support network, but many

---

1   I use the acronym LGBT in this context rather than the increasingly common LGBTQ or Queer because many older adults do not like, and may have traumatic memories triggered by, the term "queer".

LGBT older adults may not have relationships with their families of origin, and instead rely on families of choice which are often networks and relationships with people their own age. This puts LGBT older adults at greater risk of becoming isolated or lonely as their partners die, their friends become less mobile, and they cannot participate comfortably or fully in spaces in which they feel safe being open about their identity. Research is starting to show that isolation and loneliness have a significant negative impact on a person's health and well-being and can lead to measurable health disparities. There is also evidence suggesting that one of the determining factors for happiness is a robust and stable set of social relationships.[2] Much of the conversation on this topic is focused on such questions as: can elders visit one another, connect with transportation, join groups, and find social supports? Connection is a crucial aspect of reducing isolation and loneliness, but as our society ages, I want to ask whether there is a temporal aspect to isolation or loneliness. What is the impact of detaching oneself from the shared rhythms of daily, monthly, and annual life? Are isolation and loneliness connected to the sense of nearing the end of life, and what can a temporal analysis tell us about the effectiveness of different programs and activities intended to reduce isolation and loneliness?

In this chapter I put forward that one of the reasons isolation and loneliness can be harmful is that they remove older adults from temporal rhythms, making it more difficult to maintain a coherent identity or sense of self, which disconnects them from their communities and encourages reminiscence rather than looking toward future projects. By examining research from geriatric specialists as well as theories of queer temporality, the first section draws a distinction between isolation and loneliness, notes their impact on health, and outlines the reasons why LGBT older adults are more likely to experience isolation and/or loneliness than their heterosexual and cisgender peers. Specifically, many LGBT people have been barred from the typical ways in which we form and sustain families (e.g., marriage, reproductive technologies), and may also have been disowned by their families of origin. Next, I turn to the work of Simone de Beauvoir and Jean-Paul Sartre to argue that isolation is

---

2   See, for example, the information coming from the Harvard Study of Adult Development, available at http://www.adultdevelopmentstudy.org (accessed January 2018).

a social problem best approached through social justice and a critique of what we today call neoliberalism, whereas loneliness is best examined through the existentialist concern for transcendence and action. The final section analyses existing literature on interventions aimed at reducing isolation and loneliness. I argue that existentialist political commitments and philosophy can add nuance and direction to new programs that aim to prevent or reduce both isolation and loneliness. If I am correct, preventing or reducing isolation and loneliness requires much more than the occasional visit or activity. It requires both programs and interventions that provide the support and infrastructure necessary to integrate older adults, and projects that maintain their connection to a meaningful future.

Aging as an LGBT Person

Social isolation and loneliness have been linked to negative health outcomes and premature mortality. There are a number of reasons for this, including that people who are isolated or lonely often have difficulty accessing preventative medical care and experience increased stress, increased substance use, and higher rates of mental health disorders. A meta-analysis published in 2015 found that, "the risk associated with social isolation and loneliness is comparable with well-established risk factors for mortality, including those identified by the U.S. Department of Health and Human Services" (Holt-Lunstad et al. 2015, 235). The negative impacts of isolation and loneliness are often compared to those of smoking or alcohol abuse. Some researchers consider loneliness to be the psychological manifestation of isolation, but increasingly — and I think correctly — both phenomena are treated as related but nonetheless separate. Several studies have tried to tease apart the impact of being physically isolated — which may be a person's choice or preference — and feeling lonely. A study of 6500 older people published in 2013 found that "social isolation is associated with higher mortality in older men and women" but that its effect was "independent of the emotional experience of loneliness" (Steptoe et al. 2013, 5799). Another study, this time analyzing survey responses from over 11,000 people, also found that "loneliness and isolation are not highly correlated with one another" (Coyle and Dugan 2012, 1356).

Isolation often looks like living alone, having a small social network, difficulty with transportation, and generally being disconnected from other people. Loneliness, or what is sometimes referred to as subjective isolation, is an emotional and psychological state that can and does exist independently of isolation. Loneliness describes a person's sense of connection, belonging, or negative evaluation of the strength and quality of their social relationships.[3] An isolated person may choose that lifestyle and not feel lonely, while a well-connected person living in a crowded city may still feel lonely. Researchers and activists interested in isolation and loneliness often focus on older adults because many of the precipitating causes for becoming more isolated or lonely are a part of the aging process. These common causes include the death of a partner, relocation, change of role (such as retirement, or no longer parenting children who live at home), and changes in mental or physical health.[4]

There are many reasons why LGBT older adults experience higher rates of loneliness and isolation. They may not be in touch with their biological or legal families because they have been disowned, or coming out has made the relationships strained and uncomfortable. LGBT older adults often rely on a network of friends, usually around their own age and with similar difficulties with respect to mobility, transportation, or health. A 2014 survey by SAGE, the largest advocacy group for LGBT older adults in the United States, found that 40% of LGBT older adults say that their networks have grown smaller, compared to 27% of non-LGBT older adults (SAGE 2014, 9). It is quite common for LGBT older adults to be open about their LGBT identity only within a close circle of trusted people. As that circle shrinks, they feel afraid to come out to new people or providers, meaning that fewer and fewer people know that they are LGBT. The same SAGE study found that 40% of respondents in their 60s and 70s say that their health care providers do not know their sexual orientation, and two-thirds of transgender

---

    3   Specific studies may define to measure these two terms differently, the general distinction between isolation and loneliness is common across the literature. See, for example, Steptoe et al. 2013. See also, Dr. Verena Menec's blog post "Loneliness and social isolation are important health risks in the elderly," available at https://www.mcmasteroptimalaging.org/blog/detail/professionals-blog/2016/04/08/loneliness-and-social-isolation-are-important-health-risks-in-the-elderly (accessed June 2018).
    4   For a comprehensive review of the literature on aging, isolation, and loneliness, see AARP Foundation 2012.

older adults anticipate having limited access to health care as they age (SAGE 2014, 8). In a review of a large longitudinal data set, Karen Fredriksen-Goldsen and her team of researchers note:

> Older gay and bisexual men have significantly fewer children in the household than do heterosexuals and are more likely to live alone, which corroborates findings in other population-based studies. Higher rates of living alone may be related to the increased likelihood of the loss of a partner to AIDS. It is also possible that structural factors do not support committed relationships or legal marriage among same-sex partners. LGB older adults who live alone are likely at risk for social isolation, which has been linked to poor mental and physical health, cognitive impairment, and premature morbidity and mortality in the general elderly population. (2013, 1807)

One useful lens for understanding why this is the case is to look at the different temporalities afforded to people based on their identities. For example, a gay man living with AIDS in the 1980s had a very different outlook on the future and how to structure his time than a man living without the disease. A woman forced to work the night shift will engage with time differently than a woman who works during the day. Alternate temporalities are often measured against the normative temporality in which daily life is structured around the work day, and over many years is focused on raising children. That is to say that, in the United States, especially in the years following World War II, people were pressured to conform to a kind of temporal organization focused on the reproduction of the nuclear family. Everything from theories of psychological maturation to the way we structured the work place focused on rewarding people who moved from adolescence into adulthood, had children, worked through their entire adult lives, and then retired. We can think of these as normative narratives that control our relationship to time. Childhood is a time of play, adolescence that of burgeoning adventure, adulthood of responsibility and child-rearing, and these were to be followed by retirement. These normative temporalities guide who we are meant to spend our time with, and people who did not conform to this narrative are often cast as immature, failures, or morally suspect.

Alison Kafer provides another clear example of the homogenizing influence of normative temporalities. Reflecting on people living with various disabilities and the way in which they move through the world, Kafer articulates a notion of "crip time"—a "flex time" where the "flexibility... [is] not only an accommodation to those who need 'more' time but also, and perhaps especially, a challenge to normative and normalizing expectations of pace and scheduling. Rather than bend disabled bodies and minds to meet the clock, crip time bends the clock to meet disabled bodies and minds" (2013, 27). Kafer articulates the challenges faced by people living with disabilities navigating normative time. Another important aspect of her analysis is that she argues that people living with disabilities are often not seen as having a desirable future, if they have a future at all. LGBT people also have difficulty adhering to normative temporalities. While this is changing, similar to Kafer's point about disability, a person living with AIDS is often not seen as having a livable future. Additionally, because many LGBT people do not reproduce (or are not seen as capable of reproduction), they are not folded into normative temporalities that value raising the next generation.[5]

Today, LGBT people's access to institutions like marriage and reproductive technologies has given them increasing access to normative temporalities. However, LGBT people growing up and living during the middle part of the twentieth century were denied access to normative time and created alternate temporal structures and expectations. Queer theorist Jack Halberstam notes that:

> Queer time for me is the dark nightclub, the perverse turn away from the narrative coherence of adolescence—early childhood—marriage—reproduction—child rearing—retirement—death, the embrace of late childhood in place of early adulthood or immaturity in place of responsibility. It is a theory of queerness as a way to being in the world and a critique of the careful scripts that usher even the most queer among us through major markers of individual development and into normativity. (2007, 182)

Halberstam's point is that queerness is something to be valued, especially inasmuch as it affords critical positions outside of normative temporality, and this criticism is essential to understanding

---

5 To be clear, I am in no way endorsing these normative temporalities or their focus on the nuclear family. Additionally, LGBT people have always created families, raised children, and participated in many aspects of what I am calling normative temporality. Nor do I think that LGBT people should necessarily strive to match the benchmarks of normative temporality. My point is to trace the contours of the temporal expectations faced by many LGBT people living in North America over the past eighty years.

how and why many LGBT people have a different orientation to temporality. My point is that, by not having access to normative and reproductive temporality, LGBT older adults are left without formal and institutional supports as they age. Queer time may be the darkness of the nightclub, but nightclubs are most often places for the young. Whether it be queer or crip time, our bodies, identities, desires, and social contexts determine how we relate to normative temporalities (whether they be the heterosexual life course, or the demands of pace and scheduling), and the extent to which we can try to match those temporalities.

Capitalism and neoliberalism encourage a certain normative temporality and way of valuing human time and contributions.[6] This is seen most clearly in the fact that working productive members of society are considered upstanding citizens, while those who will not or cannot work are often cast as a burden on society, lazy, or morally suspect. The nuclear family allows some members of the family to work and produce wealth while relying on the unpaid labor of others, usually women.[7] LGBT people, who may not benefit from the support of a nuclear family structure and face intense discrimination in the workplace, often live at the margins of neoliberal values. Cynthia Port reminds us that LGBT elders sit at this uneasy intersection of two identities that, because of anti-LGBT bias and ageism, are often barred from the work place. Reflecting on aging she says, "no longer employed, not reproducing, perhaps technologically illiterate, and frequently without disposable income, the old are often, like queers, figured by the cultural imagination as being outside mainstream temporalities and standing in the way of, rather than contributing to, the promise of the future" (2012, 3). The LGBT older adult is doubly cast out of normative temporality, especially as it is tied to economic productivity.

LGBT older adults are isolated both by the structural reasons that impact many elders, but also because they have not had access to

---

6   For a systematic overview of how Marx understood the ways capitalism shifted our conception of temporality, see the chapter entitled "The Space and Time of Value" in David Harvey's *Marx, Capital, and the Madness of Economic Reason* (2017).

7   The classic text to make this point is Max Weber's *The Protestant Ethic and the Spirit of Capitalism*. A more contemporary analysis can be found in Nancy Fraser and Linda Gordon's chapter "A Genealogy of "Dependency": Tracing a Keyword in the US Welfare State" in Fraser's *Justice Interruptus: Critical Reflections on the "Postsocialist" Condition* (1997).

the temporal rhythms and environments that reduce isolation later in life. Sitting at the edges of the nuclear family and often unable to establish careers or economic security if they are out as LGBT, many LGBT older adults have not had access to cultural and institutional mechanisms that support the creation of multigenerational networks, and are, therefore, placed in a more precarious and isolated situation as they age. If Port is right that this positions LGBT elders as "standing in the way of, rather than contributing to, the promise of the future" (2012, 3), then we must ask: what is the promise of a future, and how does futurity impact questions of isolation and loneliness? What does the promise of a future look like inside the strictures of capitalism? In the next section, I turn to the work of Simone de Beauvoir and Jean-Paul Sartre to untangle the threads of loneliness, isolation, temporality, and neoliberalism.

The Existentialist Critique and Analysis

Simone de Beauvoir is best known for her text *The Second Sex*, but she wrote a work of comparable length and breadth on the topic of aging. *The Coming of Age* is oriented around the cultural, scientific, and philosophical facts of aging—and it is squarely political in its final diagnoses that "old age exposes the failure of our entire civilization" (Beauvoir 1972, 543). While Beauvoir does examine the phenomenology of aging and its implications for philosophy, her ultimate concern is for the ways in which our politics and economics harm older adults by creating a set of material circumstances inhospitable to their flourishing. She notes that reform will not work, because it is the "exploitation of the workers, the pulverization of society, and the utter poverty of a culture confined to the privileged, educated few that leads to this kind of dehumanization of old age" (1972, 7). For Beauvoir, the only true solution is to change our society away from one that "care[s] about the individual only in so far as he is profitable" toward a more just, egalitarian, and humane economic and political system (1972, 543).

For the existentialists such as Beauvoir and Sartre, creating meaning requires acting in a shared world. This is why, in addition to her economic critique, Beauvoir is concerned with how older adults engage in meaningful action or projects. She says, "the greatest good fortune, even greater than health, for the old person is to have his world still inhabited by projects: then, busy and useful, he escapes both from boredom and from decay. The times in which he lives remain his own… His oldness passes, as it were, unnoticed" (1972, 492–93). We can hear in this quote the existentialist commitment to recognizing that existence precedes essence. We have no inherent purpose, but create purpose through our projects and actions. There is no inherent meaning in either the human being, the human condition, or the world. Rather, it is through human action that we create meaning both for our lives and for our society. As Jean-Paul Sartre explains, "for the existentialist… man is no other than a series of undertakings, that he is the sum, the organization, the set of relations that constitute these undertakings" (1975, 359). Human beings exist in the material world, what Sartre calls *being-in-itself,* but we have the unique ability to be self-conscious, to become conscious of our existence. There is no pure consciousness; one must always be thinking of, or be conscious of, something. Sartre calls this *being-for-itself* because I, an existent entity, take myself up as the contents of my consciousness. I become a project for myself, and it is up to me to create my identity and, in collaboration with others, our shared world. Sartre asserts that "man is all the time outside himself: it is in projecting and losing himself beyond himself that he makes man to exist; and, on the other hand, it is by pursuing transcendent aims that he himself is able to exist" (1975, 368). The ability to continue in this transcendence, to project and lose yourself, is what Beauvoir calls the "greatest good fortune" for the older person.

What is unique about the older individual is that they have more history than future, and may have fewer opportunities for new projects or undertakings. As Dorothea Olkowski puts it, "for Beauvoir, life is based on self-transcendence. It is one's future oriented projects, not yet accomplished, that give life meaning… The question she presents is this: how can an aging person find joy in self-transcendence while remaining fully aware of the limitations of time?" (Olkowski 2014, 147). While the limitations of time make the existentialist perspective of aging unique, I hold that although transcendence or projects may look different for an older person, they are nonetheless still an essential part of living a good life.[8]

8   This is a topic taken up by several authors in Silvia Stoller's edited collection on Beauvoir and age, including Helen A. Fielding's excellent chapter "The Poetry of Habit," which demonstrates how certain habitual behaviors can tie into a robust sense of the future, much like a political or artistic project. For more, see Stoller (2014).

Inspired by Beauvoir, I propose that isolation points to a set of material circumstances that prevent meaningful interaction between elders and their world, while loneliness is the feeling that one cannot create meaningful projects and project a sense of self into the future. Otherwise said, isolation is a problem of social justice and capitalism, whereas loneliness requires thinking through the connection between personal identity, projects, and temporal orientation toward the past or future. What is the role of age in one's ability, capacity, or interest in projecting oneself? Is it the same for a younger person and for someone nearing the end of life? Beauvoir, reading Sartre, seems to think that the responsibility is the same. She raises the question, "what does *having* one's life behind one mean?":

> One does not possess one's past as one possesses a thing that one can hold and turn in one's hand, inspecting every side of it. My past is the in-itself that I am in so far as I have been outstripped; in order to possess it I must bind it to existence by a project; if this project consists of knowing it then I must make it present to myself by means of bringing it back to my memory. (1972, 361)

My past can only exist if I bring it into the present, and I can do this through a project or through dwelling in memory. One stereotype of older adults is that they live in the past, rehashing stories and stuck in reminiscences that prevent them from focusing on the present. On the topic of reminiscence, Beauvoir says that "again and again they turn over a few themes of great emotional value to them; and far from growing tired of this perpetual repetition, they return to it with an even greater pleasure" (1972, 372). When isolated or lonely, older adults may turn inward to create a sense of continuity and be reminded of who they are by considering who they were. It is a way to maintain a sense of a coherent identity in the face of isolation and loneliness. Rather than living in memory, Beauvoir and Sartre would endorse making the past present by tying it to our projects and future action. Beauvoir insists:

> There is only one solution if old age is not to be an absurd parody of our former life, and that is to go on pursuing ends that give our existence a meaning—devotion to individuals, to groups or to causes, social, political, intellectual or creative work. In spite of the moralists' opinion to the contrary, in old age we should wish still to have passions strong enough to prevent us turning in upon ourselves. One's life has value so long as one attributes value to the life of others, by means of love, friendship, indignation, compassion. (1972, 540–41)

As we age, we are confronted with the task of taking up the self and continuing to project it into the world of shared life. Leaving the workforce, having their children move away, and a shrinking network of friends make it harder for aging people to remain in vibrant social networks. This challenge is compounded for LGBT older adults who may not feel comfortable being out in social spaces for older people (such as senior centers or retirement communities) and who may not have relationships with their families of origin or children. Returning to the distinction between isolation and loneliness, I echo Beauvoir's sentiment that the suffering and isolation faced by older adults is the result of economic and political injustice. There is nothing intrinsic to aging that necessarily causes someone to become isolated or lonely. Isolation is the result of material conditions making one physically and socially isolated. Society does not value older adults because they are no longer productive, so we have not created robust ways to help them connect with one another and with people of other generations. Loneliness, on the other hand, is the inward turn wherein the person's past is only taken up in reminiscence and not through projects. Putting together a photo album, or reflecting on one's life to come to terms with certain events could both be seen as a kind of reminiscence-based project. That said, for something to be a project in the existentialist sense, I propose that it must be interpersonal in nature. Beauvoir's examples above—"devotion to individuals, to groups or to causes, social, political, intellectual or creative work"—all involve other people. Even something relatively private or solitary like creative activity involves an imagined and future audience. Isolation makes it more difficult for older adults to have projects, which may contribute to loneliness, but someone can still have the material and social means to create projects—meaning they are not isolated—but choose not to do so.

Sartre and Beauvoir were people of incredible energy that extended into their final years. While it is tempting to read them as proposing that all older adults must maintain the same level of engagement throughout their lives, I do not think that this is the point they would endorse. Rather, one must maintain emphasis on moving outside of oneself—taking on the project of existence and seeing oneself in projects and relationships. In the final part of the chapter below, I use the existentialist perspective to examine some concrete suggestions for preventing and mitigating isolation and loneliness.

Material and Philosophical Solutions

If, as I have argued, we recognize that isolation is a material phenomenon driven by inequality, while loneliness points to difficulty engaging in meaningful projects, it stands to reason that we must address the crises facing our aging population by engaging in both sets of problems. Researchers have evaluated various interventions that fall into roughly three categories: one-on-one interactions, group interventions, or changes to community organization and structure. Interventions may look like connecting seniors to the internet, one-on-one visits from volunteers, social adult day centers, educational events, transportation assistance, or support groups. Comparing the effectiveness of different interventions is complicated by the fact that researchers use different definitions of loneliness and isolation, various measurement tools, and disparate analytic techniques. To date, it has not been possible to determine whether one intervention or program is clearly and significantly more successful than another. In a comprehensive review of the literature, researchers at the American Association of Retired Persons (AARP) stated that, "the current understanding of what interventions are most effective in alleviating either or both objective and subjective isolation is still limited. Therefore, it is difficult to recommend one intervention technique to be more effective over another in the general population" (2012, 22). That said, the same report notes, "information to glean from these intervention studies is that it is extremely important to match appropriate interventions with people's unique circumstances, cause for being isolated, and whether they are experiencing objective, subjective, or both types of isolation" (2012, 22). In addition to removing barriers for interaction and helping people to develop stronger personal bonds, it is also important to consider how a shared project can be an opportunity for organic relationships to emerge, and effective programs or interventions can create "opportunities for so-called unintentional network building, that is, the development of friendships is a by-product of the shared activity, not the explicit purpose" (De Jong Gierveld et al. 2006, 494). While we may not know what programs or activities are the most effective, it is increasingly clear that tailoring interventions to a person's specific needs and engaging their interests are common components of successful programs.

Many people would assume that interventions to reduce isolation and loneliness necessarily involve group activities, but a recent review of the literature by Gardiner, Geldenhuys, and Gott (2016) did not find that group interventions were more effective than other interventions. In fact, these researchers noted that solitary interventions, such as caring for a pet or videoconferencing, were also effective, and that "indeed, qualitative data from this review indicate that productive engagement activities, which may be solitary, are a feature of many successful interventions" (2016, 8). This finding is in line with the review by Dickens et al. (2011), which reported that participatory interventions were most likely to be beneficial.[9]

It is important to emphasize that, for Beauvoir, it is clear that the suffering experienced by older people is not entirely or even largely because of growing older and a decline in physical health. What makes older adults suffer is largely social and economic injustice and our ageist society. Scholars and activists have the information and resources that are needed to reduce the structural causes of isolation. Increased transportation networks, free mass transit passes for older adults, accessible public spaces which are compliant with the Americans with Disabilities Act, useable and efficient paratransit systems, low-cost taxi services, and increased access to technology can all help older adults remain connected. Now is the time to begin making our communities more age friendly if we are to accommodate the growing number of older adults in North America. All of these changes can help to keep older adults in their communities for longer and to extend the amount of time they are able to live at home before needing institutionalized care. This is especially difficult for LGBT older adults because many of the spaces where LGBT people meet in the community, such as bars and LGBT centers, may not be economically or socially accessible for LGBT older people. If LGBT older adults are also economically vulnerable and not enmeshed in multigenerational networks, such as a biological family unit, it may

---

9   This study was quoted in the AARP report, where it was emphasized that "Interventions that involved active participation, which 'entailed active input from participants involving social contact (not necessarily face-to-face) rather than them simply being recipients of a service or education/training', had 80% effectiveness versus the 40% of non-participatory interventions" (2012, 23).

make it even more difficult for them to access transportation and stay connected to community.

Moving beyond the economic critique, the existentialist perspective shows us that what solitary and interpersonal interventions have in common is that they involve giving the isolated older adult a sense of agency and investment in the program or activity meant to reduce isolation and loneliness. These programs provide the support and opportunity for older adults to take up a project outside of themselves to pursue "ends that give our existence a meaning" (Beauvoir 1972, 540). When we think of the existentialists, acting to create meaning in the world often takes on the flavor of a grand project or political struggle, like joining the French resistance or writing a novel. Caring for a pet, joining an art class, or attending a lecture may not seem to be the same kind of meaning-making activity. However, my point is that for all of us, but especially for isolated and lonely older adults, these activities can provide needed opportunities to transcend their circumstances and invest themselves in something that is outside of themselves and located in the future. They can look forward to the completion of a project, or they can care for a pet to ensure that it continues to thrive. Whatever the project may be, the goal is to keep oneself rooted in a sense of linear and shared time, seeing the self and history moving toward a future, rather than rooted in the past through reminiscence.

Put otherwise, our material environments provide different manners in which we take up the project of being alive. Our environment and circumstances influence how we conceive of ourselves, the future, and our possible actions. When an older person is isolated or lonely, they may, as Beauvoir points out, come to rely on reminiscence as a way to be present to themselves. Experiencing and sensing that your future is more limited than it was in youth and adulthood may be a reason to turn away from the future and towards comforting memories. A certain shift in perspective away from the future and towards the past is a common and perhaps inevitable part of aging. The risk when someone is isolated or lonely is that the past may become their entire horizon for meaning making, and they cannot transcend the self with new or shared projects. Shifting the older adult's material environment to reduce isolation and create the possibility of projects, either in groups or alone, in which they imbue meaning, makes it possible for the isolated elder to, as Sartre observes, "los[e] himself beyond himself" (1975, 368).

Beauvoir's use of the terms "passion" and "devotion" speak to an area of important future research—specifically, researching the kinds of projects or interventions that are interesting to older adults. Many of the studies cited above note that interventions were more effective if they target specific populations, such as people who have recently lost a partner, or are home bound, or are LGBT. I imagine that this is in part because their shared experiences and difficulties can yield shared motivations or interests. If I am not passionate about, or at least interested in, a given project, I am not likely to pursue it, especially if it involves difficulty, strain, or expense. If the existentialist analysis is correct, and engaging in projects is an important intervention, we must then examine how and why certain projects are motivating to isolated and lonely people. One way to do this is to involve lonely older adults in the planning and implementation of the program. This will help ensure that they are interested, and also provide a way to establish a sense of agency and investment in it. For example, SAGE started a program called SAGE Story, which brought LGBT older adults together, gave them training on how to use audio visual equipment, and professional training on effective storytelling. After these classes, the older adults helped one another craft and record their biographies. They knew they would be safe and could speak openly about their histories because the program was run by other LGBT people and they had the opportunity to reflect on their past and reminisce, all the while creating and engaging in a project oriented around producing polished and well-crafted biographical materials. These video and audio files were then used as a part of political campaigns to push for non-discrimination legislation, thereby linking each person's history and project with a larger political ambition.

It is clear that there is no 'one size fits all' solution to reducing isolation and loneliness. As we begin to tackle this problem, I propose that looking at the case of LGBT older adults is a good place to start. Given that this is a population that is economically disadvantaged, more isolated, and facing unique social stigma, building programs intended to reduce isolation and loneliness for LGBT older adults will give us knowledge, experience, and best practices that can be applied to other communities as well. It is my hope that this existentialist analysis can help us clarify the two directions our interventions need to take. The first is political and involves investing the time and resources required to keep older adults connected to community and push back against the cultural and economic forces that would discard them once they are no longer contributing to our neoliberal economic system. The second requires activating older adults themselves in order to identify and then create opportunities to engage in meaningful projects that honor their experiences and history, but also keep them at least partially oriented toward the future. Reducing isolation and loneliness, in particular for LGBT older adults, will require that we grapple with systems and economic structures that disadvantage older adults, but also our own ageism and biases. It is a task that must be simultaneously approached on the level of systematic critique and economic justice, while also being something we commit to in our personal lives as we continue making meaning for ourselves and our communities. Existentialism is an active and future oriented philosophical system, and I hope to have shown that, far from being incompatible with aging, it can offer us lessons and inspiration to make sure that we all have the opportunities to act in the world and create our own meaningful futures at any age.

References

AARP Foundation. 2012. "Framework for Isolation in Adults Over 50." http://www.aarp.org/content/dam/aarp/aarp_foundation/2012_PDFs/AARP-Foundation-Isolation-Framework-Report.pdf

Beauvoir, Simone de. 1972. *The Coming of Age*. Translated by Patrick O'Brian. New York: G.P. Putnam's Son.

Coyle, Caitlin E., and Elizabeth Dugan. 2012. "Social Isolation, Loneliness and Health Among Older Adults." *Journal of Aging and Health* 24 (8): 1346–63. https://doi.org/10.1177/0898264312460275

De Jong Gierveld, Jenny, Theo Van Tilberg, and Pearl A. Dykstra. 2006. "Loneliness and Social Isolation." In *The Cambridge Handbook of Personal Relationships* (Cambridge Handbooks in Psychology), edited by Anita L. Vangelisti and Daniel Perlman, 485–500. Cambridge: Cambridge University Press.

Dickens, Andy P., Suzanne H. Richards, Colin J. Greaves, and John L. Campbell. 2011. "Interventions Targeting Social Isolation in Older People: A Systematic Review." *BMC Public Health* 11 (1): 647. https://doi.org/10.1186/1471-2458-11-647

Fraser, Nancy. 1997. *Justice Interruptus: Critical Reflections on the "Postsocialist" Condition*. New York: Routledge.

Fredriksen-Goldsen, Karen I., Hyun-Jun Kim, Susan E. Barkan, Anna Muraco, and Charles P. Hoy-Ellis. "Health Disparities Among Lesbian, Gay, and Bisexual Older Adults: Results from a Population-Based Study." *American Journal of Public Health* 103 (10): 1802–809. https://doi.org/10.2105/ajph.2012.301110

Gardiner, Clare, Gideon Geldenhuys, and Merryn Gott. "Interventions to Reduce Social Isolation and Loneliness among Older People: An Integrative Review." *Health & Social Care in the Community* 26 (2): 147–57. https://doi.org/10.1111/hsc.12367

Halberstam, J. 2007. "Theorizing Queer Temporalities: A Roundtable Discussion." *GLQ: A Journal of Lesbian and Gay Studies* 13 (2–3): 159–76.

Harvey, David. 2017. *Marx, Capital, and the Madness of Economic Reason*. Oxford: Oxford University Press.

Holt-Lunstad, Julianne, Timothy B. Smith, Mark Baker, Tyler Harris, and David Stephenson. 2015. "Loneliness and Social Isolation as Risk Factors for Mortality: A Meta-Analytic Review." *Perspectives on Psychological Science* 10 (2): 227–37. https://doi.org/10.1177/1745691614568352

Kafer, Alison. 2013. *Feminist, Queer, Crip*. Bloomington: Indiana University Press.

Menec, Verena. 2016. "Loneliness and Social Isolation are Important Health Risks in the Elderly." *McMaster Optimal Aging Portal*. https://www.mcmasteroptimalaging.org/blog/detail/professionals-blog/2016/04/08/loneliness-and-social-isolation-are-important-health-risks-in-the-elderly

Olkowski, Dorothea. 2014. "Letting Go the Weight of the Past: Beauvoir and the Joy of Existence." In *Simone de Beauvoir's Philosophy of Age: Gender, Ethics, and Time*. Edited by Silvia Stoller, 147–60. Berlin: de Gruyter.

Port, Cynthia. 2012. "No Future? Aging, Temporality, History, and Reverse Chronologies." *Interdisciplinary Studies in the Humanities* 4: 1–19.

SAGE. 2014. "Out & Visible: The Experiences and Attitudes of LGBT Older Adults, Ages 45-75." https://www.sageusa.org/resources/publications.cfm?ID=214

Sartre, Jean-Paul. 1975. "Existentialism Is a Humanism." In *Existentialism from Dostoevsky to Sartre*, Revised and Expanded Edition, edited by Walter Kaufmann, 345–68. New York: New American Library.

Steptoe, A., A. Shankar, P. Demakakos, and J. Wardle. 2013. "Social Isolation, Loneliness, and All-cause Mortality in Older Men and Women." *Proceedings of the National Academy of Sciences* 110 (15): 5797–801. https://doi.org/10.1073/pnas.1219686110

Stoller, Sylvia. 2014. *Simone de Beauvoir's Philosophy of Age: Gender, Ethics, and Time*. Berlin: de Gruyter.

Weber, Max. 2010. *The Protestant Ethic and the Spirit of Capitalism*. Revised Edition. Oxford: Oxford University Press.

About the author

Tim R. Johnston holds a PhD form SUNY Stony Brook and is the Director of National Projects at SAGE, the largest advocacy organization for LGBT older adults in the United States. He is responsible for directing SAGE's national training initiatives, developing training curricula, and providing consulting services to both aging and LGBT service providers. He has written scholarly and popular articles on gender and LGBT identity.

Chapter Five

Aging and Aesthetic Responsibility

Elizabeth Lanphier

Abstract

"Aging and Aesthetic Responsibility" by Elizabeth Lanphier looks at the process of aging from the point of view of the representation of the aging body, especially the aging female body, in mainstream visual arts. Lanphier seeks to establish that there is, in fact, an ethical responsibility to visually represent aged bodies, in particular, and scenes of aging, in general.

Introduction

Philosophy has an age-old preoccupation with perception (Jay 1994).[1] American culture, including its health care systems and media, has a problem perceiving age. For both philosophy and American culture, there is an obsession with the visual, and what is and is not seen. Philosophical thought has historically connected knowledge and sight: to know is, in a way, to see, and to see is to know. At the same time, contemporary U.S. culture tends to keep the elderly out of sight. According to Alasdair MacIntyre, "from Plato to Moore and since, there are usually, with some rare exceptions, only passing references to human vulnerability and affliction," including the vulnerability of being very young or very old, confronting illness, or living with a disability (1999, 1). If Western philosophy privileges the visual landscape, then what sort of challenge for an ethics of aging and an ethical responsibility toward older individuals does this present insofar as aging bodies are largely kept out of the visual landscape of American culture?

---

1   This is only one representative book-length treatment of this topic.

In this chapter I argue that there is a particular type of ethical responsibility to visually represent aged bodies and scenes of aging. Critiques of how aged bodies are, or are not, portrayed in media and mainstream culture abound, particularly with regards to the way women "of a certain age" in the United States are rendered invisible. Actor Antonio Banderas described his now ex-wife, actress Melanie Griffith, as a "victim of aging" in Hollywood (Chivers 2011, xii). Griffith herself lamented not having more movie roles, saying that "it's not because I lost my talent or became deformed. It's only because I am older" (Chivers 2011, xii). Although, notably, Griffith draws a false dichotomy between aging and deformity, this chapter will explicitly link disability scholarship with an analysis of aging.

Although these critiques of Hollywood's approach inform my argument, I appeal not to an argument for diversity or representation in mass media, but instead to an artistic responsibility to portray older bodies and lives. I make this move, in part, because of the particular ways in which we might understand an artist as uniquely responsible for her art. That a piece of artwork is both attributable and accountable to an artist provides what I will call robust accountability for said artwork on the part of the artist. Furthermore, I argue that this accountability has an ethical component in how it both reflects and shapes the social and political practices of a community.

My argument is this: our ethical communities have overlooked, failed to see, or unfairly characterized aging. I take an ethical community to be one that shares a set of values and practices. An ethical community can be broader than a cultural community, for it *could* (though does not necessarily) accommodate various cultural communities and their specific practices.[2] At the same time, an ethical community *could* (though does not necessarily) indicate something more particular than larger categories of membership, such as membership in a nation state or as member of the human species. The

---

2   Here, we might think about the ways in which a politically liberal society is meant to be pluralistic but one in which, despite such pluralism, it is possible (in theory) to arrive at an overlapping consensus, at least regarding the basic structure of society. John Rawls suggested such a pluralistic yet cohesive society is possible in *Political Liberalism* (2005). However, there is a large body of literature that responds directly and indirectly to Rawls. Iris Marion Young's *Justice and the Politics of Difference* (1990) explores the shortcomings of the traditional political liberalism views put forth by Rawls in light of social difference and histories of oppression and injustice.

failure to see within ethical communities permits injustices toward aged populations and individuals, which are essentially injustices toward most members of the community (at some point in their lives) since most individuals, hopefully, will have the opportunity to live into old age. Further, it is necessary to focus the moral imagination of the ethical community on aging and aged people to create opportunities for the community to see and understand the aging experience. This recognition helps to ensure that the aging process, and people who are aging or aged, are seen and valued within an ethical community. In order to achieve better recognition within an ethical community, aging and aged bodies ought to be the focus of at least some art, and there is a particular artistic responsibility to (accurately) portray aging and aged people, in order to render aging and aged people visible and valued within an ethical community.

This argument appeals to views within disability scholarship that advocate for the portrayal of non-normative bodies, such as disabled bodies, in art. However, my specific focus on aged bodies intends to push at something already suggested in the disability scholarship: that making visible is part of making normal. In a sense, aging and aged bodies are not non-normative bodies in a non-value-laden sense of normative. Aged bodies are the entirely normal progression of human life. Furthermore, many of us will also have disabled bodies in old-age, if we do not already. Aging (and aging-related disability) falls within, rather than outside, an expected life trajectory. However, aging (and perhaps aging-related disability) needs to be normalized within both philosophy and culture, and an ethical aesthetic responsibility is one way to achieve the value-laden normalization I make a case for here.

This chapter unfolds in three main moves. First, I address two aspects of sight. I rehearse an already well-documented problem of the invisibility of aging persons and the aged body, particularly in U.S. media and culture. This cultural absence reflects a larger social marginalization and what might be noted as a failure to value older persons in the context of U.S. society and culture. Next, I briefly consider one prominent example of the ways in which philosophy as a discipline is particularly preoccupied with sight, visibility, and seeing as the predominant means of knowing. While there may be other, necessary, interventions into how we construct and portray knowledge within the field, in several respects the history of philosophy is a history of privileging sight. Sight as knowledge provides a lens through which to read the absence of aged bodies and lives from visual representations: aging and those who are aged are not subjects to know and understand. Such a lack of visual representation is a stand-in for a lack of social, cultural, and epistemic representation.

Second, I shift my attention to moral responsibility. If the first move was to observe two problems, the second move sets the stage for a discussion of what it is to be responsible, including what it is to take responsibility for these problems, and the responsibility to solve them. Here, I draw on works in the field of moral philosophy and moral psychology by P. F. Strawson, Gary Watson, David Shoemaker, and especially Susan Wolf. Building on Wolf's (2015) argument about types of responsibility, that she calls "moral or otherwise," I suggest that responsibility even for that which appears to be a non-moral form of responsibility nonetheless reflects and generates cultural, social, and political practices within a community that necessarily have an ethical dimension. Wolf's considerations into the nature of "aesthetic responsibility" are a launch pad for deeper reflection on the ways in which artistic practices and production can participate in an ethical community.

Third, and final, I suggest an aesthetic responsibility to depict the aging, elderly body and experiences of aging. My argument is intended to do for aging bodies what Anita Silvers (2000) claims to do for disabled bodies in her piece "From the Crooked Timber of Humanity Beautiful Things Can Be Made." There, Silvers posits a unique role for art to bring disabled bodies into the literal and ethical field of vision. Similarly, there is a crucial role for art in the development of a more attuned ethical approach to aging, and, importantly, for a stronger ethics of care for aging bodies that can inform cultural and medical practices, guiding caregivers and clinicians alike. To be clear, my claim is not that all art or artists ought to take aged bodies and lives as artistic subjects. However, I do suggest that some ought to, and that artistic and aesthetic responsibility offers reasons for which individual artists, as well as individuals and communities[3] which endorse and support the arts, should reflectively consider

---

3   By individuals and communities supporting the arts, I intend to mean the institutional machinery, as well as non-institutional participation in arts more broadly. This could include donors to artists and museums, public or private grants for the arts, museum patrons or individuals who visit museums or purchase art, curators, art critics, and the like.

their own responsibility for generating ethical attention to those who have been historically kept out of sight. Such an argument is not limited to artists; it could likewise be extended to the gatekeepers of media in various forms. However, focusing on artistic responsibility locates responsibility in a specific, and productive, way. This is a first step toward social and ethical progress. Additionally, such an argument is not necessarily limited to the absence of aged bodies from visual and artistic culture, but could be relevant to various groups who are largely kept culturally out of sight.

Seeing and Knowing

Bodies in Culture and Media

Critiques of the media in Western culture, particularly U.S. culture that produces the Hollywood movie system, but also television, commercials, and print advertising (which also have international reach outside of the U.S.), often note the narrow range of bodies featured in the media. The contemporary moment is drawing attention to many of the historical exclusions of certain bodies from the media. In the wake of the Black Lives Matter[4] movement, an #OscarsSoWhite critique pointed to the absence of directors and actors of color, as well as movies with storylines about people of color, from garnering awards.[5] Feminist critiques of the narrow range of female bodies that are featured in the media are now familiar. Women on screen tend to be young, slim, and white. While we can all name exceptions to these rules, I take it to be an uncontroversial statement that U.S. media has promoted young, slender, white female bodies, and, to a lesser extent, youthful, toned, white male bodies (though with slightly more room for signs of age in males,

---

4   See https://blacklivesmatter.com (accessed 24 February 2019) for details on the movement's mission and actions.

5   See Gay (2016) and Dargis, Morris, and Scott (2016) for two sample conversations about the controversy and critique. Notably, actors, directors, costume and set designers, and writers of color have won prominent awards in 2017 (Barry Jenkins won Best Film and Best Adapted Screenplay for *Moonlight*, for which Mahershala Ali won Best Supporting Actor while Viola Davis won Best Supporting Actress in *Fences*) and in 2019 (Mahershala Ali again won Best Supporting Actor for *Green Book*, Spike Lee won Best Adapted Screenplay for BlacKKKlansman, and the film *Black Panther*, featuring a predominantly black cast and crew, won numerous awards including for Costume Design and Production Design, which were teams led by black women).

such as the trope of the "distinguished grey" hair color or the common pairing of young actresses as the love interests of older male protagonists).

In 2003, the film *Something's Gotta Give* briefly featured a completely naked Diane Keaton, then in her late 50s. That same year, an article in the *Chicago Tribune* noted a spate of films in which women actors in their 40s and 50s appeared naked on screen, suggesting a sea change from the general obsession with youthful bodies in film (Frisinger 2003). However, none of these women were over the age of 60 and could not be said to represent *aged* bodies, only aging ones (and aging bodies that still have the benefits of Hollywood trainers, dermatologists, and set lighting). The *Chicago Tribune* article referenced a love scene between older people as still being able to be sexy and steamy: the scene was between a man in his mid-fifties and a woman in her mid-thirties. While this is a departure from Ann Bancroft playing the supposedly older (yet still sexually enticing) mother of a college student against Dustin Hoffman's recent college-graduate-aged character in *The Graduate* (despite both actors in fact being in their thirties during the filming of the movie), it is not exactly the representation of men and women both *aging* on celluloid.

Public health experts have critiqued media portrayals (or lack thereof) of aging on several levels. One such critique is the way that mass media and images specifically "reflect and shape social attitudes toward older people and the treatment they receive," and "influence individual perceptions of the self and the construction of personal identity later in life" (Lumme-Sandt 2011, 45). Two objectives are noted. One is the way that images and the media influence cultural expectations of aging and aged people. The other is the way in which these factors influence an individual's own expectations for her aging experience.

The absence of images of aging, and therefore the absence of opportunities to construct and imagine aging experiences, limits open societal discussions of how we want, as a population, to grow old. Yet such open discussion and reflection would be, arguably, necessary for public health initiatives and funding for any disease (Schweda and Marchmann 2013), especially those that persons face in older age or those that prevent them from reaching these later years. The images that a society produces and privileges not only reflect and form the society's values around health care, but also inform and reinforce social values more broadly. Such values are socially constructed, which means that they can also be deconstructed, built upon, revised, or reformed. A project of ethically revising social attitudes toward aging through imagining and implementing new practices of seeing and valuing is the topic of the final section of this chapter.

Of course, there *are* examples of stories that address the aging experience explicitly on film and in mass media. Sally Chivers (2011) wrote a book-length treatment of "old age and disability in cinema" in the *Silvering Screen,* her term for the move to center stories about aging in film rather than relegating aged characters to supporting roles and storylines. Chivers underscores the ways in which older actors are expected to portray physical and mental acuity in their performances, which is a reflection on the cultural values that mainstream movies are prescribing and reinscribing to their audience (xii). She further notes that the standards are not equal for men and women, and women face greater expectations and subsequent marginalization in film. Chivers points out how in classic Hollywood films that do depict older women's stories, they are "always a horror story" (xvii).

Notably, in Chivers's analysis, the "silvering screen" focuses on old age, but not necessarily the road to, or the process of, aging itself (xvi). However, aging is not a one-time event nor a fixed state. Being old (or feeling old) might be a state in which one exists. And getting there is a daily occurrence. Aging therefore defies the dualism that is also so philosophically prevalent. Silvers suggests that it is problematic to view "normalcy and disability as definitely locked in struggle" in large part because this "constructs a dualism that tends to force all cases into one or the other category or camp" (214). But it might be even more problematic to view aging as a binary pair in which old and young are dialectically opposed. For this overlooks the aging experience, and the ways in which individuals are always already becoming older.[6]

One example of a film about an aging experience is the Sarah Polley cinematic adaptation of an Alice Munro short story, *Away from Her,* about a long-married couple in which the wife develops

---

6 Bob Dylan has the apt yet pithy line "That he not busy being born is busy dying" in "It's Alright, Ma (I'm Only Bleeding)" from *Bringing It All Back Home* (1964).

Alzheimer's disease. She moves to an assisted living facility when her husband can no longer provide sufficient care for her, where she begins a romantic relationship with another resident, as her disease causes her to forget her married life with her husband. Other films, such as *45 Years*, about a long-term marriage between older adults on the occasion of their 45th wedding anniversary portrays an aged life but through revelations about their younger pasts. The film *Still Alice* depicts the progression of early onset Alzheimer's disease, and therefore illustrates the impact of the condition on a woman much younger than what could be considered "old age".

Each of these films present complex narratives about life, love, hardship, and illness for aging adults. They also focus on educated, attractive, middle-class, married lives. No one story can tell everyone's story. And for that very reason it might be necessary to portray *more* stories and depictions of aging, aged bodies, and the lived experience of getting older. In this way, media would reflect back that age *is* something most people, who are lucky to live to old(er) age, will experience. Iris Marion Young has articulated that it is precisely because "I cannot deny that the old person will be myself" and that this aging "means my death" that "I avert my gaze from the old person" (1990, 147). As Young shows us, because we fear our mortality, and aging is part of our living and dying process, we do not wish to train our eyes on old individuals, whether they are real persons or representations of persons.

That aging, and its connection to dying, terrifies us is only an explanation, not an excuse, for ignoring it. Chivers suggests that "the silvering screen offers a potent site for the production of cultural knowledge and requires critical attention because it has a strong influence on popular thinking about late life" (2011, xviii). If Chivers is correct — and I think she is — then the work to be done is to produce more sites for the production of cultural knowledge about aging experiences not only through cinema, but also through other art forms.

Beyond a call for a greater saturation of images of aging in mass media, and finer attention to the ways in which images of aging bodies and lives are portrayed in mass culture and mainstream media, I want to raise the suggestion that there is a particularly interesting demand placed on the arts (and here I mean the fine arts, but also dramatic film, theatre, and to some extent literature) to address aging and aged bodies as artistic subjects. This is in part due to the importance of merely making aged bodies and lives visible. But as a further point, it is due to the ways in which making something the subject of art suggests that it is of *value*.

We might say that taking age, aged people, or an aging experience as an artistic topic suggests that it is worth being seen. Silvers contends that "the aesthetic is more suited to reforming than to reiterating the exclusionary practices that currently govern our gaze and contribute to the social invisibility of odd-looking people" (2000, 201). Put differently, aesthetic representations of different bodies, people, or lives train our gaze on them, render them invisible, and construct them as less (or not at all) odd.

Later in this chapter I discuss several additional, ethical reasons for why art, as well as media, ought to portray aged bodies and aging experiences. This argument is situated within, and critiques, a culture in which aged persons and aging experiences are largely kept hidden. The lack of a variety of aged bodies and experiences in art and film reflects and reproduces the marginalization and lack of valuing of older people and lives within the society. Furthermore, it reflects a failure to imagine aging in ways that could support individuals and communities preparing for, creating, and living their later lives in realistic, healthy, and fulfilled ways.

Philosophy and Seeing

The first move of this chapter was to discuss how aged bodies and lives are kept out of sight in American art and culture. The second, albeit quick, move is to consider how philosophy as a discipline has a history of preoccupation with sight and seeing. Colloquially, we can note the ways in which terms about sight are used synonymously with knowing. To confirm understanding, we might say: "I see." It is not unusual to say "seeing is believing," suggesting a connection between sight and various epistemic positions. In a social-media filled world, the appeal to document daily life has been enhanced by platforms to post pictures and images, pictures that reveal partial details of a well-curated life (replete with an internet meme of "pics or it didn't happen," suggesting that only something photographically documented is real or true). The history of philosophy explicitly and implicitly reinforces this colloquial interchange of seeing for knowing and encountering images as a way to cultivate understanding.

In Book VII of Plato's *Republic,* Socrates recounts the "Allegory of the Cave" as a tale of how the philosopher kings obtain knowledge. In this allegory, everyone is living in a cave where they only know things by the shadows they see of them on the cave wall. The cave-dwellers believe that these shadows *are* the things themselves, not realizing that they are, in fact, only shadows, i.e., distorted representations of things lit up by the fire in the cave. Only once a person emerges from the cave and into the (temporarily) blinding light of the full sun is she able to truly *see* things for what they are. And then, once she has obtained this knowledge through the true sight of objects and the world around her, she risks returning to the cave to tell her former cohabitants about her new knowledge and she is met with ridicule, doubt, skepticism, and potential harm. One does not believe what one cannot *see* for herself and these cave dwellers do not wish to be told or believe otherwise than what they themselves can see. This point about the ability to imagine otherwise than what we believe we see in plain sight is one I return to in the final section.

On the one hand, we might wish to critique the privileged relationship between seeing and knowing, to suggest other modes of coming to know and understand concepts, our environment, and other beings. Certainly, there are other ways to learn and know besides visual perception. Yet, on the other hand, seeing and being seen is about more than knowing; it is also about valuing. Making something visible suggests that it is worth being seen. Furthermore, to positively apply the cave allegory to the case of images of aging, moving such images into the light, so to speak, allows them to be brought into focus and examined, rather than seen in an incomplete and incorrect manner in the shadows. While such a movement from the shadows to the clear light of day might face initial resistance, it is a move toward a more ethical and informed society for reasons to which I now turn.

Responsibility and Ethical Practice

Seeing and Seeing Differently

Part of what happens in Plato's Allegory of the Cave is that <u>the person who represents the philosopher</u> emerges from the cave to see things in the daylight. This changed way of seeing, or seeing anew, is not welcomed by the community of cave dwellers who only see from inside the cave. We might say that this mirrors what occurs inside our ethical communities: the participants largely share a way of seeing the world. It may be just or unjust, accurate or inaccurate. Essentially the participants in the ethical community might be the cave dwellers who see the world only for the shadows cast on the wall, and this may be an incomplete or imperfect way of seeing. This partially occluded view might cause injustices to be perpetuated that cannot even be clearly perceived as such.

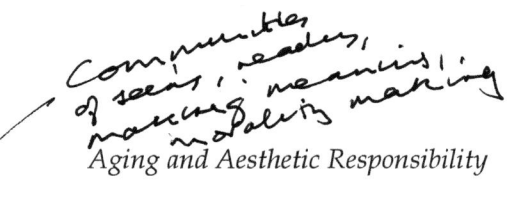

However, there are individuals and groups who, like the philosopher who emerges from the cave, are the vanguards of change. Those who emerge into a new way of seeing, or uncovering what was previously incomplete, can return to their ethical community and encourage the community as a whole, and its members individually, to see differently and see anew. It may be a matter of training attention onto what was hidden in plain sight, to use a touchstone phrase by Margaret Urban Walker (2007). That these individuals who emerge from the literal or metaphoric cave *do* return to attempt to instigate change for the better of their ethical community is notable, for this is undoubtedly the more challenging path. Yet, for these vanguards of change, it might be the case that once they see anew, and recognize that their ethical community could be different, they are compelled to bring about this change.[7]

It is possible, and arguably it is morally required, to modify ethical practices within an ethical community when the members of the community start to see such practices differently, and modify their practices in accordance with their newfound perspective. We might say that this is, in part, how moral progress functions: recognizing past or present practices as unjust, coming to see these injustices hidden in plain sight, and developing new practices to take their place. In Walker's (2007) view, morality is a community practice that is shaped, and reshaped, by those who are recognized by, who have been silenced by oppression within, or who struggle for recognition in, moral communities of practice. Social and civil rights movements have shown that this theoretical model for ethical change is also a practical one. In practice, civil rights leaders have been the

---

7 Arguably, once an individual sees differently, although working against the normative society to effect change may be the more challenging course of action (perhaps even a deadly one, when we reflect on the ways in which leaders of social change have been targets of violence and assassination), doing nothing is no longer a tenable option, either. For continuing to live within a community now recognized as unjust might also be a form of epistemic violence or social death.

vanguards of such change to push the broader ethical community to see differently, and for that they have faced ridicule, skepticism, and harm. Martin Luther King Jr. was assassinated for his role in enacting racial rights in the United States, as was Harvey Milk for his role in LGBTQ rights, to name only two of many possible such examples.

It might seem plausible that art and artists (or at least some art and artists) would be the vanguards of change. Artists are often thought of as counter-culture or challenging the mainstream, or as paving the way for what will eventually become mainstream.[8] However, Elizabeth Thomas and Julian Rappaport (1996) have noted that the formalized art world runs counter to this assumption. They say that "despite its portrayal as the bastion of avant-garde social change, much of what is legitimated as art is controlled by the most powerful and conservative forces in government and the private sector" (1996, 317). Yet, Thomas and Rappaport also note that there are opportunities for local art initiatives to work within communities to engage social change, even if these local projects do not reach the full legitimization of a recognized, commercial art world. They suggest that local art is a way for communities who face forms of exclusion (which I will interpret to include social, cultural, and economic exclusion) to exert control over their own narratives, and to "serve as a means by which a society reminds itself of the stories it wants to remember" (317).

Extending the thought from Thomas and Rappaport, while a codified commercial art world might be yet another site in which unjust systems of power exert control, the arts in general, across various media, nonetheless afford sites and modes for destabilizing imbalances of power. Notably, Thomas and Rappaport suggest that it is up to a community to determine its own narrative, and see the arts as a tool to achieve this community-driven identity and historical memory. This view of the arts as having the capacity to make and assert meaning aligns with the notion of an ethical community determining their own terms.

---

8   Certainly, this depends on the medium. There are prominent "mainstream" movies, books, and music that circulate in popular culture and are not deconstructing or reconstructing the status quo. However, there are also traditions of performance art, as well as protest music, poetry, literature, and visual art that critique and counter dominant cultural views. These are what I have in mind when I suggest the possibility for artists as the vanguards of change.

Certainly, Thomas and Rappaport view this intervention of local arts as a way of adjusting unfair practices and imbalances of power, and take local arts to be an interruption of inequities. We might say that the mainstream or commercial modes of artistic production harbor the possibility for both affirming and disrupting the status quo. Art and artists who make it can play a vanguard role for social change by drawing attention to themes, images, and subjects that have been overlooked, marginalized, or misrepresented in other areas of culture (and within the arts, as well).

My suggestion is that this role of local arts in shaping narratives and community identities is one that has the capacity to extend up to the larger community within which it operates. In this manner, art can act as a force of change, even if it is not initially welcomed as such (like our philosopher emerging from the cave). This is in part due to the ways in which art can reveal what is hidden in plain sight, and can present ideas that spark both intellectual and affective reactions from its audience. It is furthermore in part due to the nature of art as necessarily inter-subjective. There is always an exchange between the art piece and its audience, in which both art and audience co-construct meaning.

Arguably this co-constructive aspect of art renders it unstable. Its meaning cannot be fixed, but instead is a product of a collaboration between artist and receiver. While writing on a project to alter narratives about aging in older women through a series of photographic projects, Naomi Richards, Lorna Warren, and Merryn Gott make the strong claim that: "once images are made public, they become freed from the motivations and subjectivity of those responsible for their creation and enter an inter-subjective world where interpretations are open to all" (2012, 69). I take their point that meaning is collaboratively co-constructed and that meaning can be (mis)attributed by the audience. This freedom of interpretation, moreover, is the ethically rich aspect of artistic production. Rather than read inter-subjective interpretation as a free-for-all in which each viewer of a piece of art has only her private interpretation and relationship with the piece, each individual will come to make meaning about the artwork through the values, language, ideas, and culture of their community.[9]

---

9   This thought is also an echo of Wittgenstein. In *Philosophical Investigations*, Wittgenstein suggests that it is not possible for an individual to have a "private language." Language always functions within a community of speakers who construct together the communicative meaning of the language.

The ways in which the community of viewers receive a piece of art or an artistic experience, then, will reflect the community within which one already exists. An encounter with a piece of art affords a time and place for the viewer to be confronted by the values and ideas readily available within the community, whether the artwork reinforces or subverts those values. A particularly impactful artwork might spur the moral imagination to reflect anew. If an individual (or an entire community) experiences imaginative resistance when presented with art that asks them to imagine otherwise than what is readily acceptable to their preconceived notions, values, or practices, this provides an intervention into those notions, values, and practices. Such art might not overcome imaginative resistance on the part of its audience, but it could still challenge the audience to critically reflect on the fact that it has failed to imagine otherwise, *why* it has resisted imagining along with the artwork, or *whether* such resistance to imagination is, in fact, warranted. The very presence of art that takes on subjects that are often marginalized—not valued—or misunderstood provides opportunities for challenging an ethical community's moral imagination and potentially breaks down barriers and resistance to seeing differently. As Silvers suggests with regards to disability, which I hold as also true for aging, art provides the possibility for moral reform (2000, 201).

That being so, the role of art is not only to foster empathy for the art's subject in the viewer or receiver of the art work. Indeed, such empathy might be one of the roles art plays, especially when it presents a viewer with a life or subject radically different than one's own and demands recognition and consideration of this other being, experience, or perspective. But beyond creating an opportunity for empathy, art further requires of its audience its active participation in meaning-making. While this may lead an audience to fail to see the subject in significant ways or to fail to see the subject as the subject *wishes* to be seen, it also draws in the viewer or receiver as an active participant who is thus responsible for the meaning she has co-constructed.

Arguably, the co-constructed narrative between art(ist) and audience might not reflect what the artist (or, perhaps even more importantly in the case we are considering here of art about aging, the artist's subject) feels is the most accurate representation of what they intended to express. This potential misunderstanding, or incomplete understanding, is an ever-present risk in producing art for public consumption. But the reward for that risk is a greater participation into the meaning-making process, and renders the viewer accountable for the meaning the artwork produces.

In the case of art which takes aging and aged persons as subjects, both audience and artwork/artist are accountable for the meaning the art generates. Further, this renders both artist and art as active participants in the construction of narratives, ideas, and values around the aging experience. In the final section I discuss the implications for this shared responsibility in creating meaning and value. But first I briefly discuss the concept of responsibility, in order to make a case for a particular artistic responsibility with regards to the generation of community norms and values surrounding aging.

Types of Responsibility

The literature on responsibility broadly distinguishes between two types of responsibility: attribution and accountability. According to one type of responsibility, an action is attributable to a person. Say your mug fell off the table and broke. It broke after I bumped into the table and it caused the mug to fall onto the floor. I am *responsible* for your mug breaking insofar as the action of knocking over your mug is *attributable* to me. Attribution is often fairly straightforward, or at least not terribly contestable.

However, we might wonder if I am *morally* responsible in any way for the breaking of your mug. Sure, we all saw me bump into the table. But does it matter if this was an accident, done on purpose, done unknowingly (and here we might draw a distinction between occurring unknowingly out of carelessness or unknowingly for some other reason, such as a sight impairment), or done with full intent to knock your mug off the table and see if it would break? Perhaps I bumped into the table because someone shoved me backward into it, and this resulted in your mug falling and cracking. This seems, at least intuitively, different than if I walk up to the table, see your mug near the edge, and for fun see how much I have to shake the table for it to fall off and break. There is, on the whole, a cascade of possible scenarios in between these two acts, one extreme being entirely out of my control, the other entirely within my control.

In these instances, the notion of *accountability* arises as another way of thinking about responsibility. Often, the level of accountability implies a type of moral responsibility. One way to think about accountability is relating it to control — whether or not an action was in one's own control such that she can be held accountable for it. P. F. Strawson's (2008) well-known essay "Freedom and Resentment" thought through moral responsibility in the face of objections from determinists. Moral determinists believe that, since the world is pre-determined, we cannot, in fact, hold others morally responsible because they are not truly in control of their own actions.

Strawson (2008) noted that we have "reactive attitudes," namely, moral emotions, with which we respond to the quality of will we understand others to demonstrate toward us through their actions. These reactive attitudes change depending on the target of the attitude, and how we assess their responsibility for their actions. Strawson's account of reactive attitudes has yielded a robust literature on moral emotions, moral psychology, and the mechanics of blame and forgiveness, a literature that adds nuance and debate to Strawson's core ideas. For my purposes, what I take to be useful about Strawson's account is the notion that emotional responses toward others can track on to moral assessments.

Most importantly, I read Strawson as suggesting that the responsiveness of our moral assessments is flexible and contingent. It is contingent insofar as our assessments are influenced by factors that contribute to who and how something occurred. That is to say, learning more about the person(s) we are holding morally accountable can influence our attribution of accountability. And the responsiveness of our moral assessments is flexible insofar as they can be modified in light of new information about a situation, its context, and the agent(s) involved. In this regard, a Strawsonian account of moral emotions and moral responsibility is compatible with, and contributes to, my view of ethical community as one that is open to revision from within the community, in which community members see anew and modify their ethical practices.

Here, an example might be helpful. If I broke your mug because I thought it was ugly, showing disregard for your possessions, then you would likely be angry with me and resent my actions, which communicate ill will towards you. There is no excusing me for my actions. Your anger is directed toward me, and is a reactive attitude that communicates to both you and me that you hold me blameworthy. That is to say, the emotional response you have does moral work.

However, if I broke your mug because someone physically assaulted me and pushed me into the table with your mug on it, you might say that I am excused from any moral accountability for the action nonetheless attributable to me. In this scenario, you might be sad that your mug is broken, but this emotional response does not have a target: you are not sad *towards me*. And it would not be an apt response to be angry *at me* for this event (though you might feel anger toward the person who pushed me, both on my behalf for being assaulted and your own behalf for the breaking of your mug. Vicarious reactive attitudes and the distinction between anger on behalf of yourself and indignation on behalf of another, though, are a complex topic within the literature that I will not venture into here).

Moreover, should you discover that I am a toddler who couldn't even see up to the table and had bumped the table while grabbing a leg of it while trying to stand up, you might not only see this as an excuse for my actions, but also as exempting me from even being a participant in a moral community that could be accountable at all for breaking the possessions of others. This is not to say you wouldn't have any emotional response to the breaking of your mug in this scenario, but according to Strawson it would not be an apt response to feel anger towards the toddler. Here, we might imagine that you could still feel anger at the situation, but not at the person. Or if you do feel anger at a person, the target of your anger (that is to say, to whom you attribute *moral* responsibility, rather than *causal* responsibility) would be different. In this case, it is plausible that you are angry at yourself for having left the mug out where you knew the toddler could bump into it, thus holding yourself morally responsible as the target of your blame.

Strawson (2008) therefore draws a distinction between those who we take to be participants in our moral communities and hold responsible through our reactive attitudes (such as anger, resentment, indignation, and gratitude) towards them, and those who are outside the moral community, such as children or the (now contested) category of psychopaths.[10] Those inside and outside the moral community can have actions *attributed* to them, but they are not held equally *accountable* for those actions as apt targets of reactive attitudes. Furthermore, Strawson suggests that the reactive

---

10   Also see Watson (1996) and Shoemaker (2015). Watson unpacks a distinction between causal and deep responsibility, while Shoemaker breaks responsibility into three types: attributable, accountable, and/or answerable.

attitudes, or the emotional responses we have to others, are *moral* emotions that express moral content about who and how we hold others responsible through blame or praise. Yet he is also saying something about the nature of moral responsibility: moral accountability runs deeper than mere attribution for actions. If we take a Strawsonian view, to be responsible as a moral agent within an ethical community is to be accountable for our actions (and non-actions) through the blame or praise with which others respond to us.

Susan Wolf (2015) builds on Strawson's view of moral emotions and reactive attitudes, yet she questions whether there ought to be two strains of responsibility according to which accountability is more deeply moral than a weaker concept of attribution, which lacks a moral valence. Her view is one in which she accepts reactive attitudes, focusing not on the ways in which they are *moral* emotions, but instead on the ways in which they are *responsive* emotions, and signal unqualified responsibility. In her article "Responsibility, Moral and Otherwise," Wolf suggests a variety of ways in which the distinction between moral and nonmoral responsibility fails to logically cash out in the ways that our intuitions might assume. Wolf makes a case for nonmoral responsibility which, she believes, defines humanity as much as moral responsibility does. Wolf is extending the Kantian view that moral responsibility is a uniquely human feature, for as Wolf says: "the most important and deep kind of responsibility that distinguishes us as human is not limited to the moral" (2015, 141).

One case Wolf considers in the realm of nonmoral responsibility, a case upon which I build in the last section of this essay, is that of art. According to Wolf, "thinking about the extent and sense in which we hold artists responsible for their artistic creations may reveal interesting parallels to and differences from the way we think about people's responsibility for the moral good and harm they do" (129). In Wolf's examples, art is initially valued for the purposiveness of the artist in creating a work in exactly the way we see it. However, a work of art may have been produced causally at the hands of an artist, but without the intent for it to be as it is. Wolf notes that it could be the accidental splattering of paint on a canvas that produces a nonetheless pleasing aesthetic effect, or that it could have been his failing eyesight rather than his artistic vision that led El Greco to paint in the particularly dark and haunting style he did (130, 140).

What Wolf concludes from these (and other) examples of aesthetic responsibility is that it might not be *causal* responsibility that is most at stake when we think about responsibility for artistic products. She says that "it may be that there is a kind of responsibility, different and deeper than causal responsibility, that consists in the manifestation or disclosing of an intelligent self's unimpeded response to the world" (141). We might follow Wolf down this line of thinking and add that art is a mode of disclosing the self (or a way of seeing another when art takes up a subject other than the artists' own self). In other words, artistic production is both a response to the world and demands a response from the world. However, to generate a response to the world and from the world (and not merely a small subset of the most prominent or recognized persons within it), art ought to include, reflect, and be accessible to all types of people, especially those who have historically been silenced or invisible.

This interplay between art, responsibility and response exists in a world that is moral, but not only moral. To follow Wolf's line of thinking, there are deeply important nonmoral aspects of our world for which we nonetheless ought to take and recognize responsibility. This responsibility includes being responsible for the communities that we produce. These might be our moral communities, but may also be communities organized otherwise, such as artistic communities, or organized living communities. Artistic responsibility is responsibility, in part, for the production of community by responding to the world such that the members of the community can, in turn, respond to the art that is generated. To build on Wolf's idea, we take responsibility not only for our responses to the world or to art, but these responses become constitutive of our world.

So, while there may be a question as to whether responsibility need always be moral, we might want to say that the co-constructive interplay in art between artist/artwork and viewer is both exemplary and constitutive of the way communities function as engaged participants in generating meaning. Furthermore, the meanings generated within communities inform their practices, and these practices form an ethical community. Art, then, has a unique potential to reflect, challenge, and reinvent a community's ethical practices by spurring the community of participants to reflect, see differently, and establish revised practices.

In the next section I build upon each of the prior sections by bringing them together: the visual marginalization of aging persons and experiences from art and mainstream culture; the preoccupation with visibility in philosophy; the evolution of ethical communities through seeing and seeing differently; and the ways in which responsibility need not only be causal. To the last point, this is to say that responsibility need not only be evaluated with regards to attribution and accountability. Responsibility also contains the notion of *response*, being responsive to the world in which a moral agent finds herself.[11] My argument is that there is a responsibility to produce images of aging persons and experiences in order to invite a community (practical, political, and ethical) to *see* aging and to potentially see aging *anew*, in ways that value the aging experience and make it *worth seeing*, such that more ethical practices and policies are developed within and among an ethical community that is sensitive to, and involves, aging persons and their experiences.

Though we might hope that cultivating ethical practices toward aging others is a sufficient motivation for a community to take action, for some it will not be. And to those individuals, we might note that the category of aging population is one into which all of us, if we are lucky to live long lives, will eventually belong. And thus, aging is one area in which considerations for others are also, potentially, considerations for our future selves. Cultivating ethical regard for aging individuals and populations is an intersubjective practice, developing the modes through which we ought to ethically respond to others. Yet the cultivation of ethical regard for aging individuals also establishes the ethical practices with which we hope to be treated by our community when we too age. In a sense, we are establishing not only how to treat others, but how others will treat us.

---

11 Feminist ethics centers the ways in which responsibility is interconnected with the act and concept of response. Both Donna Haraway (2008) and Kelly Oliver (2001) have analyzed responsibility as "response-ability" throughout their work. See their cited work for two examples from the scholarship of each. Margaret Urban Walker (2007) highlights the aspect of response within responsibility in her framework of responsibility ethics. She notes that we have moral claims made upon us in our relationships with others, especially those who are impacted by our own choices and "we are *obligated to respond* to particular others when circumstances or ongoing relationships render them especially, conspicuously, or particularly dependent on us" (2007, 113).

Artistic Responsibility and Ethical Communities

In the realm of aging studies, fine art can provide a resource. One medical journal in gerontology established an "Images in Aging" column, created to feature fine art specifically about aging (Reynolds 2017). Yet critiques of the arts note the limited scope of images of aging on offer. Michelle Meagher presents one such critique, suggesting that in the history of art some female bodies are rendered visible, but in an "entirely negative register" (Meagher 2014, 105). We might even say that these images do harm to their subjects, and those who are members of the groups portrayed. Griselda Pollock, quoted by Meagher, describes an "artificial and frozen aesthetics of ageing" particularly of the female body in Western art (105). According to Meagher, both Pollock and Kathleen Woodward have sought to "explore how we might learn to see old women and old women's bodies differently" (105).

As already discussed, art is an inter-subjective experience in which the viewer co-constructs meaning in concert with the artwork on view. However, seeing aging bodies differently is not only about a viewer learning to see or read the body differently. This project of seeing anew also requires that the artist sees subjects differently, with sensitivity to the ways in which they portray their subject. The images themselves need to not only pedal in the tropes of witch/hag that Meagher identifies as pervading images of aging (women in particular), nor do they need to render a body in decline as (only) grotesque. The word grotesque is important here, as it connotes a distortion for effect, often a comedic one. My point is not to sanitize images of aging such that they become unrealistic. On the contrary, my point is to avoid the grotesque, which is itself a version of the exaggerated, distorted, and thus unrealistic. We tend to equate grotesque with gross, unsavory, or ugly. However, it is, at the core, a distortion from reality. This distortion could work in either a positive or negative direction. As Silvers has noted, different cultures identify particular features as either appealing or repulsive, and so the "standard against which we assess the pleasingness of any human's corporeal configuration is a constructed, or at least socially mediated, rather than natural one" (2000, 200). And if it is socially mediated, it can be remediated.

However, to achieve any of these goals requires the production of art portraying older bodies in the first place. It is necessary that *some* artists take older persons or the experience of aging as their subject. To be clear, I am not suggesting that every artist has an obligation to make aged individuals or aging the subject of their art routinely or even occasionally. Nor am I saying that any particular artist ought to take up these subjects. Part of what is valuable about art is its plurality of modes, media, expressions, topics, styles, etc. Certainly, some artists will flourish working in abstract forms that are not offering any sort of representation of bodies or persons. This richness of artistic themes and styles is part of what makes art enjoyable, challenging, and relevant. Yet I am suggesting that artistic responsibility is a type of responsibility that allows for the attribution of work to individuals, and for holding them accountable for their artistic product. Such responsibility is, arguably, easier to identify than, say, figuring out who is responsible for commercial or consumer media productions where many hands (and background cultural values that are being both created and reinforced) are involved in the output. A sitcom, a print ad in a glossy magazine, or a blockbuster film might not be attributable to one or even a clearly defined handful of individuals. They are instead a collaboration, or even a contracting out of work, in which an idea is generated by some and then executed by others, who may or may not have a say in the direction of the final product. Power, money, and hierarchy are all at play.

While power, money, and hierarchy likely influence the art world, arguably an individual artist is nonetheless generating pieces of art that she feels are authentically and uniquely their own; indeed, this is often one of the reasons that art is valuable, because of the particular vision, voice, and skill of the artist making it. And this aesthetic or artistic responsibility produces art that we might take, to borrow Wolf's phrase, as "expressive of [the artist's] soul" or "disclosive of [the artist's] self" (2015, 132) while also drawing in the viewer as, broadly speaking, participating in the community of members making meaning from the art. Meaning is made through the reactions of the audience to the art: reactions that function, like the reactive attitudes, to form judgments. Some of these judgments will be warranted, and others will need to be revised when excusing or exempting conditions are introduced, but the reactions to the works of art are themselves a mode of participation in a community.

My assertion is that our communities of practice are our ethical communities, and the practices of making and reacting to art reflect, and have a role in shaping, our ethical practices. Accordingly, individual artists can be attributable and accountable for the art they produce, but both artist and audience can pause to reflect on what, how, and why art and images are also participants in ethical communities. This could extend to a whole host of historically or contextually marginalized populations. Specifically with regards to aging, artistic responsibility is one way to shift the conversation about aged bodies: to center them and to literally bring them into focus by putting images in front of viewers. There is an imperative to bring images of aging into the light, and artists can be among the vanguards of change by doing as the philosopher cave dweller did in Plato's allegory: seeing the images for what they are instead of being content in the shadows. Although her newfound views may be unpopular, the cave dweller who breaks from her chains and sees things as they are in the daylight brings her knowledge back to those still dwelling in the cave so they can begin to see anew. Despite the difficulty she faces returning to those still living in the shadows, she understands that she has a duty to return. She remains a participant in her ethical community, reshaping it from within the community and working to actively co-construct new understanding together rather than leaving the cave and the community behind.

The co-construction of meaning is precisely what has to happen. This is the work of ethical societies constructing their values within the community of practitioners. And art brings into view people, ideas, and values that can be responded to, rejected, or reinforced by the ethical community in which the art and artist share and participate alongside others. Silvers says that "to enlarge our aesthetic responsiveness to real people… would enlarge our moral capacities" (2000, 200). We must enlarge our aesthetic responsiveness to real people, which means not only prioritizing real over ideal, but also centering the real people who have been historically excluded from full membership in the ethical community. By making aging people and their experiences visible and valued topics of artistic representation, the community recognizes older persons as full members within the community. By rendering older lives and experiences visible, an ethical community can generate co-constructed meaning about aging and the aging experience.

Following Walker's moral framework, expanding the moral community to include those who have been silenced is part of the process of seeing anew within the moral community. Full inclusion in the moral community centers the voices of aging individuals as participants, who in turn shape and participate in ethical practices attuned towards their membership in the ethical community. Artistic representation of older persons contributes to an ethical community that is better able to focus its moral imagination on the lives and experiences of older individuals in ways that can translate into better ethical practices and policies respecting aging and aged persons within the community.

Conclusion

In conclusion, I want to address two potential objections to my argument. One is from the free speech advocates who claim something like this: the artistic responsibility for which I have argued is a way of telling artists what to make their art about and this infringes on the freedom of speech to make art about whatever one desires to express. The second objection accepts the notion of artistic responsibility to portray aging, but holds that the mere making of art about aging does not necessarily entail that it will yield a positive result on the ethical communities' attitudes toward aging and aging persons. The first critic has misunderstood my argument. The second one has provided an important qualifier to it.

To the free speech advocate, my reply is that I am not suggesting that all or any particular artist must make art about aging. My point is broader: art offers a unique possibility to improve the ethical relationship between society and its aging members, and *some* art ought to address this. We might think of it as an imperfect duty—some art, some of the time, should do this. Not all art all of the time. My aim here is to open up an ethical possibility or a site of potentially fertile ethical ground.

However, I must acknowledge that the concerns of the second critic may be true for any number of reasons. Two of those reasons I consider here. One is that making aging the subject of art does not imply or require that it be a positive picture of aging. The other is that making art does not mean that it will reach an audience at all. But these two points provide a springboard for further refinement of my claim. As discussed above, Michelle Meagher, Griselda Pollock, and contemporary media critics, have all noted the ways in which art that does cast its gaze on (usually the female) aged bodies does so in unflattering ways and according to received tropes such as the witch and the hag. Or, aging is embodied in unachievable ideals, such as by casting a much younger actor to portray an older character.

My suggestion is not that art be made to portray aging in a particularly positive light, rather that it engages with aging and aged persons in a way that is not purposefully negative (i.e., grotesque, or lacking in social status or agency) nor purposefully revisionary (e.g., by depicting unrealistic ideals of beauty that defy real aging, by using much younger persons to portray or model for an older person in visual art, cinema, or photography). Essentially, I am suggesting that there is an artistic imperative to provide *realistic* rather than distorted images of old age and the aging process. Which is not to say that the art must be realist or cannot be abstract. My emphasis is that the very act of taking on realistic, lived experiences of aging and aged subjects as the focus for (some) art centers those subjects as having value. Aging and aged persons are worthy of reflection and consideration. And this consideration ought to occur in two senses: aging is a subject that demands intellectual reflection, and aged and aging individuals are ethical subjects who ought to receive just, ethical treatment and social consideration.

References

Chivers, Sally. 2011. *The Silvering Screen: Old Age and Disability in Cinema*. Toronto: University of Toronto Press.

Dargis, Manola, Wesley Morris, and A. O. Scott. 2016. "Oscars So White? Or Oscars So Dumb? Discuss." *The New York Times*. January 15.

Frisinger, Cathy. 2003. "Movies Reveal Naked Truth About Older, Sexy Women." *Chicago Tribune*. December 17.

Gay, Roxanne. 2016. "The Oscars and Hollywood's Race Problem." *The New York Times*. January 22.

Haraway, Donna J. 2008. *When Species Meet*. Minneapolis: University of Minnesota Press.

Jay, Martin. 1994. *Downcast Eyes: The Denigration of Vision in Twentieth-Century French Thought*. Berkeley: University of California Press.

Lumme-Sandt, Kirsi. 2011. "Images of Ageing in a 50+ Magazine." *Journal of Aging Studies* 5: 45–51.

MacIntyre, Alasdair. 1999. *Dependent Rational Animals*. Chicago: Open Court.

Meagher, Michelle. 2014. "Against the Invisibility of Old Age: Cindy Sherman, Suzy Lake, and Martha Wilson." *Feminist Studies* 40 (1): 101–43.

Oliver, Kelly. 2001. *Witnessing: Beyond Recognition*. Minneapolis: University of Minnesota Press.

Oxford English Dictionary. 2017. "grotesque, n. and adj." Oxford: Oxford University Press.
Plato. 1992. *Republic*. Translated by G. M. A. Grube. Indianapolis: Hackett.
Rawls, John. 2005. *Political Liberalism*. New York: Columbia University Press.
Reynolds, Charles F. 2017. "Images in Aging." *The American Journal of Geriatric Psychiatry* 26 (1). https://doi.org/10.1016/j.jagp.2017.10.005
Richards, Naomi, Lorna Warren, and Merryn Gott. 2012. "The Challenge of Creating 'Alternative' Images of Ageing: Lessons from a Project with Older Women." *Journal of Aging Studies* 26: 65-78.
Schweda, Mark, and Georg Marchmann. 2013. "How Do We Want to Grow Old? Anti-Ageing Medicine and the Scope of Public Healthcare in Liberal Democracies." *Bioethics* 27 (7): 357-64.
Shoemaker, David. 2015. *Responsibility from the Margins*. New York: Oxford University Press.
Silvers, Anita. 2000. "From the Crooked Timber of Humanity, Beautiful Things Can Be Made." In *Beauty Matters*, edited by Peg Zeglen Brand, 197-221. Bloomington: Indiana University Press.
Strawson, P. F. 2008. "Freedom and Resentment." *Freedom and Resentment and Other Essays*. New York: Routledge.
Thomas, R. Elizabeth, and Julian Rappaport. 1996. "Art as Community Narrative: A Resource for Social Change." In *Myths about the Powerless: Contesting Social Inequalities*, edited by M. Brinton Lykes, Ali Banuazizi, Ramsay Liem, and Michael Morris, 317-36. Philadelphia: Temple University Press.
Walker, Margaret Urban. 2007. *Moral Understandings: A Feminist Study in Ethics*. Second Edition. New York: Oxford University Press.
Watson, Gary. 1996. "Two Faces of Responsibility." *Philosophical Topics* 24: 227-48.
Wittgenstein, Ludwig. 2009. *Philosophical Investigations*. Translated by G. E. M. Anscombe, P. M. S. Hacker, and Joachim Schulte. Revised Fourth Edition. West Sussex: Wiley Blackwell.
Wolf, Susan. 2015. "Responsibility, Moral and Otherwise." *Inquiry* 58 (2): 127-42.
Young, Iris Marion. 1990. *Justice and the Politics of Difference*. Princeton: Princeton University Press.

About the author

Elizabeth Lanphier is a Health Care Ethics Fellow at the Center for Biomedical Ethics and Society at Vanderbilt University Medical Center. She received her PhD in philosophy from Vanderbilt University, and a Master's Degree in Narrative Medicine from Columbia University. Elizabeth previously worked in the international health and humanitarian aid sector. Her research areas span across medical, global, and feminist ethics; questions of care and justice; and shared responsibility.

Part Three

Dependence and Independence in the Context of Care and Aging

Chapter Six

Fostering a 'Community of Care': Supporting a Shared Experience of Aging in Co-housing

Magdalene Goemans

(with contributions from Lynne Markell, Sharon Irven, and Lynn Pfeffer, members of *Convivium Cohousing for Seniors*)

Abstract

"Fostering a 'Community of Care': Supporting a Shared Experience of Aging in Co-housing" by **Magdalene Goemans** explains the history and hopes of a housing project for older adults in Ottawa. As an alternative to more traditional living arrangements, the model adopted by this group is self-organization and it intends to support the goal of sharing services, as well as to act as a safeguard against social isolation.

Introduction

With the demographic shift in Canada towards an older population that is living longer, seniors will face many challenges over the next few decades. The many older adults that would prefer to age at home face limited options for affordable rental housing or home ownership (CBC News 2013; Sienkiewicz 2017), while the availability of institutional assisted living spaces for seniors has declined as costs have continued to grow (FCM 2015; Hermus, Stonebridge, and Edenhoffer 2015; CMHC 2017). The aging population also presents a substantial challenge for the Canadian health care system, with a greater number of adults requiring ongoing care for prolonged health issues in their senior years (CMA 2016).

Over the coming decades, more seniors may require extended access to supportive services, both from home-based caregivers (e.g., unpaid caregivers such as friends or relatives) as well as from external providers. With the senior cohort of recent decades having had fewer children than in previous generations, with their children often moving abroad, or with the loss of their spouses as older individuals age, the risk of social isolation for some older adults is quite significant (Turner and Findlay 2012; Hermus, Stonebridge, and Edenhoffer 2015; Mockler and Cools 2017). These types of challenges have led to calls for the development of communities tailored to seniors' needs and experiences (Province of Ontario, Seniors' Secretariat 2013; The National Seniors Council 2016).

Various models of intentional communities[1] are emerging as promising alternatives to traditional living arrangements for seniors. A 'community of care' model for seniors—also referred to as an 'aging in community' or 'co-caring' model—at its core involves a network of neighbors living in close proximity that exchange supportive services and share experiences of aging. The co-housing model is one approach to fulfilling these objectives, offering a meaningful response to the risk of social isolation among older adults in a community by strengthening connections between seniors who may more easily identify with the experiences of others in their peer group, and by recognizing the unique contributions of older adults, who may be more sensitive to each other's needs. In essence, supporting older adults in an engaged and active approach to co-care through co-housing has the potential to redefine the experience of aging (Atkins 2013; Black, Dobbs, and Young 2015; Blanchard 2013; Glass and Vander Plaats 2013; Rodman 2013).

This chapter details the efforts underway among a group of seniors organized under the name *Convivium Cohousing for Seniors*, which aims to establish a co-housing community in Ottawa, Canada, that is geared towards the needs and priorities of older adults. One key goal for the project is the establishment of a 'community of care' among residents, aiming in part at reducing their reliance upon institutional support services. The author of this chapter, a doctoral student who provided research assistance to the *Convivium* group within a community-campus partnership project based out

---

1   Shenker provides the following description of an intentional community: "Intentional communities have emerged as a result of a number of people consciously and purposefully coalescing as a group in order to realize a set of aims… These aims are not partial: they attempt to create an entire way of life, hence, unlike organizations or social movements, they are intentional communities" (2011, 6).

of Carleton University in Ottawa, has been witness to, and a participant in, the group's efforts in pursuit of a co-housing community. This chapter describes an ongoing process of community formation that is taking place among *Convivium* members prior to the actual establishment of a physical co-housing space, in which discussion around options for design, financing, and governance of the community are guided by potential co-housing residents. The present chapter examines the external support that has helped to establish and fuel the growth of this initiative, the process through which community is being formed among members as the co-housing vision takes shape, as well as the strengths and challenges associated with the efforts of the co-housing group. This examination also effectively reveals the agency and empowerment of older adults which is being manifested within this context, as the group's members take a proactive approach to accessing a housing site and supportive service options for their future seniors' community.

Scholarly Examinations of Communities of Care

A co-caring model is built on concepts of mutual support, strengthened relationships, and active and engaged participants. The 'community of care' approach is well-suited to the health and wellness needs of seniors, who have much to draw on from their own experiences as they gain a deeper understanding of each other's needs. Within such a reciprocal, caregiving context, participants who themselves require assistance may also be eager (but are not required) to contribute to others' well-being within their community of peers (Borgloh and Westerheide 2012; Glass 2016).

Co-caring models vary in size, structure, and influence. They may employ a network of services that are exchanged between neighbors or provided by other volunteers in the community, and which are supplemented by health care or wellness services administered by contracted external providers. Common informal caregiving services provided by participants include transportation to and from medical appointments, doing errands for neighbors, and taking care of individuals at home following hospitalization. External services may be funded by annual membership dues or service fees, or service credits may be provided to participants who volunteer (Atkins 2013).

Establishing a viable community of care for older adults may require significant effort, time, and financial resources (Span 2010). Scholars also assert that it is crucial that the design of seniors' co-caring communities account for the diversity of experiences, skills, and attitudes that exists among community members (Glass and Vander Plaats 2013; Black, Dobbs, and Young 2015). As members age, changes in their physical condition and needs may have significant impacts on their abilities to provide assistance to others (Atkins 2013). Others, on the other hand, may be focused on maintaining self-sufficiency and thus reluctant to accept help (Critchlow Rodman 2013).

Two common examples from the United States that support co-caring and aging in community are the NORC-SSP and Village models. A Naturally Occurring Retirement Community Supportive Service Program, or NORC-SSP, is a formal, community-scale model that involves partnerships between social and health care agencies in the provisioning of supportive services for older adults. The main goal of this type of program is to facilitate independence and aging in place within existing communities (Elbert and Neufeld 2010; Guo and Castillo 2012; Stone 2014). Compared to the NORC-SSP model, the Village model has grown out of a more grassroots, non-profit approach. Village programs typically employ a small number of paid staff (often solely in the form of a single community coordinator), but rely more substantially on the assistance of member and non-member volunteers (Accius 2010; Thomas 2011; Snelling 2012; Stone 2014). Challenges associated with the Village model include potential difficulty in ensuring sufficient and consistent funding, as well as difficulty in supporting diverse cultures and incomes among participants (Guengerich 2009; Thomas 2011; Snelling 2012).

A co-caring network for seniors may also evolve naturally within a co-housing setting, wherein the physical layout may offer both connected housing units and common spaces that promote relationship-building through communal meal preparation and group recreational activities (Critchlow Rodman 2013). The co-housing model was first conceived in Denmark and Sweden in the 1960s and 1970s as a strategy intended to suit the needs of multi-generational families. It was later applied to the seniors' housing context and gained prominence in the United States over the next few decades. In contrast to institutional retirement settings, the co-housing model offers residents a voice in the design and governance of the proposed housing community (Vestbro 1992; Bamford 2005; Durrett 2009; Lyon, Kang, and Kramp 2013). Examples of successful seniors' and senior-focused co-housing communities in Canada include Wolf Willow Cohousing in Saskatoon, Saskatchewan, and Harbourside Cohousing in Sooke, British Columbia.

The co-housing model offers several advantages, including increased efficiency and cost-savings for older adults with similar needs and priorities who live within a contained geographical area (Atkins 2013; Critchlow Rodman 2013). Although residents receive, within a home setting, support from friends in addition to caretakers, this informal caregiving is not intended to replace external professional care and services where they are needed (Span 2010). The model also provides opportunities to foster self-esteem and a sense of purpose among older adults, who actively participate throughout the process in helping others and strengthening their relationships with neighbors. This model recognizes the unique contributions of older adults, who may be more sensitive to the needs of their peers in ways that younger members of the community have not yet considered (Atkins 2013; Black, Dobbs, and Young 2015; Blanchard 2013; Glass and Vander Plaats 2013). Significantly, co-housing also offers the potential to reduce health care costs among seniors, as they face the challenges of aging together and maintain greater awareness of each other's needs (Borgloh and Westerheide 2012). The co-housing model may also assist in mitigating the risk of social isolation among older adults by deepening a sense of connectedness to community and attachment to place among individuals who may otherwise lack meaningful access to family supports (Sanguinetti 2014; Lager, van Hoven, and Meijering 2012). Co-housing also strengthens caregiving relationships between elder residents who may more easily identify with the experiences of others who are living in close proximity in their neighborhoods (Atkins 2013; Critchlow Rodman 2013; Black, Dobbs, and Young 2015; Glass 2016).

Origins of the Convivium *Group: Strategic Access to External Supports*

Convivium Cohousing for Seniors was formed as a non-profit organization in 2016 by a group of older adults living in the Ottawa area. The group maintains the primary goal of establishing a shared housing community for a network of neighbors, aged 55 or older, who will support each other as they age. As its plans for co-housing progress, *Convivium* is promoting an initiative that includes values of sustainability, diversity, equity, as well as physical and emotional health among members. The group consists of about 35 members (with a waiting list for other interested participants), with a large proportion of female members (about two-thirds), and includes some married couples. Most members fall within a middle-income demographic, and many own their own homes.

From its outset, the *Convivium* group has benefitted from its access to varied external supporters and influences. *Convivium Cohousing for Seniors* evolved out of an initiative originally known as *Innovative Housing for Older Adults in Old Ottawa East* (IHOA). Established in 2015, the IHOA initiative was formed from the efforts of a local citizen organization called *Sustainable Living Ottawa East* (SLOE). At that time, SLOE had been undertaking active efforts to incorporate a more sustainable approach into a major residential redevelopment (known as Greystone Village) of a large inner-urban greenspace property that was underway in their Old Ottawa East neighborhood. As part of this effort, SLOE formed a working group focused specifically on encouraging the allocation of seniors' housing and affordable housing within a portion of the redevelopment site, doing so in conjunction with other working groups who were promoting such sustainability measures for the site, such as energy efficiency, community connectivity, and river shoreline restoration.

With funding from the *Community Foundation of Ottawa*, in early 2015 SLOE partnered with another local organization, the *Sandy Hill Community Health Centre* (SHCHC), in efforts to encourage interested older adults within the area to assemble a common vision for seniors' housing for the redevelopment site, and to communicate this aim to the project's developer. A first gathering of older adults from the area generated significant interest, attendance, and feedback among participants, and the IHOA group formed as subsequent meetings took place over the next few months. Over time, this growing group of older adults within IHOA began to take on greater ownership of the initiative, and decided that their goal for seniors' housing would be structured around a co-housing framework. By April 2016 they had established their non-profit organization as *Convivium Cohousing for Seniors*, with the intent of further boosting the credibility of the group as it assembled proposals and applied for grants.

In the initial period of its formation, the IHOA/*Convivium* group also received research support through a community-campus engagement initiative based out of Carleton University in Ottawa; the initiative is titled "Community First: Impacts of Community Engagement" (CFICE). The CFICE project funded a research assistant—a doctoral student who is also the author of this chapter—to provide research and logistical support to the group, and to help members to articulate and communicate their objectives and overall vision for co-housing. In addition to other planning and communication support, the research assistant assisted IHOA members in fleshing out key values and physical elements to be incorporated into the co-housing project (e.g., ecological sustainability, accessibility/adaptability, connectedness to surrounding neighborhoods/supports, etc.). *Convivium* also received meaningful support from a local affordable housing consultant, who worked with group members to plan and facilitate a Financing and Ownership workshop that offered potential co-housing residents opportunities to learn about and discuss housing ownership and affordability options for the project. The consultant was subsequently hired by the group to review an offer from the developer to purchase a condominium building for co-housing on the Greystone Village site, to be discussed below.

At various points in its formation, the *Convivium* group also looked to some of the best practices of other seniors' co-housing models for inspiration. With a lack of co-housing development consultants in the Ottawa area (or within Eastern Canada generally) to assist members in developing a plan for their vision of co-living and co-care, the group sought to learn from several successful co-housing models in other areas of the country, including Pacific Gardens Cohousing in Nanaimo, British Columbia, as well as the aforementioned Wolf Willow Cohousing and Harbourside Cohousing. In April 2017, Margaret Critchlow, a driving force behind the development of Harbourside Cohousing and the originator of a course at Royal Roads University entitled "Aging Well in Community," worked directly with *Convivium* members to provide a similarly-themed workshop. Drawing on her own experience as a resident of the Harbourside community, Critchlow reiterated to seniors the advantages of the co-housing model (for example, through strengthened relationships and communication between members). Critchlow also provided guidance on decision-making processes and organizational structures to the proposed *Convivium* community, and assisted the *Convivium* group in refining its common priorities and determining the next steps in the co-housing development.

The varied external support described above aided greatly in the establishment and progress of the *Convivium* co-housing initiative. The SLOE group, with support from the SHCHC, provided an initial impetus and vision for seniors' housing in the Old Ottawa East neighborhood, as well as a venue to bring older adults in the surrounding community together to discuss possibilities for shared living and co-caring. The Community Foundation of Ottawa provided crucial, but modest, funding to the group. This was done first to support the assembly of two community workshops on design and finance and ownership, then later to cover some pre-construction costs. Lastly, the graduate research assistant, the housing affordability consultant, and the co-housing consultant all aided in the planning and execution of workshops that played important roles in fostering greater cohesion of the *Convivium* group and in expanding members' knowledge and understanding of seniors' co-housing.

Building Community as the Co-housing Vision Takes Shape

The forging of a community for *Convivium* members is an ongoing process that will come to full fruition once the physical form of their planned co-housing project is eventually established. As the group and the initiative progress, community ties are being strengthened and common values are being assembled by the development of *Convivium*'s varied structures of governance and by its formal and informal community outreach events. Workshops developed by *Convivium* have brought its members together for discussion and common learning around themes of co-housing design and ownership. Two initial workshops developed by the original IHOA group, and supported by SLOE, SHCHC, and the Community Foundation of Ottawa, were organized with extensive effort and enthusiasm by group members. A design workshop in June 2015 helped participants to prioritize co-housing design features that incorporate shared spaces for cooking, gathering, and gardening, as well as a diversity of unit types to support accessibility and adaptability. Several months later, another workshop was held to examine options for ownership within a co-housing setting and the implications for financing and affordability. That workshop revealed that participants required more information regarding basic housing costs, tenure types, and affordability measures for residents before moving forward. Subsequent workshops organized in 2016 by *Convivium* helped members refine their design ideas and establish a limited equity housing co-operative model for the development project. Surveys distributed at various points in the initiative allowed members to further clarify their preferences. These activities, along with members' participation on committees and in monthly meetings, furthered relationship-building among members, offered opportunities for participants to acknowledge each other's hopes and concerns, and helped to build shared understandings regarding the co-housing vision.

In addition to the delivery of community workshops, formal governance structures established within the *Convivium* group have played a significant role in strengthening community bonds among members. The overall management and administration of the group lies with a board of directors, whose members are guided by the organization's by-laws, as well as an inclusive decision-making process. As noted earlier, the *Convivium* group consists of approximately 35 members. Full membership costs $200 and offers members the opportunity to serve on and/or vote for its board of directors.[2] While membership does not guarantee a housing unit in the future co-housing community, those who join are expected to contribute to governance and/or provide financial and volunteer support to *Convivium*'s development. As of late 2017, another class of membership—'equity' member status—was offered to members who wished to commit more fully to purchasing a unit in the future co-housing community, by contributing more substantially to the costs of the pre-construction phase of co-housing development.

Through its formation the *Convivium* group has assembled other committees in addition to its original Design working group and Financing and Ownership working group. A Supportive Services committee has begun to refine a reciprocal caregiving model for co-housing residents, while a Membership and Communications committee maintains a contact list of *Convivium* members, facilitates

---

2   An associate membership option for a lower fee was originally offered to individuals who might, as *Convivium* had suggested, "want to observe, learn more, and eventually become full members," but this option was eventually removed.

ongoing communication through emails, and organizes various informal social events for the group. Formal governance activities are also helping to strengthen the *Convivium* community by establishing effective processes for decision-making among members, and by facilitating active networking with other organizations such as Broadening the Base, the City of Ottawa Housing branch, and the Canadian Cohousing Network. The organization's non-profit designation was also established in part to bolster their position in funding applications and broaden their access to local housing consultants.

Aspirations Moving Forward

The *Convivium* group continues to advance its efforts through the hard work, extensive knowledge, and great enthusiasm of its many members who are actively pursuing an enriched experience of aging through co-housing. This common desire to form a meaningful community is demonstrated by members' ongoing participation in the group's board of directors, and in members' meetings and informal events, as well as by their many contributions to workshop development. Through the co-housing initiative, this active group of older adults is proactively working to overcome potential vulnerabilities that come with aging. Members are establishing a clear vision for their co-housing community which is built on caring relationships between members, and which will incorporate a sustainably designed and socially vibrant space for shared experience and understanding. In a response to *Convivium*'s supportive services survey, one member articulated their overall vision for the co-caring community as "a group of people who make the conscious and sustained commitment to live in proximity in order to provide mutual support and assistance to each other in whatever way each person is able ... by having a reliable network of neighbors to count on." Some members spoke of the importance of participating in weekly rituals, such as sharing meals, as a means of fostering community, while others noted their desire for support from friends/neighbors in times of vulnerability, such as "physical challenges, illness, or death of my loved ones." Another survey participant noted, "I don't have an extended family, so I want to live with and support others and be supported by them as we age together. I need this for my own physical and social wellbeing."

Convivium members are envisioning a physical space for co-housing that:
- physically accommodates a comfortable and active process of aging within community by supporting accessibility and adaptability, and by encouraging connections between older adults within a home setting;
- allows for independence, with the comfort of knowing that others are close by to provide help when needed;
- incorporates communal areas for activities such as meal preparation, dining, gardening, and recreation;
- accommodates spaces for health and wellness services by external providers (e.g., small office space for practitioners, tub room for assisted bathing);
- offers other conveniences (e.g., provides a guest suite that is available to rent).

With regard to their vision of a co-caring community, many *Convivium* members have expressed their eagerness to exchange regular supportive services with co-housing neighbors, through activities such as shared meal preparation, checking in on neighbors, and helping others with daily errands. They have also offered more intense support to neighbors during particular times of need, for example by assisting other residents with post-hospital care. Through these and other suggested daily actions, members are actively planning for a strengthened community network within their future co-housing development.

Efforts towards refining a supportive services framework for *Convivium* did not progress as much as some would like. This delay has been attributed in part to the more intense focus taken by members in determining co-housing design and costing parameters during the first phases of the initiative, as well as the requirements for more immediate decision-making among members in response to offers for a potential co-housing site from the Greystone Village developer (this is discussed in more detail below). Some members have also suggested that there has been a lack of strong and sustained leadership specific to the supportive services effort. Overall, members anticipate that renewed discussion about supportive services will progress during the construction phase of the project.

Alongside the many accomplishments that have been part of the *Convivium* effort, there exist considerable challenges faced by the group. A main challenge for the group involves accessing a development site for the co-housing community that is centrally located, near to services and transit, and priced within a range affordable to all *Convivium* members. An original IHOA initiative was founded by the SLOE group with the intention of advocating for a seniors' housing community to be located within the Greystone Village redevelopment site in Old Ottawa East. This has proved to be quite challenging for *Convivium* to achieve, even with the extended period of direct and constructive engagement with the Greystone Village developer.[3]

Convivium next invited other developers to submit expressions of interest for the provision of a different development site and design/build team for the co-housing project. While *Convivium* ultimately did not locate a suitable development opportunity through this process, the group notes that they did gain valuable knowledge about the range of architects and builders in Ottawa that have knowledge of co-housing, as well as regarding the market context and potential risks associated with land purchases and working with a design/build team. As of the time of writing, the group would prefer to acquire an available vacant property and then hire an architect and building team to design and construct their co-housing vision according to the group's set criteria.

Through this process, the *Convivium* group has realized that it faces the continual challenge of the significant power differential that exists between its group and much larger and established private developers who are competing for the same sites in the area that are suited to a multi-unit housing development. Scanlon and Fernandez-Arrigoitia describe a similar economic situation, where co-housing groups seek out development sites in large cities within high-value, inner-urban areas, and note that "most land that is suitable for cohousing development is also suitable for other types of residential use" (2015, 119). They comment that potential co-housing residents are frequently required to make offers on land in competition with private developers, who can often submit higher bids with much larger-scale development projects and future profits in mind.

As one might expect, there have also been challenges associated with assembling a cohesive vision and unified effort towards

---

3 *Convivium* was offered another opportunity by the Greystone Village developer to purchase a turnkey building; however, this option included more units than required and a design that did not suit the priorities of the group.

co-housing development among participants. Members hold varying degrees of commitment to the project, with some primarily feeling out the possibilities associated with the initiative, and others belonging to multiple co-housing groups. Some members hold extensive career experience in planning and actively participate in setting objectives and making decisions within the group,[4] while others hold a less active interest in the development process and simply wish to purchase a set unit in the completed co-housing community. Within this varied context, *Convivium* members are required to assemble significant amounts of equity (often equity that has been accumulated over a lifetime), agree on a site, and move quickly to make decisions about purchasing a building site within limited windows of opportunity. Reflecting on this reality, one member has noted, "There is a big difference between interest and willingness to make a commitment that needs to be better understood in terms of what the issues are and how to address them." In general, it is anticipated that the size of the group will narrow as members are asked to confirm their commitment to the project and contribute more substantial funds to the co-housing development process.

These types of issues highlight one of the largest concerns voiced by *Convivium* members, namely, the lack of access to a co-housing consultant that can both assist the group throughout this process in refining co-housing design and financing objectives, and understand the multi-unit residential development environment in Ottawa. In contrast with the experiences of co-housing projects within Western Canada and the United States, as mentioned earlier there are currently no pools of knowledgeable and qualified co-housing development consultants from which to draw in the Ottawa area, or even within the wider region of Eastern Canada. With the exception of the guidance *Convivium* members received through the previously mentioned workshop hosted by Margaret Critchlow, and a meeting with residents of Wolf Willow Cohousing, there have been only limited interactions with co-housing experts. This lack of qualified guidance requires that the *Convivium* group—all of whom are volunteer members without prior co-housing experience—take on the bulk of navigating the path of continual learning and action related

4 Through extensive career experience, many members hold significant skills in setting up organizations and creating committees, organizing workshops, engaging with consultants, and assembling funding proposals.

to co-housing development, a path that for many members is unfamiliar and somewhat intimidating.

Critical Reflections on Care in Co-housing

As *Convivium* members continue the work of realizing their co-housing vision, there are several wider issues of potential concern that require further consideration. The most immediate issue involves the significant expenses incurred by residents in a co-housing project. Though there have been successes in lowering costs within some co-housing initiatives by incorporating elements such as public funding and sweat equity from residents (Fiore 1999; Fromm 2000; Hasell and Scanzoni 2000), it is commonly assumed that the co-housing model, with its additional shared living spaces and other amenities, will be more expensive to construct and operate. As a result, occupancy in a co-housing community is often limited to persons of means within a homogenous group of middle-class or upper-income residents (Ruin 2015).

Convivium members increasingly recognize the substantial costs associated with establishing a co-housing community, particularly within a location that will appeal to a broad base. Affordability for residents—an early goal set out by the SLOE group and the SHCHC—has proven to be a significant constraint for the project,[5] as members discover that co-housing may ultimately require a more substantial financial commitment than conventional housing. This realization led some earlier members to leave the group, while some others have pressed for efforts to advocate for public subsidies for the project. As time goes on, the costs of developing a co-housing project in areas best suited to the needs of seniors (for example, with easy access to amenities and public transportation) continue to escalate; as one *Convivium* member has noted, "turns out, everyone else wants to live in those locations too."

The costs associated with co-housing also often require that prospective residents commit significant funds to a project for the purposes of covering consulting and legal expenses prior to the actual construction of a housing community. Members must have ready access to capital and be somewhat able to bear certain levels of financial risk (Fromm 2000; Williams 2008). *Convivium* members

5   A more extensive discussion of affordability issues within the *Convivium* initiative can be found in Ballamingie, Goemans, and Martin (2017).

hope to assemble a development team (e.g., a lawyer, an architect, a builder) prior to securing a site, which may require an accumulated financial commitment from the group of up to $50,000. The group has unsuccessfully sought out opportunities for external funding for this phase of the process, and, as of the time of writing, the group has not received resource support from any level of government to assist in the advancement of their co-housing vision. Given the context of a dwindling supply of affordable housing available to Canadians over the last two decades, the challenge of accessing financial assistance for the *Convivium* project reflects a wider absence of public policy, programs, or subsidies at all levels of government to support ownership (versus rental) of affordable housing for middle- or lower-income households.

Another area for reflection involves the intentional restriction within the *Convivium* group to adults over 55 years of age, which sets a condition of perpetual age segregation within the housing community. Scholars have noted several potentially negative aspects associated with age segregation within seniors' housing, including possible loneliness and isolation among residents (due to the loss of direct connections to family members or to the vitality of the local community), or experiences of boredom or despair as residents age (Addae-Dapaah 2008; Percival 2001). The grouping of senior residents into a distinct area may be perceived as superficial or forced, and not reflective of the diversity that exists within communities (Waldron et al., 2005). In addition, older adults face uncertain futures regarding the ways in which personal circumstances and health may change over time as they age. As *Convivium* members grow older together, the relatively narrow range of ages among residents may result in a significant proportion requiring increasing care over the same period, limiting members' ability to exchange supportive services with one another. This may require that a greater proportion of supportive services be provided by external agencies, resulting in overall increased costs for services for residents.

It is also important for residents to unpack their impressions of, and commitment to, a model of 'reciprocal' caregiving among group members. Fiore notes concerns from some scholars about caregiving relationships premised "solely or primarily in terms of their usefulness in achieving one's own personal end(s)" (1999, 256). The form in which the *Convivium* co-housing community and its supportive services model is taking shape, with its predominance of female members, also highlights the gendered dimensions of care in older age. Women commonly take on a multitude of unpaid/informal care roles; for elder females, who are often dealing with their own concurrent health and wellness issues, providing care to others may generate significant additional emotional and physical strain (Hirst 2005; Dahlberg, Demack, and Bambra 2007; Pinquart and Sorensen, 2007; Hiel et al., 2015). One *Convivium* member has noted that a next step in planning for supportive services will require that more specific standards of care and availability among members be negotiated in advance—for example, with regard to members' willingness to participate in the preparation of meals versus more intimate care, such as changing dressings for neighbors. Overall, many *Convivium* members have acknowledged these types of challenges, while others believe that the group has not adequately considered or planned for these concerns.

In dealing with these issues, there are also opportunities within the seniors' co-housing model to help alleviate some of the challenges associated with informal caregiving. At a basic level, informal caregiving within a co-housing context may offer a promising (and potentially cost-effective) alternative to institutional care for seniors, which is often structured around imposed schedules and services which may not match the distinct needs of individual residents (Fiore 1999). Such informal care may provide a more suitable option for residents who require mild to moderate assistance (e.g., a friendly daily check-up, or help with home care after routine surgery) in contrast to more intense health care interventions. Within such an environment, members are cared for by friends, and residents—not corporations—make decisions about care.

The co-housing context also offers moments between members for the social and emotional support that is so very necessary for informal caregivers. Elder caregivers in co-housing settings may form deeper relationships and foster family ties with each other through "shared meanings and memories" (Jarvis 2011, 572) that exist among "age peers" (Barker 2002, 166), who hold a similar appreciation for the care they receive and a genuine desire to help others (Percival 2001; Portacolone and Halpern 2016). This type of caregiving exchange also holds the potential to build on participants' sense of empowerment, belonging, and self-esteem, and to help members more fully recognize the value of their own caregiving efforts (Morris, Morris, and Britton 1989; Fiore 1999; Rutman 1996; Pinquart and Sorensen 2007).

Conclusion

As this initiative progresses, the members of the *Convivium* group continue to infuse a great deal of accumulated knowledge, interest, and enthusiasm into the pursuit of their planned co-housing community. Their active participation in the design and governance of the co-housing initiative has contributed a sense of purpose that, as one member has noted, "is so lacking in retirement homes where everything is done for you." Along with its successes, the group deals with ongoing challenges largely through the sustained volunteer efforts of its members, albeit with some modest additional support from the outside. One *Convivium* member has suggested that, in retrospect, there existed a substantial degree of naivety among members regarding the true amount of persistence and self-education required to participate in this type of process. Members also acknowledge the struggles of working through this effort without co-housing experts in Ontario to help them, within a context that requires members to develop an extensive expertise in the residential design/build context for a one-time development project. As a further step forward, the group is engaging the services of a local social housing development consultancy with experience in developing multi-unit housing for community organizations.

Despite these constraints, the *Convivium* group is focused on moving forward, as members excitedly pursue their plans for a seniors' co-living and co-caring community. Based on the co-housing model, this community of care would bring together neighbors with mutual interests and common experiences of aging wherein members can appreciate the diversity of perspectives that its residents possess. The physical design would complement this approach by offering shared spaces in which residents could strengthen relationships and build on lessons learned regarding the advantages and realities of being part of a co-housing community. The exchange of supportive services among *Convivium* residents would most likely be initiated at a modest scale, and grow over time. Members of this community of care would also probably need to rely on other caregiving and funding support, as well as an external service coordinator, if required. Ideally, members would adequately recognize each other's contributions, encourage each other to accept additional support when needed, and acknowledge the changing needs and capacities among members over time.

Through this examination of the growth of the *Convivium* initiative, it is evident that there is a community forming among *Convivium* members even prior to the establishment of a physical co-housing space. These burgeoning bonds are the result of the substantial volunteer hours among prospective co-housing residents that have gone into the creation of this group, of the development and ongoing work of committees, and of other formal and informal opportunities to come together to build friendships, understanding, and expertise. It has also involved dealing with challenges together as they arise. For some members, the sense of community within the *Convivium* group has not yet been forged as deeply as originally hoped. While ongoing informal events such as summer picnic get-togethers and monthly dinner gatherings have offered members many meaningful opportunities to build relationships and exchange ideas through relaxed conversation over meals, members have also noted that it is the day-to-day planning, communication, and joint learning that takes place within *Convivium*'s various formal committees that has helped to forge the strongest bonds between members. As one *Convivium* member has stated, "Community building is not just about showing up with a casserole when a fellow member is under the weather ... it is taking the time to think things through and propose ideas and solutions for the benefit of the whole community." By this measure it appears likely that the *Convivium* group will continue to strengthen communal ties as it works towards establishing its co-housing community through a process that aims to support a vibrant and connected experience of aging.

References

Addae-Dapaah, K. 2008. "Age Segregation and the Quality of Life of the Elderly People in Studio Apartments." *Journal of Housing for the Elderly* 22 (1–2): 127–61.

Accius, J. C. 2010. *The Village: A Growing Option for Ageing in Place*. Washington, DC: AARP Public Policy Institute.

Atkins, S. 2013. "We're Better Together: The Gifts, Responsibilities, and Joys of Ageing in Community." *Generations* 37 (4): 92–96.

Ballamingie, P., M. Goemans, and G. Martin. 2018. "Supporting Local Civic Engagement through a 'Community First' Approach to Foster Broader Social Inclusion in Development." In *Toward Equity and Inclusion in Canadian*

Cities: Lessons from Critical Praxis-Oriented Research, edited by F. Klodawsky, J. Siltanen., and C. Andrew, 111–34. Montreal: McGill-Queen's University Press.

Bamford, G. 2005. "Cohousing for older people: Housing innovation in the Netherlands and Denmark." *Australasian Journal on Ageing* 24 (1): 44–46.

Barker, J. C. 2002. "Neighbors, Friends, and Other Nonkin Caregivers of Community-Living Dependent Elders." *Journal of Gerontology* 57 (3): 158–67.

Black, K., D. Dobbs, and T. L. Young. 2015. "Ageing in Community: Mobilizing a New Paradigm of Older Adults as a Core Social Resource." *Journal of Applied Gerontology* 34 (2): 219–43.

Blanchard, J. 2013. "Ageing in Community: The Communitarian Alternative to Ageing in Place, Alone." *Generations* 37 (4): 6–13.

Borgloh, S., and P. Westerheide. 2012. "The Impact of Mutual Support Based Housing Projects on the Costs of Care." *Housing Studies* 27 (5): 620–42.

Canada Mortgage and Housing [CMHC]. 2017. "Seniors' Housing Report: Ontario."

Canadian Medical Association [CMA]. 2016. *The State of Seniors Health Care in Canada*.

CBC News. 2013. "Canadian boomers want to stay in their homes as they age." October 24. http://www.cbc.ca/news/business/canadian-boomers-want-to-stay-in-their-homes-as-they-age-1.2224171

Critchlow Rodman, M. 2013. "Co-caring in Senior Cohousing: A Canadian Model for Social Sustainability." *Social Sciences Directory* 2 (4): 106–13.

Dahlberg, L., S. Demack, and C. Bambra. 2007. "Age and Gender of Informal Carers: A Population-based Study in the UK." *Health and Social Care in the Community* 15 (5): 439–45.

Durrett, C. 2009. *The Senior Cohousing Handbook*. Gabriola Island, BC: New Society.

Elbert, K. B, and P. S. Neufeld. 2010. "Indicators of a Successful Naturally Occurring Retirement Community: A Case Study." *Journal of Housing for the Elderly* 24: 322–34.

Federation of Canadian Municipalities [FCM]. 2015. *Seniors and Housing: The Challenge Ahead*. Ottawa: Federation of Canadian Municipalities.

Fiore, R. N. 1999. "Caring for Ourselves: Peer Care in Autonomous Aging." In *Mother Time*, edited by Margaret Urban Walker, 245–60. Lanham, MD: Rowman & Littlefield.

Fromm, D. 2000. "American Cohousing: The First Five Years." *Journal of Architectural and Planning Research* 17 (2): 94–109.

Glass, A. P., and R. S. Vander Plaats. 2013. "A Conceptual Model for Ageing Better Together Intentionally." *Journal of Ageing Studies* 27: 428–42.

Glass, A. P. 2016. "Resident-Managed Elder Intentional Neighborhoods: Do They Promote Social Resources for Older Adults?" *Journal of Gerontological Social Work* 59 (7–8): 554–71.

Guengerich, T. 2009. *Neighbors Helping Neighbors: A Qualitative Study of Villages Operating in the District of Columbia*. Washington: AARP.

Guo, K. L., and R. J. Castillo. 2012. "The U.S. Long Term Care System: Development and Expansion of Naturally Occurring Retirement Communities as an Innovative Model for Ageing in Place." *Ageing International* 37: 210–27.

Hasell, M. J., and J. Scanzoni. 2000. "Cohousing in HUD housing – problems and prospects." *Journal of Architectural and Planning Research* 17 (2): 133–45.

Hermus, G., C. Stonebridge, and K. Edenhoffer. 2015. *Future Care for Canadian Seniors: A Status Quo Forecast.* Ottawa: The Conference Board of Canada.

Hiel, L., M. A. Beenackers, C. M. Renders, S. J. W. Robroek, A. Burdorf, and S. Croezen. 2015. "Providing Personal Informal Care to Older European Adults: Should We Care about the Caregivers' Health?" *Preventative Medicine* 70: 64–68.

Hirst, M. 2005. "Carer Distress: A Prospective, Population-based Study." *Social Science and Medicine* 61: 697–708.

Jarvis, H. 2011. "Saving Space, Sharing Time: Integrated Infrastructures of Daily Life in Cohousing." *Environment and Planning* A, 43: 560–77.

Lager, D., B. van Hoven, and L. Meijering. 2012. "Places that Matter: Place Attachment and Wellbeing of Older Antillean Migrants in the Netherlands." *European Spatial Research and Policy* 19 (1): 81–94.

Lyon, M., M. Kang, and J. Kramp. 2013. "Case Study of Senior Cohousing Development in a Rural Community." *Journal of Extension* 51 (6): 1–7.

Mockler, P., and A. C. Cools. 2017. *Getting Ready: For a New Generation of Active Seniors.* Ottawa: Senate of Canada.

Morris, L. W., R. G. Morris, and P. G. Britton. 1989. "Social Support Networks and Formal Support as Factors Influencing the Psychological Adjustment of Spouse Caregivers of Dementia Sufferers." *International Journal of Geriatric Psychiatry* 4: 47–51.

National Seniors Council. 2014. *Report on the Social Isolation of Seniors.* Ottawa: Government of Canada.

National Seniors Council. 2016. *Who's at Risk and What Can Be Done About It? A Review of the Literature on the Social Isolation of Different Groups of Seniors.* Ottawa: Government of Canada.

Percival, J. 2001. "Self-esteem and Social Motivation in Age-segregated Settings." *Housing Studies* 16 (6): 827–40.

Pinquart, M., and S. Sorensen. 2007. "Correlates of Physical Health of Informal Caregivers: A Meta-Analysis." *Journal of Gerontology: Psychological Sciences* 62B (2): 126–37.

Portacolone, E., and J. Halpern. 2016. "'Move or Suffer': Is Age-Segregation the New Norm for Older Americans Living Alone?" *Journal of Applied Gerontology* 35 (8): 836–56.

Province of Ontario, Seniors' Secretariat. 2013. *Ontario's Action Plan for Seniors.* Toronto: Queen's Printer for Ontario.

Ruiu, M. L. 2015. "The Effects of Cohousing on the Social Housing System: The Case of the Threshold Centre." *Journal of Housing and the Built Environment* 30: 631–44.

Rutman, D. 1996. "Caregiving as Women's Work: Women's Experiences of Powerfulness and Powerlessness as Caregivers." *Qualitative Health Research* 6 (1): 90–111.

Sanguinetti, A. 2014. "Transformational Practices in Cohousing: Enhancing Residents' Connection to Community and Nature." *Journal of Environmental Psychology* 40: 86–96.

Scanlon, K., and M. Fernandez Arrigoitia. 2015. "Development of New Cohousing: Lessons from a London Scheme for the Over-50s." *Urban Research and Practice* 8 (1): 106–21.
Shenker, B. 2011. *Intentional Communities (Routledge Revivals): Ideology and Alienation in Communal Societies*. London: Routledge.
Shin Choi, J. 2004. "Evaluation of Community Planning and Life of Senior Cohousing Projects in Northern European Countries." *European Planning Studies* 12 (8): 1202–16.
Sienkiewicz, A. 2017. "With a Wave of Seniors Coming, Why Many are Choosing to 'Age in Place' in Toronto Condos." *CBC News*. May 25. http://www.cbc.ca/news/canada/toronto/with-a-wave-of-seniors-coming-why-many-are-choosing-to-age-in-place-in-toronto-condos-1.4129912
Snelling, S. 2012. *The Village Movement: Redefining Ageing in Place*. https://www.nextavenue.org/village-movement-redefining-aging-place/
Span, P. 2010. "Living Together, Ageing Together." *The New York Times*. September 9.
Stone, R. 2014. "What Are the Realistic Options for Ageing in Community?" *Generations* 37 (4): 65–71.
Thomas, M. 2011. "Villages: Helping People Age in Place." *AARP The Magazine*. May/June.
Turner, A., and L. Findlay. 2012. *Informal Caregiving for Seniors*. Catalogue no. 82-003-X. Ottawa: Statistics Canada.
Vestbro, D. U. 1992. "From Central Kitchen to Community Cooperation: Development of Collective Housing in Sweden." *Open House International* 17 (2): 30–38.
Waldron, V. R., R. Gitelson, D. Kelly, and J. Regalado. 2005. "Losing and Building Supportive Relationships in Later Life: A Four-Year Study of Migrants to a Planned Retirement Community." *Journal of Housing for the Elderly* 19 (2): 5–25.
Williams, J. 2008. "Predicting an American Future for Cohousing." *Futures* 40: 268–86.

About the author

Magdalene Goemans completed her doctoral degree in the Department of Geography and Environmental Studies at Carleton University in 2019. While pursuing thesis research related to climate change adaptation, she gained considerable knowledge of seniors' co-housing issues through her involvement as a research assistant in a community-campus partnership initiative based at Carleton University. Within a Social Sciences and Humanities Research Council of Canada-funded project entitled Community First: Impacts of Community Engagement, Magdalene provided research support to a neighborhood initiative that aims to establish a seniors' co-housing community in the Ottawa area.

Chapter Seven

Dependency and Vulnerability in the Twenty-First Century: The Swedish Case

Hildur Kalman

Abstract

"Dependency and Vulnerability in the Twenty-First Century: The Swedish Case" by **Hildur Kalman** illustrates the impact of regulations on the provision of care for older adults. Even if Sweden is perceived as having generous welfare policies, Kalman's paper is concerned with the noticeable move toward the marketization of care and its impact on the care recipients, more specifically, older adults who require intimate care.

Introduction

Disability and the frailties of old age put many people in need of various forms of intimate home care, for example, undressing, using the toilet, changing adult diapers or incontinence pads, showering, washing intimate parts of the body, brushing one's teeth, shaving, and so on (cf. Carnaby and Cambridge 2006, 20). The challenge of maintaining personal dignity and integrity during home care services thus reaches its extremes when intimate care is involved — and yet little attention is being paid to this hidden, off-the-radar world. Today, much more attention is being given to the challenges presented by demographic changes and by an aging population, and a strong focus has been put on active and 'successful aging' (Katz and Calasanti 2015, 26). At the same time, this strong and narrow focus risks hiding the bodily and functional limitations that arise with age and which can make us vulnerable and dependent upon intimate support and care.

In this chapter, the vulnerability intrinsic to being dependent on others for one's personal and intimate care is examined in the context of present-day Sweden, which is to say in relation to significant changes in the Swedish welfare system that have occurred over the last few decades. This contextualization works as a base for reflection upon the results and experiences gained from recent observational studies of intimate care in home care services.

Dependent and Vulnerable

Approximately 164,000 people over the age of 65 (of an approximate total population of 1.8 million) were granted home care services in Sweden in 2012 (Socialstyrelsen 2013c). Among those under the age of 65, there are approximately 30,000 persons who receive home care services or personal assistance due to disabilities, a majority of whom receive help with intimate and personal care (Försäkringskassan 2011; Socialstyrelsen 2013b).

Intimate care, a cornerstone in Swedish social welfare, entails particular challenges for the recipients of care as well as for care workers, both in terms of how the care itself is to be performed and how to manage feelings of, for example, anxiety and embarrassment (Twigg 2000; Clark 2009; O'Lynn and Krautscheid 2011). Set betwixt and between home and institutional, private and professional settings, the situation and the relations involved in intimate care as a part of home care services are particularly precarious, and this very situation is a much-neglected area of research.

Partly in response to scandals which have highlighted deficiencies in elderly and social care, concepts such as dignity, influence, and participation have been adopted in Swedish legislation—e.g., the Social Services Act (SFS 2001: 453)—and have been put forth in national guidelines alongside a new emphasis upon person-centered care (see, e.g., SOU 2008: 51; SOFS 2012: 3). How exactly person-centered care is to be implemented, not least with respect to intimate care, is, however, "seldom given more substance than through the aforementioned concepts of influence and participation," and thereby we risk overlooking "the dependency and vulnerability of those in need of intimate care in home care services" (Andersson and Kalman 2017, 220). Thus, as is the case with similar guidelines in other countries, such relatively abstract concepts are promoted without clear operational guidelines as to how to translate them into practice, and this is especially the case with respect to intimate care (see, e.g., Socialstyrelsen 2013a; cf. Carnaby and Cambridge 2002).

The 1992 reform of elder care (Socialstyrelsen 1996) prioritized enabling older people to continue living at home in spite of conditions such as disability, frailty, illness, or dementia. One result of this reform was a 25% reduction in the number of beds set aside for elder care in residential homes within a period of a mere eleven years—this despite an increase in the number of citizens aged 65 and upwards over the same period of time (Szebehely and Ulmanen 2012). This has had the effect that those now receiving home care services are, on average, living in poorer conditions than before, and that only those in need of a great deal of help receive such services, all of which constitute a severe challenge to home care service as a whole.

Challenges for/in Intimate and Personal Care

Intimate care has low status as a form of care work, even among social service professionals, and is a domain surrounded by prejudices, presuppositions, and idealizations—with connotations colored by gender and ethnicity (cf. Andersson 2007, 2012; Carnaby and Cambridge 2002; Isaksen 2002; Twigg 2000). The more intimate the task, the more disliked among staff. The most disliked task of all is the cleaning-up of body products without any personal contact with the service users (Carnaby and Cambridge 2002; cf. Isaksen 2002; Twigg 2000).

Furthermore, attitudes regarding intimate care differ significantly between laymen and those who have had the actual experience of receiving or performing intimate care (Isaksen 2002; Clark 2006; Inoue, Chapman, and Wynaden 2006; O'Lynn and Krautscheid 2011; Andersson 2012). In one study of laypersons' attitudes regarding intimate care, noteworthy differences in attitude were found between those who at some point had had the experience of being a recipient of intimate care and those who had not (O'Lynn and Krautscheid 2011). Similar differences in attitude have been reported by care workers, who relate that the attitudes of laymen, such as friends and relatives, vary from disbelief to admiration. The same care workers also report that other workers within social care seemingly do not recognize the central place of intimate care in their jobs (Carnaby and Cambridge 2002).

Historically, care and care work has been associated with the female gender, and is to date a female-coded field of practice largely dominated by women, in respect to the number working in that sector. These historical associations with the female gender have also contributed to the low social status given to such work, and the reflection of that low status in the quality of wages; care work has long been thought to rest on inborn female qualities rather than on education. Even so, these associations with the female gender may be comparatively positive for women, to the extent that men in care work may be confronted with negative expectations and be questioned as to their level of knowledge. The low status and low wages of care work in home care services also make it an area of work in which many immigrants find employment. In 2012, the most common occupation of immigrant women was within the care work sector (> 50%), and among immigrant men it was the third most common (approximately 25%) (SCB 2014). However, the above-mentioned prejudices and idealizations grace immigrant women with positive expectations—i.e., of being 'caring' by nature—whereas in the attitudes of fellow staff, immigrant men are commonly positioned on the lowest rungs of the home care services hierarchy (Andersson 2012).

It is non-professional groups (such as assistant nurses, nurse assistants, and home-helpers) who perform most intimate care work. In home care services, this is even more the case: according to the latest available national report, the percentage of staff with formal education in home care services in Sweden declined from 56% in 2003 to less than 50% in metropolitan districts in 2006 (Socialstyrelsen 2003, 51; 2006). More recent reports show that the situation remains severe in parts of Sweden. This means that many care workers have received little or no formal or in-house training in intimate caregiving and are at risk of being left to devise their own methods or coping strategies (cf. Carnaby and Cambridge 2002; Clark 2006, 15, 128; Inoue, Chapman, and Wynaden 2006, 566; Sörensdotter 2008, 236).

Thus, professional groups (i.e., professionals or semi-professionals) are, broadly speaking, not present at the front lines where the most substantial intimate and personal care is to be found. Where home care services are concerned, trained social workers can be found acting as administrators, supervisors, and as the care managers who perform needs assessments. But at the front lines, neither trained nurses nor trained social workers are to be found, and, at the best of times, intimate care is actually performed by assistant nurses or home-helpers. It is also a form of work that, both historically and presently, has been afforded a low status and defined as dirty (body) work (Isaksen 2002; Twigg 2000). This may be one of the reasons for the relative lack of attention in nursing and social work research on intimate home care services, in comparison to research on, for example, residential care or care provided in hospitals. Further, what may be effective routines in residential or hospital care cannot be presumed to be optimal ways of performing intimate and personal care in someone's home. What is largely lacking in studies of the field are first-person accounts of intimate care, both from vulnerable citizens in need of personal and intimate care and from caregivers working on the front lines of home care services.

Home Care Services Set in a Larger Context: The Transformation of the Swedish Welfare State

The Nordic Welfare states, and Sweden among them, have "often been described as generous and universal in the sense that the state takes extensive responsibility for care and offers services to all social groups," and care for older and disabled people has often been described as a core area of the Nordic model (Andersson and Kvist 2015, 276). However, while a senior citizen may be assigned home care services after a care manager, employed by the local authorities, has assessed their needs, the law does not actually include detailed regulations, nor does it confer citizens with rights to specific services (Meagher and Szebehely 2013). The law which regulates elder care services is the Social Services Act (SFS 2001:453), a goal-oriented framework law which ensures a general right to assistance if needs "cannot be met in any other way" (chapter 4, § 1).

Over the last few decades, the Swedish elder care system has undergone significant changes. First of all, and as mentioned above, one of the consequences of the reforms of elder care in 1992 (Socialstyrelsen 1996) was a 25% reduction in the number of beds in residential homes for the care of the elderly, to the effect that those now receiving home care services are, on average, in worse condition than they have been in the past (Szebehely and Ulmanen 2012). At times, the reform of 1992 has thus been dubbed "compulsory care/confined to home" whenever elders have been refused care in residential homes, or even the possibility of moving into such a home (Persson, Holmberg, and René 2016, 6).

Moreover, a substantial transformation of Swedish elder care has taken place, both as a consequence of the marketization of care and as a result of legislation. Previously, elder care could be described as "universal, that is, comprehensive, publicly financed, mainly publicly provided, high-quality services" that were "available to all citizens according to need rather than ability to pay" (Szebehely and Trydegård 2012, 300). But even though Swedish elder care can still be described as part of a universal, social, and democratic welfare system in which care is seen as a social right and is mainly financed through tax revenues, a "transformation of elder care in later years has been influenced by neoliberal politics, which emphasize economic efficiency and cost reduction through competition" (Andersson and Kvist 2015, 275). Thus, under the influence of New Public Management ideology, a certain marketization of care has been established in Swedish public elder care, with emphasis being placed on reduced costs and (more) effective care. As a consequence, ideas derived from the commercial sphere of life have gradually been introduced into the public service, but "the marketization within public elder care can at best be described as a quasi-market, since it differs from conventional markets: markets for elder care are established by the public sector and providers compete to be contracted" (Andersson and Kvist 2015, 277).

Throughout the transformation of Swedish elder care, the notion of choice has been given a preeminent place at the table, and in 2009 the Act on the System of Choice in the Public Sector (in Swedish: Lagen om valfrihetssystem, hereafter referred to as LOV [SFS 2008:962]) was introduced. LOV provides municipalities and county councils with the opportunity to expose their publicly provided services to market competition. By way of this change, so-called users of public services would also be enabled to choose the care company that would provide them care.

The Ideology/Ideological Shifts and their Consequences

In an analysis of the policy process leading to the adoption of LOV, Andersson and Kvist (2015) demonstrate that the problem which was meant to be solved by the legislation was a lack of choice in publicly financed elder care. This was "articulated as a key to increased quality, empowerment of users and good care" (Andersson and Kvist 2015, 275). Choice was repeatedly mentioned—and then often in relation to empowerment, diversity, and quality. Individual choice was understood as being 'intrinsically good'—and was therefore to be "the dominant factor shaping the activities of publicly funded welfare services"—in order for these to "be more closely attuned to individual circumstances and to satisfy individual preferences and priorities" (Andersson and Kvist 2015, 279).

The actual freedom of choice was, and is, however, rather limited. Elders are allowed to choose between different care companies, but they can neither choose the content of care (that is to say what specific tasks will be performed), nor who the person(s) attending to their needs will be. Given that the care is publicly financed, all interventions provided for the elders need to be means-tested by a care manager, who makes the actual decisions concerning intervention. Furthermore, exactly how the law is interpreted and implemented varies between municipalities, for local politicians standardize the form of interventions within their jurisdictions, resulting in differing guidelines.

This reform also rests on the assumption of an active and rational citizen exerting a customer's right to choose a company to provide care services. The same reform thus turns a blind eye to the fact that, over our life-spans, there are ever present, albeit changing, states of dependency. The vulnerability of dependency is not only part and parcel of the human condition in general, but especially so for those in need of home care services. The logic of choice championed by the LOV reform "turns elders in need of care into customers, and like customers, they are expected to make their own choices, which stand in opposition to the logic of care" (Andersson and Kvist 2015, 280; cf. Mol 2008). When struck by ill health, we are frequently unable to act as calculating individuals making rational choices. The "abstract individualism" which underpins the rhetoric of freedom of choice in care is an ideology underpinned by false notions about the human condition, writes Lindman (2017, 44). When choice comes to be seen as an end in itself, both the anxious and unsettling position of dependency and the specific circumstances that characterize care for those who are dependent are neglected.

It has been shown that even while the elderly, in general, appreciate an opportunity to choose care providers, they do not find the choice of providers to be particularly important. As, for instance, Andersson (2007) has shown, elders are more interested in having an influence over the content of care than they are in choosing a care company. Importance is ascribed to having an influence over what help one is to get, and how it is to be performed, and the persons that will perform the care are important for the users as well (Hjalmarsson and Wånell 2013, 13). What actually matters to elders is preserving some control over one's everyday life in spite of one's need of help (Wikström 2005, 144).

It is also important to note that one of the factors which influence elders' choice of home care services is the fact that it is a service which many of them do not even want, for their favored choice would be to be able to continue managing on their own. Thus, many of those who do have home care services have not applied for this service themselves; rather, someone else did so on their behalf. According to one study (Hjalmarsson and Norman 2004), almost half of care recipients started receiving home care services after being hospitalized. In such cases it was the hospital staff who had originally contacted social services. Several of the elders in the study had suffered strokes or had had accidents such as serious falls, and therefore arranging for home care services was a matter of some urgency, for the patients involved were not able to return to their homes without having a care package put into place. Only one third of the interviewees in the study had themselves taken the initiative to apply for home care services, sometimes after having been prompted to do so by their children (Hjalmarsson and Norman 2004).

Moreover, in one study (Meinow, Parker, and Thorslund 2011), researchers analyzed a nationally representative sample of Swedes aged 77+ for the prevalence of the cognitive, physical, and sensory resources associated with the capacity to make and to carry out informed choices concerning medical and social care providers. The results suggest that "those elderly people who are most dependent on care services and who could benefit most from a 'good choice'" are also those who have the highest prevalence of the cognitive and physical limitations associated with an incapacity to act as rational consumers of care services (Meinow, Parker, and Thorslund 2011, 1289). According to a report from the Swedish National Board of Health and Welfare, as many as one-third of those who had chosen elder care providers were not even aware of, or did not remember, having done so. The choice had often been made when struck by ill health and in a most difficult phase of life, wherein even becoming a recipient of home care services was a life-changing experience in itself (Socialstyrelsen 2004).

In line with the above, even as the opportunity to change providers is generally appreciated, very few older people ever actually exert this right (Svensson and Edebalk 2010, 27). For older persons with an extensive need for care due to poor physical and/or mental health, the choice to change providers both implies a substantial and difficult effort, and involves taking the risk of putting oneself in an uncertain position wherein an existing relationship with a provider is endangered.

Thus, to summarize, the effort to assess and compare different providers will often be beyond the abilities and capacities of someone who, due to frailty or ill health, is already in an uncertain and unsettled position of dependency, and is frequently without any relatives to aid them in making such choices. As Andersson and Kvist (2015, 281) conclude, the neoliberal changes have imposed a market-rationale for decision-making, and normatively construct individuals as entrepreneurial actors in every sphere of their lives—which also implies that they bear full responsibility for their actions, and therefore also for their choices.

The welfare model of the Nordic countries has often been described as 'women-friendly' as the state's extensive responsibility for care has meant that women no more than men have had to choose between work and family, and as women's participation in the labor market provides for economic autonomy. In recognition of this, Andersson and Kvist (2015), in their analysis of the LOV policy process, also studied the professed values of heightened equality and diversity which were to be outcomes of marketization and freedom of choice. They found that "diversity" mainly referred to the "encouragement of multiple actors in elderly care," and was not "used in relation to social stratification in any sense" (281). Similarly, they found that "equal treatment" and "non-discrimination" were articulated and understood "only in relation to the different providers of care services" (281), and, further, that "gender equality" was mainly understood as increased female entrepreneurship (282). The premised understanding was therefore that increased competition in the elder care market would create better opportunities for women to establish small businesses, and that this would be equivalent to improved working conditions within elder care (and would also result in greater status and better career opportunities for women). Of course, any transformation in the elder care system affects more women than men, for "a majority of the users, informal carers, eldercare workers and managers of care for the elderly are women" (282). Paradoxically, though, in a case study of local-level elder care outsourcing, Sundin and Tillmar (2010) found that elder care could be said to have been masculinized after the reform. This came about as small companies, mostly owned by women, were driven out of the market by larger companies, mostly owned by men, and thus men came to be the owners and managers of most care companies, whereas the actual elder care work was still predominately performed by women.

At the Frontlines: A Tension between Legislation/Guidelines and Practice

Now, let us turn back to the frontlines of home care services where intimate care is actually performed and provided to some of society's most unprivileged and vulnerable groups: the frail, the elderly, and disabled persons. What happens when the abstract concepts and buzzwords such as choice, dignity, participation, and influence become embodied in various practices, and are then experienced in the real world? Do recipients of home care services exert their freedom of choice more in the home care setting than when choosing care company providers?

Even while many guidelines underscore the importance of person-centered approaches by which care recipients are expected to be able to instruct care workers, earlier research on the performance of intimate care has shown that both care workers and care recipients fall silent during the performance of intimate care. Researchers also warn of the risks involved in approaching intimate care in a task-oriented manner, to the effect that care recipients' bodies cease to be private (Clark 2009; Wiersma and Dupuis 2010).

In their own research on home care services, researchers too have tended to fall quiet regarding certain matters—and even after concluding that intimate care is usually passed over in silence. Even in the few studies of home care services in which interviews have been performed, researchers often fall silent when approaching the matter of intimate care tasks, despite having noted the evasive answers or silence on the subject on the part of both staff and care recipients

(Andersson 2007, 152 ff.; Sörensdotter 2008, 230 ff.). This silence, and the fact that many of those in need of help with intimate care are not even capable of giving instructions, heightens both the challenge and the need for ethical awareness (cf. Mol 2008).

While legislation and guidelines (SFS 1993:387; 2001:453; SOU 2008:51; Socialstyrelsen 2011, 2012; SOFS 2012:3) emphasize participation and influence, two recent observational studies of home care service by Katarina Andersson and myself (Kalman and Andersson 2014; Andersson and Kalman 2017) have shown that staff and care recipients often resort to silence while, for example, the washing of intimate body parts is taking place. Instead of giving instructions, or exchanging questions and answers, we found strategies such as objectification, distancing, and routinization were used in the interaction between care workers and care recipients. The objectification strategies that we found resemble those described in earlier studies of medical and nursing practice, where they have been interpreted as ways of counter-balancing the intimacy implied in the care given, and safeguarding the integrity of the person (Emerson 1970; Menzies 1977[1970]; Heath 1986, 45 ff., 106; Frankel 1993; Måseide 2008, 371; cf. Goffman 1971). These results challenge the professed ideals, for the practice of objectification on the part of the care recipients comes forth as a participatory strategy.

Studies of Intimate Care in Home Care Services — Daytime and Night-Time

Let us look closer at the results of our two participant observation studies: the first, of daytime (2014), the other, of night-time (2017) home care services. Most of the earlier studies of intimate care have used written narratives or interviews with staff or nursing students (see, e.g., Twigg 2000; Carnaby and Cambridge 2002; Grant, Giddings, and Beale 2005; Clark 2006; Inoue, Chapman, and Wynaden 2006; England and Dyck 2011; Twigg et al. 2011). There are a few exceptions, though, such as the studies of Clark (2009) and Calveley [neé Clark] (2012), in which she used participant observations of intimate and personal care. However, those studies were performed in residential care homes and not in home care services. Given that evasive answers are prevalent when interviewing staff on the more intimate parts of bodywork, such as matters of touching and nakedness (Sörensdotter 2008, 228), we considered it important to use participant observation. Observations in both of our studies, daytime and night-time, were carried out as one of the researchers followed teams of care workers in two districts in one of the largest municipalities in mid-Sweden, with approximately 200,000 inhabitants. The empirical material was gathered by way of 'shadowing', which emphasizes observation on the part of the researcher (see Czarniawska 2007, 56).

During the daytime study (Kalman and Andersson 2014), care workers were thus shadowed by one of the researchers in their daily work routines in the homes of elderly clients. A total of 37 visits, to a sum of 23 care recipients, were made on four different days by following seven different care workers (three men and four women). Most of the recipients of intimate care were women between ages 65 and 95. Out of 37 visits, 18 included intimate care to a total of ten care recipients, and considerably more time was spent on the visits that included intimate care. Field notes and personal reflections were written directly after each visit, and the notes commonly contain observations on such matters as procedures, verbal exchanges, postures, and positioning (2014, 404).

During the analysis, two overarching themes emerged: strategies for framing and contextual aspects of care, respectively. In general, the more intimate the parts of the body being washed, the more the talk would turn to other body parts, either in order to shift focus or just to keep the dialogue going and avoid silence. Both care workers and care recipients alike seemed to avoid silence as long as possible during intimate care. But when the space for providing care was really narrow, or when bodily fluids were dealt with, both parties often fell silent. The changes in the conversation between care workers and care recipients seemingly served to create a certain distance, corresponding to the degrees of intimacy in the situation. Generally, it seems that when the levels of intimacy were quite pronounced—such as when washing intimate body parts in narrow spaces—speaking of other topics did not suffice in creating the desired distance, thus moving the participants to resort to silence instead (Kalman and Andersson 2014, 408–9; cf. Sörensdotter 2008, 228 ff.).

Another strategy identified was that of a rather extensive eye discipline on the part of the care worker, as well as the care recipient. The more intimate the body part involved in the performance of care, the more both parties avoided looking at that body part. The challenge of heightened intimacy in these close situations was thus counter-balanced by a distance achieved through glances that were clothed and which, in the words of Goffman, avoided the "penetration of the eyes" (1971, 45–46) (Kalman and Andersson 2014, 409).

In the next step of the analysis the results were compared to the results of earlier and influential studies of medical and nursing practice, which have shown how professionals and their clients, by way of routines, social interaction, and other means, create frameworks of interaction which sustain professional distance in situations that would otherwise be counted and experienced as intimate (Kalman and Andersson 2014, 405). In our study, interactional strategies such as objectification, distancing, and routinization were identified and suggested to be strategies that help sustain care recipients' dignity.

> The more intimate the body parts and the touch, the more precarious the situation, the more need there was for a simultaneous creation of distance. A matter-of-fact stance on the part of both the care workers and most care recipients signaled a dominant definition of the context as a care situation. Intimate body parts then seemed to be dealt [with] just like any other body parts, thus preventing any private and sexual connotations. (Kalman and Andersson 2014, 410–11)

Seemingly insensitive to the business at hand, the care recipients became minimal participants in the activity while intimate care was being performed. This, however, seems to be contrary to the ideals articulated in Swedish legislation and guidelines, since practices of objectification on the part of the care recipients routinely come forth as an interactional participatory strategy.

The strategies for handling intimacy identified in our study displayed both similarities and dissimilarities to those forms of professional framing identified in earlier studies, whereas the contextual aspects for providing a frame for care differed in important aspects. Several challenges to professional framing of intimate care were thus highlighted in our studies of both daytime and night-time home care services (Kalman and Andersson 2014; Andersson and Kalman 2017; cf. Glasdam et al. 2013).

It was often the case that care workers were providing care in homes that were not adapted for such work. Bathrooms and toilets were often very narrow, and care recipients were severely disabled. Therefore, the use of toilet buckets was frequent, or the washing of intimate parts of the body might take place in the senior's bedroom or sitting room (Kalman and Andersson 2014, 407). Given that intimate care was being provided in a setting that was neither fully a home nor a workplace, and given that many of the professional resources that are provided by a medical setting were lacking, the relationship between care worker and care recipient in intimate care became particularly precarious (cf. England and Dyck 2011; Glasdam et al. 2013). Adding to the situation, the staff wore work clothes that identified them as coming from home care services, which did provide an overarching frame for the interaction. But given that such clothes do not signal the level of one's education, the staff is neither afforded the status nor the distance that a hospital uniform might confer (Andersson and Kalman 2017, 407; cf. Dahl 2000).

Another challenge is that daily care, such as washing intimate parts of the body, does not easily lend itself to technical language, which in medical practice works as a kind of neutralizer when intimate contact needs to be balanced by distance. Lacking recourse to technical language, both staff and care recipients often choose to remain silent regarding sensitive subjects. In home care services many guidelines underscore the importance of person-centered approaches in which care recipients are expected to instruct the care worker as to how they want things to be done. But it is difficult for a care recipient to describe how he or she wishes to have intimate body parts washed or dried and simultaneously keep a distance from the situation at hand. Furthermore, in a medical setting, there is often a right procedure to follow during an examination, whereas a home care setting may present care recipients with difficulties—both in terms of knowing what to expect and how to respond to whatever routines are employed during intimate care. Care workers, too, experience problems: they frequently do not know "what routines and responses are 'right'" in the minds of particular care recipients, nor, in general, "whose and what standards of 'right'" should be applied (Kalman and Andersson 2014, 411–12). Thus, what may function as effective routines within, for example, the context of hospital care, cannot be presumed by default to be optimal for the performance of intimate and personal care within someone's home—neither optimal for the care recipient, nor for the care workers involved.

Turning now to the study of night-time home care services (Andersson and Kalman 2017), the same procedure of shadowing was applied while following two experienced teams of night-time care workers working from 9.30pm to 8.00am. A total of 84 visits were observed during the two separate and remarkably burdensome nights: one team making 53 visits and the other 31, with a great deal of time spent travelling between visits. The majority of the care recipients had severe impairments due to illnesses and age-related disabilities and/or dementia.

When compared to the character of daytime home care services, the night-time care work was not specifically marked by being set in someone's home. From the researcher's perspective, the way that staff entered houses, apartments, and bedrooms to care for recipients who were often asleep, resembled the way that staff walk from room to room on a ward. This impression was reinforced by the fact that many bedrooms had piles of the accoutrements needed for intimate care, such as boxes of diapers and bed sheets (Andersson and Kalman 2017, 225). The two teams used strikingly similar routines, and we identified a combination of strategies being employed during intimate care interactions, such as routines, ritualization, objectification, and dis-attention. The care work was marked by everyday professional routines that revealed themselves in the manner in which diapers were changed, help with the bedpan was given, etc. In the absence of dialogue, care workers and care recipients aligned themselves to the task at hand. "The care recipients presented relevant body parts for help" and the care workers "rendered themselves to seemingly be no more than a pair of hands doing their work" (Andersson and Kalman 2017, 226). For those who were asleep, or almost asleep, smooth routines seemed "to serve to balance the transgression of intimate thresholds. The distancing and balancing effect of small talk, jokes, and the like during daytime, was at night-time accomplished by smooth routines" (Andersson and Kalman 2017, 228).

Implications

To summarize the present-day context and the consequences for home care services, care recipients in home care services are being framed as free agents and consumers of welfare services in national legislation and guidelines, regardless of their actual levels of dependency and poor health. This emphasis on free choice has pushed the responsibility for care onto elderly people and their relatives. While free choice is effectively limited to choosing the company which will provide care, the care recipients cannot choose the content of care, and many of those in need of care cannot make, or have not made, the choice themselves, for their need for help frequently comes at an acutely difficult time—often while being struck by ill-health. In guidelines concerning the provision of care, key words such as participation and influence are often bandied about. However, our observational studies of home care services have highlighted a tension between, on the one hand, the ways in which care recipients are conceptualized in present-day political thinking and guidelines, and, on the other hand, the strategies and practices used during interactions between care recipients and care workers, when integrity and intimacy are most at stake.

Despite the fact that the care almost seems as if it were being performed on bodies in a line, the objectifying practices which were observed during the studies were interpreted as strategies for maintaining the care recipient's dignity. This indicates a severe disjunction between actual practices and the notion of a person-centered approach that has been proclaimed in the ideals of participation and influence, as stipulated in the law and the national guidelines (Andersson and Kalman 2017, 229). A paradox is revealed by the tension between the ideal rational-choice consumer as presumed in guidelines, who exerts influence through participation, and the silent, distanced care recipient of our studies. While national guidelines are abstract and vague, the actual practice of intimate care during home care service visits is performed under dismal and difficult conditions, during which care workers and care recipients are left to resolve the challenges of intimate care on their own. This disjunction between abstract ideals and actual practices marks the need for further research—research in which the voices of care recipients and the care workers laboring at the frontlines of home care services are heard. It also calls for a renewed political discussion.

References

Andersson, K. 2012. "Paradoxes of Gender in Elderly Care: The Case of Men as Care Workers in Sweden." *NORA* 30 (3): 166–81.

———. 2007. "Omsorg under förhandling: om tid, behov och kön i en föränderlig hemtjänstverksamhet." ["Care under Negotiation: Concerning Time, Needs and Gender in a Public Elderly Home Care Service in Transformation"]. PhD diss., Umeå University.

Andersson, K., and H. Kalman. 2017. "Strategies to Handle the Challenges of Intimacy in Night-time Home Care Services." *European Journal of Social Work* 20 (2): 219-30. https://doi.org/10.1080/13691457.2016.1188779

Andersson, K., and E. Kvist. 2015. "The Neoliberal Turn and the Marketization of Care: The Transformation of Eldercare in Sweden." *European Journal of Women's Studies* 22 (3): 274-87. https://doi.org/10.1177/1350506814544912

Calveley, J. 2012. "Including Adults with Intellectual Disabilities who Lack Capacity to Consent in Research." *Nursing Ethics* 19 (4): 558-67.

Carnaby, S., and P. Cambridge. 2006. *Intimate and Personal Care with People with Learning Disabilities*. London: Jessica Kingsley.

___. 2002. "Getting Personal: An Exploratory Study of Intimate and Personal Care Provision for People with Profound and Multiple Intellectual Disabilities." *Journal of Intellectual Disability Research* 46 (2): 120-32.

Clark, J. 2009. "Providing Intimate Continence Care for People with Learning Disabilities." *Nursing Times* 105 (6): 26-28.

___. 2006. "Providing Intimate Care: The Views and Values of Carers." *Learning Disability Practice* 9 (3): 10-15.

Czarniawska, B. 2007. *Shadowing and Other Techniques for Doing Fieldwork in Modern Societies*. Malmö: Liber.

Dahl, H. M. 2000. *Fra kitler til eget tøj: diskurser om professionalisme, omsorg og køn* [*From Smock Frock to your Own Clothes: Discourses on Professionalization, Care and Gender*]. Aarhus: Politica.

Emerson, J. P. 1970. "Behaviour in Private Places: Sustaining Definitions of Reality in Gynecological Examinations." *Recent Sociology* 2: 74-97.

England, K., and I. Dyck. 2011. "Managing the Body Work of Home Care." *Sociology of Health and Illness* 33 (2): 206-19.

Frankel, R. M. 1993. "The Laying on of Hands: Aspects of the Organization of Gaze, Touch, and Talk in a Medical Encounter." In *The Social Organization of Doctor-Patient Communication*, Second Edition, edited by A. D. Todd and S. Fisher, 71-107. Norwood, NJ: Ablex.

Försäkringskassan [Social Insurance Agency]. 2011. Statlig personlig assistans - resultat från undersökning av gruppen assistansberättigade. ["State Personal Assistance: Results from a Survey of the Group Receiving Assistance Allowance."] *Socialförsäkringsrapport* [*Social Insurance Report*] 18.

Glasdam, S., N. Henriksen, L. Kjær, and J. Praestegaard. 2013. "Client Involvement in Home Care Practice: A Relational Sociological Perspective." *Nursing Inquiry* 20 (4): 329-40.

Goffman, E. 1971. *Relations in Public: Microstudies of the Public Order*. New York: Basic Books.

Grant, B., L. Giddings, and J. Beale. 2005. "Vulnerable Bodies: Competing Discourses of Intimate Bodily Care." *Journal of Nursing Education* 44 (11): 498-504.

Heath, C. 1986. *Body Movement and Speech in Medical Interaction*. Cambridge: Cambridge University Press.

Hjalmarsson, I., and E. Norman, eds. 2004. *Att välja hemtjänst* [*To Choose Home Care Services*]. Stockholm: Socialstyrelsen.

Hjalmarsson, I., and S. E. Wånell. 2013. *Valfrihetens LOV: En studie om vad Lagen om valfrihet betyder för den som har hemtjänst, för kommunen och för utförarna*

[*The Act on System of Choice: A Study of what the Act on Freedom of Choice in Care Implies for the One Receiving Home Care Services, for the County and for the Providers*]. Stockholm: Stiftelsen Stockholms läns äldrecentrum.
Inoue, M., R. Chapman, and D. Wynaden. 2006. "Male Nurses' Experiences of Providing Intimate Care for Women Clients." *Journal of Advanced Nursing* 55 (5): 559-67.
Isaksen, L. W. 2002. "Masculine Dignity and the Dirty Body." *NORA* 10 (3): 137-46.
Kalman, H., and K. Andersson. 2014. "Framing of Intimate Care in Home Care Services." *European Journal of Social Work*. Special Issue: Active Ageing and Demographic Change. 17 (3): 402-14. https://doi.org/10.1080/13691457.2014.885882
Katz, S., and T. Calasanti. 2015. "Critical Perspectives on Successful Aging: Does it 'Appeal more than it Illuminates'?" *The Gerontologist* 55 (1): 26-33.
Lindman, M. 2017. "Vårdreformen och valfrihetens abstrakta individualism" ["The Reform of Care and the Abstract Individualism of Freedom of Choice"]. *Hufvudstadsbladet* 24 Sept. https://www.hbl.fi/artikel/vardreformen-och-valfrihetens-abstrakta-individualism/
Meagher, G., and M. Szebehely, eds. 2013. *Marketisation in Nordic Eldercare: A Research Report on Legislation, Oversight, Extent and Consequences*. Stockholm: Department of Social Work, Stockholm University.
Meinow, B., M. Parker, and M. Thorslund. 2011. "Consumers of Eldercare in Sweden: The Semblance of Choice." *Social Science and Medicine* 73 (9): 1285-89.
Menzies, I. E. P. 1970 [1977]. *The Functioning of Social Systems as a Defence against Anxiety: A Report on a Study of the Nursing Service of a General Hospital*. Reprint. London: Tavistock Institute of Human Relations.
Mol, A. 2008. *The Logic of Care: Health and the Problem of Patient Choice*. Abingdon, Oxon: Routledge.
Måseide, P. 2008. Profesjonar i interaksjonsteoretisk perspektiv [Professions in the Perspective of Interaction Theory]. In *Profesjonsstudier* [*Studies of Professions*]. Edited by Anders Molander and Lars Inge Terum, 367-85. Oslo: Universitetsforlaget.
O'Lynn, C., and L. Krautscheid. 2011. "'How Should I Touch You?': A Qualitative Study of Attitudes on Intimate Touch in Nursing Care." *American Journal of Nursing* 111 (3): 24-31.
Persson, B., M. O. Holmberg, and I. Réne. 2016. "Nej till tvångsvård i hemmet" ["No to compulsory care/confined to home!"]. *Svenska Dagbladet*. January 10. https://www.svd.se/nej-till-tvangsvard-i-hemmet-for-de-aldre
Sundin, E., and M. Tillmar. 2010. "Masculinisation of the Public Sector: Local-level Studies of Public Sector Outsourcing in Elder Care." *International Journal of Gender and Entrepreneurship* 2 (1): 49-67.
Svensson M., and P-G. Edebalk. 2010. *Kundval i äldreomsorgen. Stärks brukarens ställning i ett valfrihetssystem?* [*Choosing as a Customer in Elder Care Services. Is the Position of User Strengthened in a System of Freedom of Choice?*]. Stockholm: SKL.
Szebehely, M., and G-B. Trydegård. 2012. "Home Care for Older People in Sweden: A Universal Model in Transition." *Health and Social Care in the*

Community. Special issue: Reforming Home Care in Ageing Societies. 20 (3): 300–309. https://doi.org/10.1111/j.1365-2524.2011.01046.x
Szebehely, M., and P. Ulmanen. 2012. Åtstramningens *pris* [The Price of Cutdowns]. Report. Stockholm University.
Sörensdotter, R. 2008. "Omsorgsarbete i omvandling: genus, klass och etnicitet inom hemtjänsten" ["Caring in Transition: Gender, Class and Ethnicity in Home Help"]. PhD diss., Stockholms universitet.
Twigg, J. 2000. *Bathing: The Body and Community Care*. London: Routledge.
Twigg, J., C. Wolkowitz, R. L. Cohen, and S. Nettleton. 2011. "Conceptualising Body Work in Health and Social Care." *Sociology of Health and Illness* 33 (2): 171–88.
Wiersma, E., and S. L. Dupuis. 2010. "Becoming Institutional Bodies: Socialization into a Long-term Care Home." *Journal of Aging Studies* 24 (4): 278–91.
Wikström, E. 2005. "Inflytandets paradoxer: möjligheter och hinder för självbestämmande och inflytande i hemtjänsten" ["The Paradoxes of Having Influence: Possibilities and Impediments for Exerting Self-determination and Influence in Home Care Services"]. Licentiate thesis, Växjö University.

Laws and Official Reports Cited

SCB [Statistics Sweden]. 2014. *Yrkesstrukturen i Sverige 2012: Yrkesregistret med yrkesstatistik* [*The Occupational Structure in Sweden 2012: Occupational Statistics based on the Swedish Occupational Register*].
SFS 1993:387. *Lag om stöd och service till vissa funktionshindrade* [*Act concerning Support and Service for Persons with Certain Functional Impairments*].
SFS 2001:453 *Socialtjänstlagen* [*The Social Services Act*].
SFS 2008:962. *Lagen om valfrihetssystem* [*The Act on System of Choice in the Public Sector*].
SFS 2010:110 *Socialförsäkringsbalken* [*Social Insurance Code*].
Socialstyrelsen [The National Board of Health and Welfare]. 1996. *Ädelreformen – slutrapport* [*Ädel reform – final report*]. Reports No: 1996-15-2.
___. 2004. *Att välja hemtjänst* [*To Choose Home Care Services*]. Available at: www.socialstyrelsen.se
___. 2003. *Kompetensförsörjning inom vård och omsorg om äldre och funktionshindrade – Del II – Faktagrund och beräkningar* [*Provision of Competence in Care of Older People and Disabled – Part II – Basis of Facts and Calculations*].
___. 2006. *Kompetensförsörjning inom kommunernas vård och omsorg om äldre – Lägesrapport* [*Provision of Competence in Community Care of Older People – Progress Report*].
___. 2011. *Hur lokala värdighetsgarantier inom äldreomsorgen kan utformas* [*How Local Guarantees concerning Dignity can be Designed*].
___. 2012. *Äldreomsorgens nationella värdegrund – ett vägledningsmaterial* [*National Core Values in Eldercare – A Guidance*].
___. 2013a. *Lokala värdighetsgarantier – en vägledning med utgångspunkt från ansökningar om prestationsersättning 2012* [*Local Guarantees concerning Dignity – A Guidance based on Applications for Payment for Achievements 2012*].

___. 2013b. *Personer med funktionsnedsättning – vård och omsorg 1 oktober 2012* [*Care and Services Input to Persons with Impairments 1 October 2012*].
___. 2013c. *Äldre – vård och omsorg den 1 oktober 2012* [*Care and Services to Elderly Persons 1 October 2012*].
SOFS 2012:3 *Socialstyrelsens allmänna råd om värdegrunden i socialtjänstens omsorg om äldre* [*General Advice on Core Values for Elder Care in Social Services from the National Board of Health and Welfare*].
SOU 2008:51 *Värdigt liv i äldreomsorgen* [*Life with Dignity in Elderly Home Care Services*].

About the author

Hildur Kalman is Professor of Social Work and Reader in Philosophy of Science at Umeå University, Sweden. She has earlier served as Director of the National Research School in Social Work, Sweden, and as Coordinator of the Graduate School of Gender Studies at Umeå Centre for Gender Studies, Umeå University. Her work critically evaluates the outcomes of changes in the Swedish welfare system for home care services in Sweden with a focus on how users' power may be neutralized when dependency on care is clothed in terms of clients and customers.

Chapter Eight

Caring across Borders: Lessons from Transnational Families

Marta Rodríguez-Galán

Abstract

"Caring across Borders: Lessons from Transnational Families" by **Marta Rodríguez-Galán** shares the story of the author's mother's rapid decline due to an early onset of Alzheimer's. Moving from her personal story of caring for her mother from a distance, Rodríguez-Galán casts a wider net and reviews the policies, among which immigration policies, that affect transnational families when it comes to caring for aging family members.

Introduction

New family structures extending across various countries and continents are a byproduct of globalization, one that has significant effects on both providing care to elders and the more defining care practices. For immigrants, the decision-making process on how best to care for their aging parents is not an easy one, as they must confront legal and policy hurdles, coupled with the social, moral, and ethical dilemmas surrounding their caregiving options. In this context, transnational families caring for the elderly seem to occupy a liminal space that has not been sufficiently investigated by either mainstream social gerontology or the literature on diversity and aging. It would appear as though research and theory in this field have been almost exclusively concerned with families living within the same nation. I contend that a sharper focus on transnational families and aging is vital to understanding not only their particular experiences, but also in order to shed more light on the meaning of intergenerational bonds and of the very notion of family itself.

In this chapter, I will first review the existing literature and current policies affecting transnational families in several Western countries, studies emanating primarily from North America, Western Europe, and Australia. My intention is to present the particular circumstances of selected families and the issues and challenges confronting them as transplants in another nation. Second, I will identify gaps and propose new areas for research and scholarship. I have to admit that my interest in this subject is not simply an academic one, as I am myself involved in transnational family care. Therefore, I will intersperse my review of the literature with some vignettes and insights drawn from my own experiences. Ultimately, I aim to begin to unravel how my own family's story and the stories of other immigrants are embedded in the greater contexts of family ethics, cultural change, social welfare state systems, and immigration laws.

Defining Transnational Families

Transnational families have been defined as "families that live some or most of the time separated from each other, yet hold together and create something that can be seen as a feeling of collective welfare and unity, namely 'familyhood', even across national borders" (Bryceson and Vuorela 2002, 18). Others have defined this phenomenon as the "globalization of kinship" (Deneva 2012, 108). This definition implies that families that extend across national borders provide the same types of support as proximate families, including emotional, financial, and instrumental support (Merla 2015). For example, in the 1990s, U.S. sociologists began to take notice of family transformations brought about by the increase in the number of immigrant women coming to the United States (especially those from Latin America) to perform domestic and caregiving work, while leaving their own children behind in the care of others. These women represent a new variation of motherhood that, to a degree, transgresses traditional gendered notions (Hondagneu Sotelo and Davila 2005) and they have become part of a "global care chain" (Eckenwiler 2011), which has resulted in a "care drain" (Hoschild 2003) in sending countries. Similarly, a small number of studies have begun to examine the implications of the globalization of kinship in elder care, as well as the roles of older immigrants themselves in providing child and domestic work for their immigrant children. In the sections that follow, I will focus on examining the continuities and transformations of elder care in a transnational context.

Family Ethics and Aging: Transformations in Filial Piety and Familism

Vignette I: The dilemmas of immigration and intergenerational solidarity

> The weekly phone calls were practically all we had to stay connected between Christmas and summer break, when I was able to save enough money from my graduate student stipend to visit my parents in Spain. But we made the most of those phone chats in order to stay abreast of how everyone was doing, the state of local politics in my hometown and, of course, the jokes. My mother had a quick and witty sense of humor, infused with a big dose of corniness; she would look forward to amusing me with the latest joke or piece of trendy Spanish popular culture. Mom indeed was a skillful conversationalist, or as she liked to put it, God had granted her the "Don de gentes" – the gift of congeniality. But at some point that I cannot pin down exactly, our conversations started to change. For example, she began to repeat the same stories almost obsessively, and the only piece of current news on which she would now comment was the weather, which she still enjoyed watching on TV displayed on a big map with pictures of clouds, the sun, thunder, and drops of rain. "Mañana el huevo frito," a fried egg for tomorrow – she would jokingly announce, meaning that she saw a white cloud with a big yellow sun in the middle – mostly sunny, but with some clouds. My mother was not yet 60 years old when she began to show the first symptoms of mild cognitive impairment.
>
> In 2007, when my mother entered the unforgiving journey of dementia, I was an A.B.D. student of sociology on a student visa (about to expire), working on my dissertation and with aspirations of becoming an academic in the United States. As such, I found myself confronting a personal conundrum for which none of the research articles and books on aging I had read could fully prepare me. Many thoughts flooded my mind during those months, and even years, as I tried to find some resolution. First of all, I was trying to understand what was really happening to my mother. There seemed to have been an incessant series of questions that I was suddenly pondering. For example, if this is dementia, what kind? Furthermore, why did it attack my mother so early? What health implications does this diagnosis have for me as a daughter? But perhaps the most difficult question and moral and ethical dilemma facing me was how to reconcile my social location and personal circumstances with what I had aspired to become. As a daughter, a "legal alien" in the United States from a Spanish working-class background, would it be

possible to reconcile my own professional goals with the sense of obligations and commitment that I felt I owed my parents? What is best for my family? And especially, how would I be able to ensure that my mother received good care? Furthermore, as a sociologist, I also began to wonder how other immigrants had confronted similar challenges. Moreover, I was endeavoring to unravel the riddle of what caring for aging parents means in a transnational context.

The scholarship suggests that obligations towards elders may be one of the oldest forms of family contract (Mengwei 2016), although cross cultural variation exists with respect to who specifically becomes the primary caregiver for a frail elder. Among East Asian families, filial piety is embedded in Confucian traditions that define and outline the obligations of children towards parents. It is important to note that such responsibilities include physical, financial, and emotional support. Although the sense of obligation seems to remain strong, the content of the care provided is altered by transnational offspring, for whom direct physical care is not feasible. Instead, these children tend to emphasize the emotional and symbolic aspects of support, such as "checking in" on parents by maintaining regular communication (Mengwei 2016). Similarly, a strong sense of identification with family (or *familismo*) and deference towards elders is commonly observed among Latinos. Among Peruvians and Moroccans in Spain, providing emotional support and sending remittances help to improve care conditions of aging relatives who remain in the country of origin. Escriva observes:

> although migration has often been blamed for separating families and disrupting family care resources, studies such as those collected in the book edited by Saraceno (2008) and our own research prove that under specific conditions migration helps to provide better assistance to those in need, even to improve communication and a sense of value between generations. (2013, 285)

Thus, the emotional ties between parents and children may not only be maintained, but may even be strengthened in transnational families. Social class, age, and the availability and affordability of formal services and social welfare infrastructure also influence the type of care provided across borders. For instance, among older Filipino immigrants in Canada, sending remittances to elder family members in the Philippines constitutes the primary form of elder care. These families are also more likely to have extended family in the home country to offer other types of supports to the old, and to promote the development of fictive kin relationships for elders living in the adopted country (Ferrer, Brotman, and Grenier 2017).

Middle-class Taiwanese families who are part of the one-child policy generation have been able to experience greater social mobility by investing in their only child's education, a phenomenon that even included "parachute children"—children who are sent to live without their parents in a Western country in order to improve their educational opportunities. Today, the parents of these upwardly mobile offspring believe that the financial dependence of elders on their children is neither necessary nor realistic, and they are more likely to endorse a more modern and democratic relationship between the two generations (Sun 2012, 153–57). Along the same lines, Taiwanese immigrants in the United States are also reinterpreting what filial piety means in the global context:

> I used to think that filial piety was to be near your parents and look after them. Now I realize the importance of successfully managing your own life, not to let parents worry about you, and make them proud. I think this is also a form of filial piety. (Wen, female, 33, married, legal assistant) (Sun 2012, 9)

It is evident here that while filial piety continues to represent a sense of obligation towards the older generation, its interpretation is more akin to North American notions of intergenerational solidarity such as "intimacy-at-a-distance"; in other words, both generations maintain residential autonomy, while staying emotionally connected. In addition, filial piety is achieved through other symbolic forms of support, which include bringing honor to the family name by becoming successful in a "better country" (Sun 2012).

Immigrants create new strategies for enacting the normative expectations of elder care, but opportunities to do so are shaped by the resources both in the destination country and the country of origin. For example, for Salvadoran refugees living in Australia, "transnational care" entails the ability to travel, having a social network in El Salvador, spending time in the home country, education, and knowledge (especially learning new technologies, as well as English), and regular communication (Merla 2015). Communication technologies, such as video conference technology, internet calling, messaging, and others, play a significant role in the ability of immigrant families to maintain contact as well as emotional bonds.

However, social inequalities with respect to access to such technologies in poor countries, such as El Salvador, pose more challenges to lower income families from those developing nations. For instance, in El Salvador only 9.3% of the population are internet users and only 5.1% have a personal computer, which indicates that internet communication between Salvadoran immigrants in Australia and their aging parents in El Salvador is scarce (Merla 2015).

Similarly, among working-class Polish immigrants living in Iceland, some traditional practices of elder care remain unchanged (primarily through family remittances), while others are modified and yet others are completely new. Modified practices include regularly checking in on parents through Skype, arranging help with domestic chores for parents, arranging medical help, paying bills on-line, and internet shopping, among other acts. New elder care practices include helping parents financially (traditionally, it is the other way around), acquiring new technological devices for parents, arranging medical consultations in Iceland, and introducing parents to the virtual world of the internet. Moreover, these migrants provide unpaid work during vacations instead of just taking time for themselves, during which they help parents with shopping, cleaning, repairs, and gardening (Krzyowski and Mucha 2014).

The gerontological literature as a whole is filled with analyses of the gendered dynamics of family caregiving. In fact, daughters and wives outnumber by far any other family care taker (Bracke, Christiaen, and Wauterickx 2008). These gender inequities are also present in the transnational context. Less is known about the particular experiences of female migrants and their transnational families, but evidence from various international communities shows that they follow a similar pattern. For example, Wilding and Baldassar (2009) found that female migrants from Italy and Ireland living in Australia are more likely than their male counterparts to reduce work expectations in order to assist their families. They also tend to feel guilty because they cannot provide physical care on a regular basis for their aging parents back home. On the other hand, the case of men is different in that they define their caregiving role for aging parents as an extension of the culturally expected role of "breadwinner," and thus use work as the means to support the economic needs associated with caregiving (e.g., international travelling, sending remittances). Although a gendered, albeit somewhat modified division of labor is still present in transnational families, the "newness" of this form of family organization allows for transgressions of gender norms not normally approved of in traditional cultures, such as grandfathers taking care of grandchildren (Deneva 2012) and single women living alone as breadwinners in the adopted society (Krzyowski and Mucha 2014).

Family Reunification and Social Welfare Policy

Beyond culture and family ethics, immigrants' decisions regarding elder care options are greatly influenced by the welfare and immigration policies in the sending and receiving countries. A brief cross-national overview of these policies would allow us to see the legal and policy challenges to family reunification and elder care.

The United States and Australia

In comparison to other countries, the United States still has a more "generous" family reunification immigration policy, but elder migration remains a difficult task. Although children can sponsor their parents, this implies that they are also financially responsible for all of their care needs for five years after reunification in the United States. After that time, the parents may be eligible to receive Medicare, Medicaid, and other entitlement programs. Still, because of the high cost of medical care and long-term care for seniors in the United States, this five-year moratorium is unaffordable for most low income and middle-class immigrants. This precarious form of migration may lead to either the bankruptcy of the sponsor in the event of illness, or to the "abandonment" of parents in the country of origin, where limited family and government support is available to them. Those who are undocumented would be in an even more precarious position to cope with the demands of elder caregiving (Angel and Angel 2015; U.S. Citizenship and Immigration Services 2018). Moreover, if President Trump's new immigration proposals are successful, only children and spouses will be eligible for sponsorship in the future.

Australia has a reunification policy similar to that of the United States, but the period during which children are fully responsible for the welfare costs or "assurance of support" of parents is set at 10 years for parent visa holders. Additionally, in order for one to sponsor a parent or grandparent, the government uses a "balance of family test," which requires that at least half of the siblings must live permanently in Australia (Australian Government Department of Home Affairs 2018).

Canada

In Canada, parents and grandparents cannot be sponsored through the regular family reunification program. However, in 2011, the government launched the "Parent and Grandparent Supervisa" program granting applicants multiple visa entries to visit family members for a 24-month period, in order to eliminate the backlog in Family Sponsorship applications. Nonetheless, parents/grandparents are still ineligible for government assistance and their children are ultimately fully responsible for their care and financial support. Ilyan Ferrer concludes:

> At worst, this type of policy disrupts family dynamics by placing considerable burden on sponsors to care for their parent's financial, social, and physical well-being. The unbalanced power dynamics also pushes older parents into potentially vulnerable positions where they are structurally dependent on their adult children for financial and social support. These invisible realities warrant further attention from policy makers, practitioners, and scholars especially in terms of how these types of policies impede caring relationships both locally and transnationally. (2015, 265)

In 2014, Canada revamped its family reunification policy, significantly restricting sponsorships of parents and grandparents. Before 2014, the Minimum Necessary Income threshold was sufficiently low that it was feasible for low-income families to sponsor a family member. After 2014, there was a 30% rise in the threshold. Similarly, the dependency period rose from 10 to 20 years, making it virtually impossible for an older parent to ever receive Canadian government benefits. Eligibility for permanent residency was also set at 20 years (with the exception of the province of Quebec, where it is still 10 years). According to the government's immigration page, these changes were needed to protect Canadian taxpayers. Moreover, the number of applications per year was capped at 5,000, but that number has since been raised to 10,000 under Prime-Minister Justin Trudeau (Government of Canada Immigration 2018).

Europe (example: Switzerland)

For non-EU/EFTA citizens there is no legal basis for family reunification per se. Obtaining permission necessitates a special status granted under immigration law in each country. In most cases, the request for reunification is granted for "humanitarian" reasons.

In general, immigrants contemplate family reunification right after a major life event disrupts transnational family dynamics. Vuille, Bolzman, and Hirsch (2013) identified three main types of reasons for family reunification with parents:

1) *An aging parent needs help*
This may be due to changes in health; becoming a widow/widower; a lack of family support in the country of origin; changes in health due to accident, disease, or simply due to advancing age. Isolation may also be a concern, as there may be a fear of not being able to receive needed services or to financially afford them. In some situations, an older migrant has returned to the country of origin, only to find themselves a stranger in their own country.

2) *The immigrant son or daughter needs help from (a) parent(s)*
In this case, typically, the son or daughter cannot afford child care or he/she needs help balancing the demands of work, family, and/or education (Vuille, Bolzman, and Hirsch 2013). There is a relatively prolific body of research describing the role of older parents in helping their immigrant children with housework and child care (Kalavar and Van Willigen 2005; Treas 2008).

3) *Changes in the socio-political context of the country of origin*
Changes in the socio-political context of the country of origin can make maintaining contact with parents more difficult. This may be caused, for instance, by a civil war or by widespread violence in the country of origin. In these kinds of situations, children may be able to sponsor parents for "humanitarian" reasons, or elders may obtain refugee status.

Perhaps due to the above-mentioned legal and policy constraints, the migration of older parents remains an infrequent phenomenon. In fact, reliable statistics or substantive studies of the United States, Australia, Canada, and the European Union are sparse. In Switzerland, for example, parent migration accounts for only 1% of all family reunification cases (Vuille, Bolzman, and Hirsch 2013). A brief comparative overview of family reunification policies for parents/grandparents across various receiving Western countries shows that this type of immigration is still rare and envisioned only as an exception to the typical influx of younger immigrants. When it does happen, immigrant families are forced to provide for all the needs of elders for a prolonged period of time, thus discouraging low-income and moderate-income families from pursuing this type of reunification.

The United States, the United Kingdom, and other Western receiving countries are currently engaged in polarizing debates regarding immigration. For instance, President Trump has made repeated appeals to change family reunification policies and severely restrict the "chain migration" of extended family members that has been, historically, more characteristic of the United States. In this political context, Canada is often cited as an example of the route the United States may take in toughening family reunification laws. If passed, these policies would only contribute to placing the burden of elder care entirely on the immigrant families who would, once again, be expected to "take care of their own" without assistance from the receiving society. Given the gendered dynamics of family caregiving, these policies will also incur significant opportunity costs for immigrant women in particular.

Vignette II: Transnational Family Care for my Spanish Mother with Early Onset of Dementia

> *My mother was never fully aware that I had finally graduated with a PhD, nor could she accurately verbalize that she had dementia, but she understood the importance of both. To her, dementia felt as if she was very, very old, even though she was not; and a PhD was like climbing to the top of a job ladder. In her own way, my mother understood that there had been important new developments in our lives. And then she declared: "Ahora mandas tú," [now you are in charge], "you were the youngest daughter and, growing up, everyone else in the family tried to tell you what to do; but now you are in charge, and I will follow your wishes." With these words, and her humorous style, my mother repositioned my role within the family.*

I do not consider myself a caregiver in the traditional sense of the word, nor in the way that this role is construed in the majority of gerontological literature (Tremont and Davis 2014). My own non-traditional, informal caregiving situation most closely parallels the findings of Keefe and Fancey (2000) regarding the roles of family caregivers whose loved ones have entered formal long-term care: I may not be directly giving care, but I am still very involved in my mother's care. In 2006, just two years before a full-blown, worldwide economic recession struck, the administration of the socialist President of Spain, José Luis Rodríguez Zapatero, passed the *Ley 39/2006 de Promoción de la Autonomía Personal y Atención a las Personas en Situación de Discapacidad* [Law 39/2006 for the Promotion of Personal Autonomy and Attention to Persons in a Situation of Disability (referred to henceforth as L.A.D.)]. This new law effectively created for both the citizens and residents of Spain a new social right, alongside health care, education, and pensions: the right to receive social services (Rodríguez 2011). The aim of the L.A.D. was to either support or supplement informal caregiving, allowing applicants the option of either receiving services at home or for families to receive a monetary allowance to allow them to make their own caregiving arrangements. Moreover, access to services became universal in all the autonomous communities, with municipalities becoming responsible for their provisions, and users contributing a co-payment based on their current income. This law supports the cultural orientation toward *familismo,* and the preference of Spaniards for receiving services at home rather than in institutional settings (Roldán García, Garcí Giráldez, and Nogués Sáez 2013). In addition, while it significantly reduces the cost of caring for the dependent in a formal residential setting, it also improves the quality of life of the dependent person, and may even help create much-needed jobs (Rodríguez 2011).

As my mother's legal guardian, my father (a retired factory worker) applied for, and was granted, services for my mother. He opted for receiving home health services, to which he would have to contribute 25% of the cost. However, when the austerity measures of the new conservative president Manuel Rajoy took effect, this co-payment rose to 75%. In addition to the co-payments for social services, there were also new co-payments for retirees' medications. A few months before the general election of December 2015, the co-payment for home care was reduced back to the original 25%. These co-payments for drugs and social services, in combination with the high unemployment rate in Spain, could have an effect on the use of services for the aged and disabled, with family members discontinuing services and opting for full-time care for the dependent person. Fortunately for us, however, Spain does have a better social service infrastructure than the poorer nations from which many other immigrants originate, such as Latin America, African nations, and newer members of the European Union.

Caring for the Primary Caregiver in the Transnational Context

These days, I am only able to have phone conversations with my father, for my mother can no longer speak and is also bedridden. These phone conversations represent the main vehicle for my ability to provide some form of long-distance companionship, and emotional and informational support for him (the primary caregiver), from cooking and nutrition tips, to interpreting medical and legal documents, to planning a family vacation. In addition to this, every year I spend a minimum of eight weeks of vacation time in Spain, helping out my parents. However, I constantly worry about how best to support my parents as they age and their health deteriorates given that both my brother and I have migrated elsewhere (my brother to the United Kingdom and I to the United States).

I became an American citizen in March 2017, just a few months after President Trump's election. My new citizenship status grants me the possibility of sponsoring my parents, but I find myself financially and practically unable to do so. The cost of health insurance for both of my parents, and of long-term care assistance for my mother, would make it impossible to make ends meet, even with all of our resources combined. Thus, my own family case highlights the extreme difficulty of family reunification with older parents, even for middle-class professionals from relatively wealthy nations.

In this chapter, I have presented an overview of transnational family care, the transformations it implies for family ethics, a cross-national comparison of family reunification policies affecting the elder care options available to transnational families, as well as my own family experiences in navigating these structural and cultural hurdles. Although there is a relatively sizable body of research on the experiences of elders (usually the "young old") who have already reunited with their children; there is still a vacuum of data, research, and theory that could shed light on the experiences of transnational children caring for elders. On the one hand, my exploration of the literature on this topic has shown the adaptability, ingenuity, and resilience displayed by transnational families. However, in an era of profound economic anxiety, cuts in welfare systems, and the perception that immigrants are a burden to national economies through family reunification, personal and ethical conundrums such as mine will only continue to haunt the children who have migrated.

References

Angel, Ronald J., and Jacqueline L. Angel. 2014. *Latinos in an Aging World: Social, Psychological, and Economic Perspectives*. London: Routledge.

Australian Government Department of Home Affairs. https://immi.homeaffairs.gov.au/visas/getting-a-visa/visa-listing/contributory-parent-143. Accessed March 2019.

Bracke, Piet, Wendy Christiaens, and Naomi Wauterickx. 2008. "The Pivotal Role of Women in Informal Care." *Journal of Family Issues* 29 (10): 1348–78.

Bryceson, Deborah, and Ulla Vuorela. 2002. "The Transnational Family: New European Frontiers and Global Networks." In *Transnational Families, Migration and the Circulation of Care: Understanding Mobility and Absence in Family Life*, edited by L. Baldassar and L. Merla, 315–22 London: Routledge.

Deneva, Neda. 2012. "Transnational Aging Carers: On Transformation of Kinship and Citizenship in the Context of Migration among Bulgarian Muslims in Spain." *Social Politics* 19 (1): 105–28.

Eckenwiler, Lisa. 2011. "Women on the Move: Long-term Care, Migrant Women, and Global Justice." *IJFAB: International Journal of Feminist Approaches to Bioethics* 4 (2): 1–31.

Escrivá, Angeles. 2013. "Asset Accumulation and Transfer for Old Age: A Study on Peruvian and Moroccan Migration to Spain." *European Journal of Ageing* 10 (4): 279–87.

Fancey, Pamela, Janice Keefe, Robin Stadnyk, Emily Gardiner, and Katie Aubrecht. 2012. "Understanding and Assessing the Impact of Nursing Home Approach to Care and Physical Design on Residents and their Families: A Synthesis of the Literature." *Seniors Housing and Care Journal* 20 (1): 99–114.

Ferrer, Ilyan. 2015. "Examining the Disjunctures between Policy and Care in Canada's Parent and Grandparent Supervisa." *International Journal of Migration, Health and Social Care* 11 (4): 253–67.

Ferrer, Ilyan, Shari Brotman, and Amanda Grenier. 2017. "The Experiences of Reciprocity among Filipino Older Adults in Canada: Intergenerational, Transnational, and Community Considerations." *Journal of Gerontological Social Work* 60 (4): 313–27.

Government of Canada Immigration Services. http://www.cic.gc.ca/english/helpcentre/answer.asp?qnum=1330&top=14. Accessed February 2018.

Hochschild, Arlie Russell. 2003. *The Commercialization of Intimate Life: Notes from Home and Work*. Berkeley: University of California Press.

Hondagneu-Sotelo, Pierrette, and Avila, Ernestine. 1997. "'I'm here, but I'm there': The Meanings of Latina Transnational Motherhood." *Gender & Society* 11 (5): 548–71.

Kalavar, Jyotsna M., and John Van Willigen. 2005. "Older Asian Indians Resettled in America: Narratives about Households, Culture and Generation." *Journal of Cross-Cultural Gerontology* 20 (3): 213–30.

Keefe, Janice, and Fancey, Pamela. 2000. "The Care Continues: Responsibility for Elderly Relatives Before and After Admission to a Long-term Care Facility." *Family Relations* 49(3): 235–44.

Krzyżowski, Łukasz, and Janusz Mucha. 2014. "Transnational Caregiving in Turbulent Times: Polish Migrants in Iceland and their Elderly Parents in Poland." *International Sociology* 29 (1): 22–37.

McDonald, Lynn. 2011. "Theorising about Ageing, Family and Immigration." *Ageing and Society* 31 (7): 1180–201.
Merla, Laura. 2015. "Salvadoran Migrants in Australia: An Analysis of Transnational Families' Capability to Care across Borders." *International Migration* 53 (6): 153–65.
Rodríguez, Pilar Rodríguez. 2006. "Los Servicios de Ayuda a Domicilio (SAD) o de atención domiciliaria. Conceptualización y objetivos." In *Los servicios de ayuda a domicilio: planificación y gestión de casos: manual de formación para auxiliaries*, edited by Pilar Rodríguez Rodríguez and Carmen Valdevieso Sánchez, 21–30. Madrid: Editorial Médica Panamericana.
Roldán García, E., T. García Giráldez, and L. Nogués Sáez. 2013. *Los Servicios Sociales en España*. Madrid: Síntesis Editorial.
Sun, Ken C. 2012. "Fashioning the Reciprocal Norms of Elder Care: A Case of Immigrants in the United States and their Parents in Taiwan." *Journal of Family Issues* 33 (9): 1240–71.
Treas, Judith. 2008. "Transnational Older Adults and their Families." *Family Relations* 57 (4): 468–78.
Tremont, Geoffrey, and Jennifer Duncan Davis. 2014. "The Role of Caregivers in the Treatment of Patients with Dementia." In *The Neuropsychology of Cortical Dementias*, edited by Chad A. Noggle and Raymond S. Dean, 393–422. New York: Springer.
Tu, Mengwei. 2016. "Chinese One-child Families in the Age of Migration: Middle-class Transnational Mobility, Ageing Parents, and the Changing Role of Filial Piety." *Journal of Chinese Sociology* 3 (1): 1–17.
U. S. Citizenship and Immigration Services. https://www.uscis.gov/family/family-us-citizens/parents/bringing-parents-live-united-states-permanent-residents. Accessed February 2018.
Vuille, Marilène, Claudio Bolzman, and Elisabeth Hirsch Durrett. 2013. "Professional Stances and Personal Values in the Realm of Transnational Family Reunification with Older Parents: Social Work Practice in an Emerging Field." *European Journal of Social Work* 16 (3): 407–26.
Wilding, Raelene, and Loretta Baldassar. 2009. "Transnational Family-work Balance: Experiences of Australian Migrants Caring for Ageing Parents and Young Children across Distance and Borders." *Journal of Family Studies* 15 (2): 177–87.

About the author

Marta Rodríguez-Galán is Associate Professor of Sociology at St. John Fisher College, where she also directs the Gerontology program. For over a decade, she has been conducting research on aging and health with a particular focus on Hispanic/Latino communities in the United States. She is currently researching civic engagement among low-income older Latinos and the experiences of Latina grandmothers and great-grandmothers raising grandchildren.

Part Four

Critical Perspectives on Aging

Chapter Nine

Missing Voices in Aging-Well Frameworks: A Postcolonial Analysis

Lauren Brooks-Cleator and Audrey Giles

Abstract

"Missing Voices in Aging-Well Frameworks: A Postcolonial Analysis" by **Lauren Brooks-Cleator** and **Audrey Giles** proposes a post-colonial critique of dominant aging-well frameworks (i.e., active and successful aging) that are used to inform policy and practice related to older adults' health and well-being. The paper provides a critical discussion of dominant aging-well frameworks through a postcolonial theoretical lens, which is used to examine the historical and ongoing impact of colonialism on Indigenous peoples. The authors call for the construction of new, inclusive, and culturally safe aging-well frameworks and policies.

Introduction

The Indigenous population in Canada[1] is much younger than the non-Indigenous population. Despite the young age of this population, however, the number of Indigenous older adults is rapidly growing. Between 2001 and 2011 the population of Indigenous seniors (aged 65 years and over) in Canada doubled: seniors

---

1   Our chapter is focused on Indigenous populations in Canada. Notably, we understand that Indigenous peoples globally, and nationally, are diverse and have different values, beliefs, cultures (etc.) and we do not want to homogenize their experiences. Due to the limited amount of research related to Indigenous perspectives on aging, however, we include some research on this topic from Australia and the United States. We felt that such inclusion is appropriate because of the shared past and present experiences of colonialism between Indigenous peoples in Canada, Australia, and the United States. As such, unless otherwise stated, when discussing Indigenous older adults in this chapter we are referring to the Canadian context.

comprised 4% of the Indigenous population in 2001 and grew to 6% in 2011 (O'Donnell, Wendt, and National Association of Friendship Centres 2017). Additionally, the population of Indigenous older adults now comprises over 2% of the total older adult population in Canada (Statistics Canada 2018). While this may seem to be a small number, it is becoming increasingly important for researchers, decision-makers, service providers, and community members to work together to support Indigenous older adults as they age. Despite the increasing number of Indigenous older adults, Beatty and Berdahl noted that "Aboriginal seniors are among the most neglected societal class...[and are in] more challenging and dependent situations at an age when they should expect to be well treated and taken care of properly by both their families and governments" (2011, 1). Indeed, authors have noted that there is a dearth of research concerning the Indigenous older adult population (Beatty and Berdahl 2011; Wilson, Rosenberg, Abonyi, and Lovelace 2010), especially research that shares Indigenous older adults' perspectives (Lewis 2014; Pace and Grenier 2017).

Indigenous older adults face numerous health and social issues and represent one of the most marginalized groups in Canada. The Health Council of Canada (HCC) identified that despite the diversity of Indigenous older adults in Canada, members of this group share many similar health and social concerns resulting from colonization and colonial acts, such as the Indian Act, residential schools, forced relocation to reserves or remote northern communities, and the Sixties Scoop:[2] food insecurity, poor housing, elder abuse, outmigration of young adults (for older adults living in rural communities), and low literacy skills (HCC 2013). Research has also demonstrated that many Indigenous older adults do not trust the mainstream health care system due to systemic racism and discrimination against Indigenous peoples (HCC 2013). These

---

2   Racial discrimination, which positions Indigenous populations as inferior to non-Indigenous, white populations, is the driving force of these various colonial policies and practices in Canada (Loppie, Reading, and de Leeuw 2014). These policies and practices, all built on the basis of Western superiority and Indigenous inferiority, have resulted in many disparities in the distribution of resources and opportunities, which in turn have affected the overall health and well-being of many generations of Indigenous peoples, contributed to the loss of Indigenous cultures and languages, and taken away land and resources from Indigenous peoples (Loppie, Reading and de Leeuw 2014).

health and social factors influence Indigenous older adults' "health status, quality of life, ability to fulfill their traditional roles, and life expectancies" (Baskin and Davey 2015, 48). Despite these challenges, however, many researchers and Indigenous older adults themselves have acknowledged, partially in response to the deficit-based understandings of health, this population's significant resiliency and the meaningful roles that they hold in their communities (Browne, Mokuau, and Braun 2009; Ginn and Kulig 2015; HCC 2013; Hopkins et al. 2007; Lewis 2014).

The experiences of Indigenous older adults with aging and being well in older age ought to be recognized as being worthy of considerable attention from researchers, service providers, policymakers, and community members alike, not only because of the health and social inequities that they face, but because they bring another perspective to aging-well research—a perspective that is often missed. In addition to this, it is crucial that we recognize and address Indigenous older adults' histories with colonialism, as these histories have shaped their life course. This is especially important because aging research is typically embedded in a Western, Eurocentric perspective (Hopkins et al. 2007; Lewis 2011) that does not privilege non-Western perspectives on aging, such as those of Indigenous older adults (Lewis 2011). Very few researchers have addressed aging well for this population (Pace and Grenier 2017). While some have demonstrated the differences between Rowe and Kahn's (1987) model of successful aging and Indigenous perspectives on aging (Lewis 2011; Pace and Grenier 2017), the multiple frameworks for aging well have not been analyzed using a postcolonial lens, which privileges the voices of those who have been colonized. Consequently, in this chapter, we conduct a postcolonial analysis of the frameworks that describe aging well in order to demonstrate that Western knowledge of aging and health is privileged in the dominant aging-well frameworks. While these frameworks leave out the voices of many groups, a postcolonial analysis allows us to examine how aging-well frameworks specifically miss the voices of those who have been negatively affected by the ongoing impacts of colonialism, such as Indigenous older adults in Canada, which limits their opportunities for being well in older age.

We begin by outlining the postcolonial theoretical lens that we apply throughout this chapter. We then provide a brief overview of the multiple frameworks for aging well, with an emphasis on active aging and successful aging. Following this, we conduct a postcolonial analysis of aging-well frameworks by 1) exploring the historical context in which the current cohort of Indigenous older adults has aged, 2) identifying whose knowledge is privileged in aging-well frameworks, and 3) examining who has the opportunity to age well. We then discuss how disparities within current aging-well frameworks can be addressed through the inclusion of Indigenous older adults' perspectives on aging and the development of a culturally safe aging-well framework. Importantly, as researchers we recognize our position as settler Canadians. While we cannot speak for Indigenous older adults and their experiences, we hope that this postcolonial analysis demonstrates the importance of including their voices in future research, especially research related to aging well.

Postcolonial Analysis

A postcolonial analysis encourages researchers to use a postcolonial theoretical lens to analyze the history and legacy of colonialism and to critically examine the structural inequities linked to the effects of colonization, all of which is particularly relevant for this chapter given the role of colonialism in Canada and its impact on Indigenous older adults' lives (Browne, Smye, and Varcoe 2005; Reimer Kirkham and Anderson 2002). Importantly, the "post" in postcolonialism does not refer to the fact that we have moved past a point where legacies of colonialism are still intact, but rather it refers to the "emergent, new configurations of inequities [that] are exerting their distinctive effects" (Browne, Smye, and Varcoe 2005, 20), such as the health and social inequities that are faced by Indigenous older adults. As such, postcolonial theory combines the knowledge systems of those who have endured colonialism with a political critique of their lived experiences (Young 2001). Concerning Indigenous peoples in Canada, specifically, a postcolonial lens enables researchers to examine the unequal power relations that currently exist between Indigenous and non-Indigenous peoples and to recognize and critique the socio-historico-political structures that influence Indigenous peoples' health and social conditions (Browne, Smye, and Varcoe 2005). Researchers conducting postcolonial critiques and analyses seek to understand the historical context of colonialism and how these past circumstances have shaped — and continue to shape — present-day conditions (Young 2001).

Common Frameworks for Aging Well

There are many concepts that are commonly used in aging-well literature and policies, such as "successful" and "active aging". These concepts focus on "the need for self-discipline, which stresses individual responsibility to 'age well' and moderate the burden of welfare risk" (Angus and Reeve 2006, 145). Aging-well frameworks are premised upon the role of individual agency and lifestyle, with limited focus on the role of the social determinants of health (Katz and Calasanti 2015). Angus and Reeve (2006) argued that if aging-well policies and programs continue to ignore the social and cultural structures in which seniors live their lives, these policies and programs will be unsuccessful because they only address a small portion of the aging experience. These concepts identify what it means to "age well" and guide the development of community initiatives that support seniors to do so, e.g., the World Health Organization's (WHO) Age-Friendly Communities framework (International Longevity Centre-Brazil 2015). Katz and Calasanti discussed how aging-well frameworks have "been churned into theoretical paradigms, health measurements, retirement lifestyles, policy agendas, and antiaging ideals" (2015, 1). Indeed, while there are multiple concepts with which to describe the process of aging well, active and successful aging have become the dominant frameworks that are employed to describe "good" aging and to address seniors' health and social needs.

Successful Aging

Prior to the development of Rowe and Kahn's widely known definition of successful aging, researchers typically understood aging as a time of deterioration and disease during which age-related cognitive and physical changes were normal (1987). Rowe and Kahn proposed a definition of successful aging that included 1) the low probability of disease and disease-related disability, 2) high cognitive and physical functional capacity, and 3) active engagement with life, in which all three components are interrelated (1987). This definition of successful aging represented a paradigm shift in that it suggested that many of the effects of aging were actually due to the effects of disease and the risk of disease (Pruchno, Wilson-Genderson, and Cartwright 2010); however, by focusing so strongly on individual choice and lifestyle for achieving success and health in advanced age, they moved aging further away from the social determinants of health (Katz and Calasanti 2015). There has been significant new research that develops further measurements of successful aging. For example, functional ability or disability have become the most common aspects of measuring successful aging, which typically involve self-reports of activities of daily living, instrumental activities of daily living, or functional abilities (Pruchno, Wilson-Genderson, and Cartwright 2010).

Since Rowe and Kahn's (1987) original definition of successful aging, "social gerontologists have grappled with the ways in which successful aging has and has not captured the personal, social, economic, and political contexts of aging" (Martinson and Berridge 2015, 59). In their systematic review of the critiques of successful aging, Martinson and Berridge (2015) found that the main concerns with successful aging as a concept included 1) the need to include missing criteria, such as subjective criteria, spirituality, leisure activity, etc., 2) the lack of perspectives from older adults, particularly from diverse cultural perspectives, 3) the individualized, neoliberal, biomedical view of aging, and 4) the unrealistic portrayal of old age.

Active Aging

Active aging and healthy aging are closely associated in that "active ageing should incorporate and mutually support healthy ageing and healthy life expectancy" (Walker and Maltby 2012, S123). Active aging emphasizes the importance of a life course perspective and does not solely focus on later life issues; it is a concept that is relevant to all stages of life (Walker 2002; Walker and Maltby 2012). The "active" part of active aging does not merely relate to being physically active; it involves being active in many aspects of life. Active aging is built on the concepts of successful and productive aging and emphasizes the strong link between activity and health, and it identifies the importance of healthy aging (Walker 2002). It is a concept that addresses older people's participation and inclusion in society as full citizens with an emphasis placed on quality of life and physical and mental well-being (Walker 2002). In 2002, the

World Health Organization (WHO) released *Active Ageing: A Policy Framework* in order to address the growth of the older adult population and to help guide action plans that promote healthy and active aging. The framework was later built upon by the International Longevity Centre Brazil (ILC-Brazil) in 2015. At the policy level, it addresses how social institutions are to support and enable people to take opportunities throughout their lives that contribute to their well-being in later life (ILC-Brazil 2015). Active aging is "the process of optimizing opportunities for health, lifelong learning, participation and security in order to enhance the quality of life as people age" (ILC-Brazil 2015, 39).

Active aging is a multidimensional approach that understands aging as being influenced by the individual, the community, and society (Bowling 2008; Walker and Maltby 2012) and as something that is the responsibility of both individuals and society (Walker 2006). Active aging proponents argue that older people are active participants in society and focus on the diversity of older adults' contributions, not just their economic productivity (Walker and Maltby 2012). In contrast to the early understandings of successful aging, active aging researchers take less of a biomedical approach to aging. Instead, they focus on enhancing the quality of life without reducing the concept of aging well to simply avoiding disease and decline and maintaining independence. To further build upon the successful and active aging discussions, and to strengthen the many critiques of the aging-well discourses in Western societies, our postcolonial analysis offers a viewpoint of the personal, social, economic, and political contexts of aging that place Indigenous peoples' experiences at the center of analysis.

Postcolonial Analysis of Aging-Well Frameworks

While both active and successful aging have been continuously critiqued and refined, by understanding the historical context of Indigenous older adults' lives and further analyzing concepts of aging well using a postcolonial theoretical lens we can demonstrate that Western knowledge of aging is privileged in the dominant aging-well frameworks and that, as a result, groups who continue to be influenced by colonialism, such as Indigenous older adults in Canada, have limited opportunities to age well.

Historical Context

With any study that focuses on participants' experiences and perspectives, it is important to consider the historical contexts that have influenced their lives. When examining a certain age group, researchers need to realize that the experiences of one cohort are not the same as previous cohorts and will not be the same as subsequent cohorts; each cohort deals with specific events and transitions over time, which can impact its members' health and well-being later in life.

The current cohorts of Indigenous older adults have had many significant life experiences which are related to the impacts of colonialism. They are "survivors who have experienced much loss, in the face of threats to the health and longevity of Indigenous people" (Waugh and Mackenzie 2011, 30). It is important to examine the historical circumstances that have informed Indigenous older adults' current health and social circumstances. In examining current aging-well frameworks, it becomes apparent that there is no recognition of how historical circumstances related to colonialism may shape Indigenous older adults' experiences with, understandings of, and ability for successful or active aging. The historical relationship that Indigenous older adults in Canada have had with colonial and racist policies and practices, such as the Indian Act, residential schools, the Sixties Scoop, and others, cannot be ignored since it has shaped this population's experiences with aging and health (Reading and Wien 2009). Many members of the current generation of Indigenous older adults are survivors of these hideous colonial acts. For example, Baskin and Davey (2015), in their study with 12 female Indigenous Elders and seniors in Toronto, showed how their participants' experiences with aging could not be understood without addressing their experiences of residential schools. Thus, Indigenous older adults' perspectives on aging well and the health and social disparities that they face as they age cannot be understood without considering how colonial acts have contributed to alienation, depression, substance abuse, and loss of language and culture for many individuals and families (HCC 2013; Reading and Wien 2009; Truth and Reconciliation Commission of Canada [TRC] 2015).

Whose Knowledge is Privileged?

Bowling and Dieppe (2005) argued that aging-well frameworks incorporate elements of both the biological and scientific models of aging, and that they are aligned and legitimized through a close association with a scientific model, which is very highly privileged in Western/Eurocentric societies (Estes and Binney 1989). In Western cultures, the aging-well discourse is mainly conducted at the biological level which privileges disease-free, active older individuals, and which does not fit with cultures that privilege other, non-biological ways of being well in older age, especially those ways related to the social and community context. Within aging-well frameworks, scientists are depicted as the experts on aging who can claim knowledge about old age (Parker et al. 2014; Vincent 2006). In Indigenous cultures, there are other experts who hold and share knowledge on living well. An Elder is chosen by community members and is "a cultural and spiritual guide and who has insights, understandings, and communication abilities to transmit the wisdom of previous generations" (Baskin and Davey 2015, 47). Their perspectives on aging are also important, as they play pivotal roles in the health and well-being of their communities (Collings 2011; Ginn and Kulig 2015; Lewis 2014; Waugh and Mackenzie 2011). For example, Ginn and Kulig's (2015) research focused on First Nations grandmothers' definitions of health and ideas on health promotion, because studies have demonstrated the importance of Indigenous grandmothers' leadership in their communities due to their strength, resiliency, and wisdom. They noted that Indigenous grandmothers "possess traditional knowledge, know their communities and families, and are well positioned to work collaboratively to negotiate change" (2015, 12). Thus, they are invaluable resources for strengthening their communities, sharing cultural traditions, and promoting health and well-being. The expertise of Elders, however, is not recognized and their knowledge of being well in older age is absent from Western aging-well frameworks.

The reliance on scientific expertise increases the power of a Western-dominated knowledge system, which encourages neoliberal, individualistic values to influence lay people's beliefs and policymakers' decisions. The knowledge system in which aging-well frameworks are built is the same one in which the colonial socio-historico-political structures originate, and which continue to impact Indigenous peoples' lives. Through analyzing the dominant knowledge of aging well, we can clearly recognize that missing from these frameworks are non-Western, Indigenous perspectives of aging. Ignoring these perspectives perpetuates colonial attitudes.

Additionally, research has demonstrated that much of what we know about aging well comes from researchers who have studied those who have reached advanced ages (Pruchno, Wilson-Genderson, and Cartwright 2010). While it is important to consider aging well from the perspectives of the elderly, we must note that such a perspective overlooks segments of the population with lower than average Canadian life expectancy. For example, life expectancy for the total Canadian population is 80 for men and 84 for women (WHO 2016), while for Inuit men and women it would be 64 and 73, respectively (Statistics Canada 2015). Métis and First Nations populations also have lower than average life expectancy: "73–74 years for men and 78–80 years for women" (Statistics Canada 2015, 1). Thus, members of Indigenous populations in Canada are less likely to reach advanced age and, as such, are less likely to be represented in aging-well research.

Who has the Opportunity to Age Well?

The focus of successful and active aging on "autonomy and productivity as the route to a fulfilling old age smacks of a form of cultural imperialism which may have limited validity" (Estes, Biggs, and Phillipson 2003, 73). Aging-well frameworks privilege Western understandings of aging as a linear process and limit aging well to those who have not experienced the ongoing impacts of colonialism. Here, we show how current aging-well frameworks, such as the successful and active aging frameworks discussed previously, are often in contrast to the holistic views on aging that are held by many Indigenous older adults, which can further marginalize this population and limit their opportunities for aging well. In addition to viewing aging as a cyclical, rather than linear, process (Baskin and Davey 2015), Indigenous views on aging have been identified as being inclusive of mental health, emotional well-being, and physical health, but also community engagement and spirituality (Collings 2001; Ginn and Kulig 2015; Hopkins et al. 2007; Lewis 2011; Lewis 2014; Pace and Grenier 2017; Waugh and Mackenzie 2011). The effects of colonialism, however, have created an environment where Indigenous older adults frequently face a health care system that does not privilege their holistic views of aging and health, thus resulting in a system that cannot adequately address the health disparities that Indigenous peoples face (de Leeuw, Lindsay, and Greenwood 2015).

Researchers have shown that Indigenous older adults define staying healthy throughout the aging process as multidimensional — that is, as a balance between physical, mental, emotional, and spiritual health (Ginn and Kulig 2015; Pace and Grenier 2017; Waugh and Mackenzie 2011). Interestingly, Ginn and Kulig (2015) found in their participatory action research study with seven First Nations grandmothers (aged 48 to 80 years) in a small city in Alberta, Canada, that physical health was not defined in accordance with the dominant Western view of avoiding loss, decline, chronic disease, and disability. Instead, the grandmothers noted that physical health included role-modelling for their families and communities on how to be healthy, educating community members and non-Indigenous health care providers in order to bridge gaps between cultures, and living off-reserve, for this provided access to increased health and opportunities to be present for their grandchildren (Ginn and Kulig 2015). For these grandmothers, mental health included 1) knowing who could be trusted and who could not, 2) problem solving, 3) enjoying life through humor by letting go of negative influences, and 4) building on past experiences in order to learn how to be grateful and develop self-confidence (Ginn and Kulig 2015). Emotional health included resilience and surviving the trauma of residential schools, staying positive, constructively addressing racism through their experiences with it, and educating others about cultural differences (Ginn and Kulig 2015). Finally, spiritual health included having faith and praying, using knowledge gained from their own Indigenous culture, as well as from Western cultures, and following their dreams and intuitions (Ginn and Kulig 2015).

While aging-well frameworks, such as active and successful aging, prioritize quality of life and physical and mental well-being (Rowe and Kahn 1987; Walker 2002), Ginn and Kulig's (2015) work demonstrates how some aspects of aging well are not represented in Western aging-well frameworks, such as role-modelling, resilience, and spirituality, to list a few. Not considering these other important factors of aging well can limit the extent to which Indigenous older adults receive the culturally safe (Ramsden 1993) care and support that they need. Culturally safe care occurs when Indigenous peoples feel empowered and in charge of decisions concerning their health, and when their present-day realities are considered within the historical context of colonization (Brascoupé and Waters 2009).

Studies outside of Canada have shown that not only is individual health important for Indigenous older adults to be well in older age, but so too is the health of their families and communities. In contrast, the dominant Western frameworks of aging well solely emphasize individual health and independence (Pace and Grenier 2017; Waugh and Mackenzie 2011). Here, we provide an example of how aging well for Indigenous older adults focuses on more than just individual health and independence. In his study in rural Alaska with 25 Alaskan Native Elders aged 61 to 93, Lewis (2014) found that avoiding having to relocate away from their families and remaining in their own homes were key factors in successful aging. Additionally, the participants in his study noted that successful aging also involved having a reciprocal relationship with their families, wherein they are supportive of each other, and wherein the older adults teach and lead future generations and share their knowledge and wisdom (Lewis 2014).

Again, in contrast to Western frameworks of aging well, successful aging for Indigenous older adults is also related to community support through inclusion. For example, in a study from Sydney, Australia, with Indigenous Australians aged 45 and above, many participants discussed that community engagement allowed them to connect with other community members and with their culture, and reduced their sense of social isolation (Waugh and Mackenzie 2011). They also mentioned the importance of being able to share their knowledge and pass on cultural traditions to both their families and the community, as it provided them with feelings of importance and worthiness (Waugh and Mackenzie 2011). It is clear that the reciprocal nature of family relationships and community support is important for Indigenous older adults. Considering the historical and present-day marginalization that Indigenous older adults have faced, and their resilience in light of it, it is especially important for researchers to embrace Indigenous older adults' perspectives.

Creating Culturally Safe Approaches to Aging Well

Research on aging well has typically focused on non-Indigenous populations. While some researchers have addressed aging from the perspectives of Indigenous older adults, research that privileges marginalized groups' experiences and perspectives on aging remains rather limited. Increased research *with* Indigenous older adults can help to create more culturally relevant and culturally safe approaches to aging well. Since cultural safety is becoming an increasingly popular way to address the health and social inequities faced by Indigenous peoples (Brascoupé and Waters 2009), this is an area of research that is particularly important. Additionally, privileging their perspectives and respecting the role and knowledge of Elders can contribute to resisting colonialism by deconstructing the ways in which dominant knowledge systems inform and privilege "expert" Western knowledge in aging-well frameworks. As such, conducting research into understanding Indigenous older adults' perspectives on aging well is relevant and important for addressing health inequities in Indigenous communities that have resulted from the effects of colonialism. Hopkins et al. argued that diverse cultural approaches to aging and health are needed because cultural beliefs influence life choices, and knowledge of these beliefs is "essential in forming health policy and health promotion programs to meet the growing needs of aging minority populations" (2007, 43).

In light of this, researchers should consider more inclusive and empowering research methodologies, such as community-based participatory research (Dickson and Green 2001; Holkup et al. 2004; Israel et al. 1998; Wallerstein and Duran 2006). This methodology privileges participants' knowledge and involves collaboration and shared ownership of the research, which aligns with the key aspects of post-colonialism. For example, Lewis (2011) used a community-based participatory research approach to understand successful aging with Indigenous older adults in Bristol Bay, Alaska. Research privileging older Indigenous peoples' perspectives would give researchers and practitioners "the contextual knowledge for developing interventions and health care programs" (Lewis 2011, 547). While Indigenous older adults have been engaged in health research (Krieg and Martz 2008) and there is significant literature on the importance of the inclusion of Indigenous peoples in health research (Anderson 2008; Maar et al. 2009; Monchalin, Lesperance, and Logie 2016; Zehbe et al. 2012; Ziabakhsh et al. 2016), Indigenous older adults' engagement is limited in the field of gerontology and in aging-specific research, especially research that addresses aging-well frameworks, such as active and successful aging (except for the few studies that we have highlighted in this chapter).

Conclusion

Colonialism has had many long-lasting impacts on the lives of Indigenous older adults, including many social and health inequities; however, despite the marginalization that this population has faced, Indigenous older adults have demonstrated remarkable strength and resilience. To ensure that community initiatives that support older adults' efforts to age well address the particular needs of Indigenous older adults, their perspectives need to be considered within aging-well frameworks, such as successful and active aging (Hopkins et al. 2007; Lewis 2011). To demonstrate this need for privileging Indigenous older adults' knowledge, we provided a postcolonial analysis of current aging-well frameworks, including successful and active aging, which have become the dominant frameworks to describe "good" aging in order to address seniors' health and social needs. We have shown how Indigenous perspectives on aging are seldom a part of the overall discussions on aging well, particularly due to the Western-dominated knowledge system that informs prevalent ideas of aging well and the representation of Indigenous perspectives in aging-well frameworks. Additionally, we have demonstrated how, by not addressing aging well from a social determinants of health perspective that includes colonialism, opportunities for aging well are limited for Indigenous peoples. It is of vital importance to consider Indigenous older adults' histories, for understanding aging from their perspectives is "necessary if we are to understand the ways in which culture shapes the experiences of aging" (Lewis 2011, 542).

While there is some applicability of current understandings of aging well to Indigenous perspectives of aging, there are numerous other factors that are excluded from these frameworks, such as emotional well-being, mental health, spiritual health, family support, and social and community engagement (Ginn and Kulig 2015). As such, there is a pressing need to conduct further research with

Indigenous older adults to understand how they define aging well, their historical context of aging, how these perspectives are shared within the Indigenous older adult population, and to accept alternative understandings of aging well. With increasing calls to achieve reconciliation between Indigenous peoples and the rest of Canada and create meaningful and respectful relationships (TRC 2015), we cannot miss the voices of Indigenous older adults in discussions about our aging society and what it means to reach "good" old age.

References

Anderson, Kim. 2008. "Notokwe Opikiheet—'Old Lady Raised': Aboriginal Women's Reflections on Ethics and Methodologies in Health." *Canadian Woman Studies* 26 (3-4): 6-14.

Angus, Jocelyn, and Patricia Reeve. 2006. "Ageism: A Threat to 'Aging well' in the 21st Century." *The Journal of Applied Gerontology* 25 (2): 137-52. https://doi.org/10.1177/0733464805285745

Baskin, Cyndy, and Caitlin Davey. 2015. "Grannies, Elders, and Friends: Aging Aboriginal Women in Toronto." *Journal of Gerontological Social Work* 58 (1): 46-65.

Beatty, Bonita, and Loleen Berdahl. 2011. "Health Care and Aboriginal Seniors in Urban Canada: Helping a Neglected Class." *The International Indigenous Policy Journal* 2 (1): 1-16. https://doi.org/10.18584/iipj.2011.2.1.10

Bowling, Ann. 2008. "Enhancing Later Life: How Older People Perceive Active Ageing?" *Aging and Mental Health* 12 (3): 293-301. https://doi.org/10.1080/13607860802120979

Bowling, Ann, and Paul Dieppe. 2005. "What is Successful Ageing and Who Should Define it?" *BMJ* 331 (7531): 1548-51. https://doi.org/10.1136/bmj.331.7531.1548

Brascoupé, Simon, and Catherine Waters. 2009. "Cultural Safety: Exploring the Applicability of the Concept of Cultural Safety to Aboriginal Health and Community Wellness." *Journal of Aboriginal Health* 5 (2): 6-41.

Browne, Annette, Victoria Smye, and Colleen Varcoe. 2005. "The Relevance of Postcolonial Theoretical Perspectives to Research in Aboriginal Health." *Canadian Journal of Nursing Research* 37 (4): 16-37.

Browne, Colette, Noreen Mokuau, and Kathryn Braun. 2009. "Adversity and Resiliency in the Lives of Native Hawaiian Elders." *Social Work* 54 (3): 253-61. https://doi.org/10.1093/sw/54.3.253

Collings, Peter. 2001. "'If You Got Everything, it's Good Enough': Perspectives on Successful Aging in a Canadian Inuit Community." *Journal of Cross-Cultural Gerontology* 16: 127-55.

de Leeuw, Sarah, Nicole M. Lindsay, and Margo Greenwood. 2015. "Rethinking Determinants of Indigenous Peoples' Health in Canada." In *Determinants of Indigenous Peoples' Health in Canada: Beyond the Social*, edited by Margo Greenwood, Sarah de Leeuw, Nicole M. Lindsay, and Charlotte Reading, xi-xxix. Toronto: Canadian Scholars' Press.

Dickson, Geraldine, and Kathryn L. Green. 2001. "Participatory Action Research: Lessons Learned with Aboriginal Grandmothers." *Health Care for Women International* 22: 471–82.

Estes, Caroll L., Simon Biggs, and Chris Phillipson. 2003. *Social Theory, Social Policy, and Ageing: A Critical Introduction.* Berkshire: Open University Press.

Estes, Caroll L., and Elizabeth A. Binney. 1989. "The Biomedicalization of Aging: Dangers and Dilemmas." *The Gerontologist* 29 (5): 587–96.

Ginn, Carla S., and Judith C. Kulig. 2015. "Participatory Action Research with a Group of Urban First Nations Grandmothers: Decreasing Inequities through Health Promotion." *The International Indigenous Policy Journal* 6 (1): 1–16. https://doi.org/10.18584/iipj.2015.6.1.4

Health Council of Canada [HCC]. 2013. *Canada's Most Vulnerable: Improving Health Care for First Nations, Inuit, and Métis Seniors.* Toronto: Health Council of Canada.

Holkup, Patricia A., Emily M. Salois, Toni Tripp-Reimer, and Clarann Weinert. 2007. "Drawing on Wisdom from the Past: An Elder Abuse Intervention with Tribal Communities." *The Gerontologist* 47 (2): 248–54.

Hopkins, Scarlett E., Pat Kwachka, Cécile Lardon, and Gerald V. Mohatt. 2007. "Keeping Busy: A Yup'ik/Cup'ik Perspective on Health and Aging." *International Journal of Circumpolar Health* 66 (1): 42–50. https://doi.org/10.3402/ijch.v66i1.18224

International Longevity Centre-Brazil [ILC-Brazil]. 2015. *Active Ageing: A Policy Framework in Response to the Longevity Revolution.* http://ilcbrazil.org/portugues/wp-content/uploads/sites/4/2015/12/Active-Ageing-A-Policy-Framework-ILC-Brazil_web.pdf

Israel, Barbara A., Amy J. Schulz, Edith A. Parker, and Adam B. Becker. 1998. "Review of Community-Based Research: Assessing Partnership Approaches to Improve Public Health." *Annual Review of Public Health* 19: 173–202. https://doi.org/10.1146/annurev.pubhealth.19.1.173

Katz, Stephen, and Toni Calasanti. 2015. "Critical Perspectives on Successful Aging: Does it 'Appeal more than it Illuminates'?" *The Gerontologist* 55 (1): 26–33.

Lewis, Jordan P. 2011. "Successful Aging through the Eyes of Alaska Native Elders: What it Means to be an Elder in Bristol Bay, AK." *The Gerontologist* 51 (4): 540–49. https://doi.org/10.1093/geront/gnr006

———. 2014. "The Role of Social Engagement in the Definition of Successful Ageing among Alaska Native Elders in Bristol Bay, Alaska." *Psychology and Developing Societies* 26 (2): 263–90. https://doi.org/10.1177/0971333614549143

Loppie, Samantha, Charlotte Reading, and Sarah de Leeuw. 2014. *Aboriginal Experiences with Racism and its Impacts.* Prince George: National Collaborating Centre for Aboriginal Health.

Loomba, Ania. 2005. *Colonialism/Postcolonialism.* Abingdon: Routledge.

Maar, Marion, Barbara Erskine, Lorrilee McGregor, Tricia L. Larose, Mariette E. Sutherland, Douglas Graham, Marjory Shawande, and Tammy Gordon. 2009. "Innovations on a Shoestring: A Study of a Collaborative Community-based Aboriginal Mental Health Service Model in Rural Canada." *International Journal of Mental Health Systems* 3: 1–12. https://doi.org/10.1186/1752-4458-3-27

Martinson, Marty, and Clara Berridge. 2015. "Successful Aging and its Discontents: A Systematic Review of the Social Gerontology Literature." *The Gerontologist* 55 (1): 58–69.
Monchalin, Renee, Alexa Lesperance, Sarah Flicker, Carmen Logie, and Native Youth Sexual Health Network. 2016. "Sexy Health Carnival on the Powwow Trail: HIV Prevention by and for Indigenous Youth." *International Journal of Indigenous Health* 11 (1): 159–76. https://doi.org/10.18357/ijih111201616011
O'Donnell, Vivian, Michael Wendt, and the National Association of Friendship Centres. 2017. *Aboriginal Seniors in Population Centres in Canada*. Ottawa: Statistics Canada.
Pace, Jessica E., and Amanda Grenier. 2017. "Expanding the Circle of Knowledge: Reconceptualizing Successful Aging among North American Older Indigenous Peoples." *The Journals of Gerontology: Series B* 72 (2): 248–58. https://doi.org/10.1093/geronb/gbw128
Parker, Sara, Rose Khatri, Ian G. Cook, and Buan Pant. 2014. "Theorizing Aging in Nepal: Beyond the Biomedical Model." *Canadian Journal of Sociology* 39 (2): 231–54. https://doi.org/10.29173/cjs22252
Pruchno, Rachel, Maureen Wilson-Genderson, and Francine Cartwright. 2010. "A Two-Factor Model of Successful Aging." *Journal of Gerontology: Psychological Sciences* 65B (6): 671–79. https://doi.org/10.1093/geronb/gbq051
Ramsden, Irihapeti M. 1993. "Kawa Whakarukruhau: Cultural Safety in Nursing Education in Aotearoa." *Nursing Praxis in New Zealand* 8 (3): 4–10.
Reading, Charlotte, and Fred Wien. 2009. *Health Inequalities and Social Determinants of Aboriginal Peoples' Health*. Prince George: National Collaborating Centre for Aboriginal Health.
Reimer Kirkham, Sheryl, and Joan M. Anderson. 2002. "Postcolonial Nursing Scholarship: From Epistemology to Method." *Advances in Nursing Science* 25 (1): 1–17.
Rowe, John W., and Robert L. Kahn. 1987. "Human Aging: Usual and Successful." *Science* 237: 143–49. https://doi.org/10.1126/science.3299702
Statistics Canada. 2015. *Life Expectancy*. http://www.statcan.gc.ca/pub/89-645-x/2010001/life-expectancy-esperance-vie-eng.htm. Accessed September 2017.
___. 2018. *Census of Population, 2016, Catalogue no. 98-400-X2016155, [Table]*. http://www12.statcan.gc.ca/census-recensement/2016/dp-pd/dt-td/Ap-eng.cfm?LANG=E&APATH=3&DETAIL=0&DIM=0&FL=A&FREE=0&GC=0&GID=0&GK=0&GRP=1&PID=110588&PRID=10&PTYPE=109445&S=0&SHOWALL=0&SUB=0&Temporal=2017&THEME=122&V-ID=0&VNAMEE=&VNAMEF=. Accessed March 2018.
Truth and Reconciliation Commission of Canada. 2015. *Honouring the Truth, Reconciling for the Future: Summary of the Final Report of the Truth and Reconciliation Commission of Canada*. http://publications.gc.ca/collections/collection_2015/trc/IR4-7-2015-eng.pdf
Vincent, John A. 2006. "Ageing Contested: Anti-Ageing Science and the Cultural Construction of Old Age." *Sociology* 40 (4): 681–98. https://doi.org/10.1177/0038038506065154

Walker, Alan. 2002. "A Strategy for Active Ageing." *International Social Security Review* 55 (1): 121–39.

———. 2006. "Active Ageing in Employment: Its Meaning and Potential." *Asia-Pacific Review* 13 (1): 78–93. https://doi.org/10.1080/13439000600697621

Walker, Alan, and Tony Maltby. 2012. "Active Ageing: A Strategic Policy Solution to Demographic Ageing in the European Union." *International Journal of Social Welfare* 21: S117–S130. https://doi.org/10.1111/j.146802397.2012.00871.x

Waugh, Elizabeth, and Lynette Mackenzie. 2011. "Ageing Well from an Urban Indigenous Australian Perspective." *Australian Occupational Therapy Journal* 58: 25–33. https://doi.org/10.1111/j.1440-1630.2010.00914.x

World Health Organization [WHO]. 2002. *Active Ageing: A Policy Framework.* Geneva: WHO.

———. 2016. *Life Expectancy and Healthy Life Expectancy: Data by Country.* http://apps.who.int/gho/data/view.main.SDG2016LEXv?lang=en. Accessed March 2018.

Wilson, Kathi, Mark W. Rosenberg, Sylvia Abonyi, and Robert Lovelace. 2010. "Aging and Health: An Examination of Differences between Older Aboriginal and non-Aboriginal People." *Canadian Journal on Aging* 29 (3): 369–82. https://doi.org/10.1017/S0714980810000309

Young, Robert J. 2001. *Postcolonialism: An Historical Introduction.* Malden: Blackwell.

Zehbe, Ingeborg, Marion Maar, Amy Nahwegahbow, Kayla S. M. Berst, and Janine Pintar. 2012. "Ethical Space for a Sensitive Research Topic: Engaging First Nations Women in the Development of Culturally Safe Human Papillomavirus Screening." *Journal of Aboriginal Health* 8 (1): 41–50.

Ziabakhsh, Shabnam, Ann Pederson, Natasha Prodan-Bhalla, Diane Middagh, and Sharon Jinkerson-Brass. 2016. "Women-centered and Culturally Responsive Heart Health Promotion among Indigenous Women in Canada." *Health Promotion Practice* 17 (6): 814–26.

About the authors

Lauren Brooks-Cleator is a Postdoctoral Fellow in the School of Social Work at Carleton University. She recently completed her PhD in Human Kinetics at the University of Ottawa, which explored understandings of aging well with First Nations and Inuit older adults in Ottawa, Canada.

Audrey R. Giles is a Full Professor in the School of Human Kinetics at the University of Ottawa. She works with Indigenous communities to examine the nexus between culture/gender/place as they relate to health promotion and injury prevention.

Index

accountability
    attribution and, 120
    control and, 113–18
    moral responsibility and, 113–14, 116
active aging, 190–91
Active Aging: A Policy Framework (WHO), 191
acute care model, hostile strangers and, 19
aesthetic responsibility
    to depict aging/aged, 102, 106–107
    to prolong older bodies and lives, 100, 101
affect
    empathy/sympathy/compassion and, 51
    moral conduct and, 50
affordable housing consultant, 133, 139–40
aged/aging bodies
    kept out of visual landscape, 6, 99, 100, 107
    value, creating, 107
ageism, 30
    LGBT and, 88
    older people as Other, 79
    suffering and, 94
ageist views, 31–32
    of young towards elderly, 79
Aggarwal, N., 33
aging
    active, 190–91
    catastrophizing of, reducing, 52–53
    disability and, 41, 42
    as disease, 30
    ethical communities, 100–101
    excluded from media portrayals, 103–108
    existentialism and, 89–93
    fear of and care, 57
    fear of dying and, 106
    images of, 121–22, 123
    LGBT persons, 84–89
    living in past and, 91
    normalizing through art, 101
    older people as burden, 76
    philosophy and, 2, 3
    as process, 105
    projecting self into shared life, 92
    successful, 189–90
    values, creating, 107
    vulnerability and, 31
aging in community, *see* community(ies) of care model
aging well, 3
aging-well frameworks, 189
    Indigenous, 195, 196
    Indigenous grandmothers, 193
    individual vs community, 196
    life expectancy, 194
    opportunity to age well, 194–96
    postcolonial analysis of, 191–94
    privileged knowledge, 193–94
    scientific model vs Elders, 193
    Western, 195–196
"Allegory of the Cave" (Plato), 108, 109
Alzheimer's disease, 106. *See also* dementia
    Carpe Diem and, 37–38

American Association of Retired Persons (AARP)
    interventions, understanding of, 93
American culture
age, problem perceiving, 99, 100, 107
Andersson, Katrina, 158
anti-LGBT bias, 88
Apostolova, Iva, 4, 12, 41, 61
Applewhite, Ashton, 79
Arendt, Hannah, 50
artist, seeing aging bodies differently, 119
artistic responsibility, 117
    attribution and accountability and, 120
    ethical communities and, 119–22
    free speech and, 122
    images of aging and, 121–22
    realistic images of aging, 123
artistic subjects, creating value, 107, 108
art(s)
    aged/aging, producing images of, 106–107
    causal responsibility and, 117
    co-construction of meaning, 111–13, 119, 120–21
    disclosure of self, as, 117, 120
    ethics of care, promoting, 102
    as force of change, 111–12
    imaginative resistance to, 112
    as intersubjective experience, 111, 119
    making meaning, 110, 112–13, 120–21
    moral reform, possibility for, 112
    normalizing aging through, 101
    social change and, 110–11
attribution
    accountability and, 120
    moral responsibility and, 113, 116
autonomy
    aging and, 31
    as goal, critique of, 43–45
    interdependence and, 29, 49–50
    judgment and, 50
    not independence, 5, 49, 58
    and reality, 49–50
    relational, 29–30
    responsiveness to other, 49
    of self, 50
Away from Her, 105

Bancroft, Ann, 104
Banderas, Antonio, 100
Beauvoir, Simone de
    The Coming of Age, 89
    having one's life behind, 91
    passing and interventions, 96
    projects, importance of, 89–90, 91–92
    suffering and injustice, 92
    suffering, reasons for, 94
Bennett, Marilyn
    duty to die, 77, 78
Benveniste, Emile, 17
Bleakley, Alan, 27–28
(em)bodied rationality, 50
bodies in culture and media, 103–107
body, false illusion of control over, 19
Brooks-Cleator, Lauren, 10–11, 185, 202
Building Hospitable Communities for Aging, 1
burden, older people as, 76

Callahan, Daniel, 5, 75, 78n5
capitalism, 88
care
    avoiding ableist view of, 55
    moral remainders and, 53–58
    needs vs rights, 54, 55–56
    praxis of, 59
    tension embedded in, 54–55
    vulnerability vs authority, 54
care drain, 169
care crisis, 53–54
care ethics, 41
    participatory epistemology and, 43
    social criticism of, 53–56
    caring for primary caregiver, 179
Carpe Diem, 37–38, 37n11

Index

CFICE, 133
Chivers, Sally, 105, 106, 107
chronically ill, acute care model and, 19, 28
Cloutier, Sophie, 3, 4, 15, 40
co-caring model, *see also* community(ies) of care model
    services offered, 129
co-caring network, 130
Code, Lorraine, 47
cognitive/conative limitation(s), 52
co-housing model, 8, 128, 130–31
    advantages of, 131
    affordability issues, 140–41
    Canadian examples, 131
    significant expenses for members, 140, 141
colonialism, effects of, 186, 194–95, 198
commodification of care, 56
community
    role of, 42
    self-coping and, 46–47
community-based participatory research, 197–98
community building, 134–36, 143, 144
"Community First: Impacts of Community Engagement" (CFICE), 133
Community Foundation of Ottawa, 132, 134
community identity
    local art initiatives and, 110–11
community(ies) of care model
    defined, 128
    examples of, 130–31
    scholarly examinations of, 129–31
compassion
    fundamental moral attitude, 59
    heightened moral attention and, 51
conatus (Spinoza)
    anti-dualism, 42, 45, 46
    defined, 42
    relational ontology and, 7, 8, 44–45

Convivium Cohousing for Seniors, 128, 131–34
    acquiring development site, 137–38
    age segregation issues, 141
    based on co-housing model, 143
    best practices, 133–34
    building community, 134–36, 143, 144
    challenges, 137–40
    cohesive vision and efforts, 138–39
    community of care, establishing, 128, 143–44
    competing with developers, 138
    design workshop, 134
    equity needed, 139
    external supports and influences, 132–34
    formal governance structure, 135, 136
    lack of qualified guidance, 138–39, 143
    membership and communications committee, 135–36
    origins of, 131–34
    ownership workshop, 134–35
    physical space for, 137
    reciprocal caregiving, 141–42
    supportive services committee, 135
    supportive services framework, 137
    types of membership, 135, 135n2
    vision for community, 136
crip time (Kefer), 86–87
Critchlow, Margaret, 133–34
culturally safe care, 195–96, 197–98

Damasio, Antonio, 51
daytime study, Sweden
    eye discipline, 159–60
    frameworks for interaction, 160–61
    home care services, 158–61
    silence, 158
    silence vs technical language, 161

death, *see also* end of life
    decline and (Kass), 65–69, 72–72, 73
    fear of, 106
    hostility towards, 19–20
    loss of social presence as preparation for, 68–70
    nature of, 71
de Beauvoir, Simone, *see* Beauvoir, Simone de
de Grey, Aubrey, 30
dementia, 2
    increase in cases, 29
Derrida, Jacques
    ethics of hospitality, 16
    hospitality as chain, 19
    receptiveness to stranger, 22, 23
    unconditional hospitality, 23
    xenos, 17, 20n4
desire, Spinoza on, 43, 46
Dickens, Andy P., 94
disability(ies)
    aging into, 41, 42, 56
    loss of ability from aging, 45
    as natural state of being, 59
    normative temporalities and, 87
    portraying in art, 101
    realizing ubiquity of, 57–58
    as repression of *conatus*, 47
    Spinoza and, 42
    viewed as norm, 55
disabled
    aesthetic responsibility to depict, 102
    crip time and, 86–87
    Donovan, Josephine, 51n3
double stranger, 19–20
duty to die, 6, 77–78
    criticisms of, 78
duty to public care, 55–56
Dylan, Bob, 105n6

elders, obligations towards, 171–74
El Greco, 116
(em)bodied rationality, 50
embodied existence (Spinoza), 45
embodied rationality (Spinoza), 46
Emmanuel, Ezekiel, 78–79

Emmerman, Karen, 53
empathy
    fundamental moral attitude, 59
    replaces impartiality, 54
    vs sympathy, 50–51
end of life, valuing, 72–73
epistemic modesty, 52
ethical community(ies)
    aging, treatment of, 100–101
    art, images and, 121
    artistic responsibility and, 119–22
    defined, 100–101
    focusing moral imagination of, 101
    moral emotions/responsibility and, 114–15
    seeing and moral progress, 109–10
    ways of seeing, 109
ethical regard, cultivating, 118
ethical responsibility to represent aging bodies, 6–7, 100
ethics of care, art and, 102
ethics of hospitality, 20–22
    bioethics, form of, 17
    defined, 16
    vs ethics of care, 18–19
    ethics of contrariety and, 24–25
    feeling of being at home, 33–34
    fluidity of borders/boundaries, 31–32
    hospitable communities for aging, building, 30–34, 34–39
    hospitality and health care, 26–30
    practice of hospitality, 16–20, 30
    reciprocity and, 21
    recognition and hostility, 20–22
    respecting other temporalities, 33
    responsibility to care, 31
    transformation and, 22
existentialism
    aging, critique/analysis of, 89–93
    creating meaning, 89–90

fading out (Kass), 69–70
family caregiving, gendered dynamics of, 173–74
family reunification
    Australia, 174–75
    Canada, 175
    Europe, 175
    social welfare policy and, 174–80
    United States, 174
Farrelly, Lorraine, 34
    Hogeweyk village comments, 37
    total care philosophy and, 31
feelings as reflected responses, 51
feminist ethics, 118n11
Ferrer, Brian, 175
Fielding, Helen A., 90n8
filial piety, 171, 172. *See also* intergenerational solidarity
Floriani, Ciro Augusto, 19, 28, 29
fluidity of borders, contact between generations and, 32
45 Years, 106
Francis, Leslie, 47, 48, 49
Fredriksen-Goldsen, Karen, 86
free speech, 122
Fukuyama, Francis
    enforced loss of social presence, 76
    generational succession, 74
    generational warfare, 76–77

Gardiner, Clare, 94
Gauthier-Mamaril, Élaina, 4, 41, 61
Geldenhuys, Gideon, 94
gendered dynamics of family caregiving, 173–74
generational life events, 74
generational succession, 74–75
generational warfare, 76–77
Giles, Audrey, 10–11, 185, 202
global care chain, 169
globalization of kinship, 169
Goemans, Magdalene, 7–8, 127, 147
González-Serna, Galdán José Maria, 26–27
Gott, Merryn, 94, 111
grandmothers, Indigenous, 193

Greystone Village, 132, 133, 138, 138n3
grieving
    mortality, 43
    skill of, 52
Griffith, Melanie, 100
grotesque, avoiding, 119
Gruen, Lori, 52

Halberstam, Jack
    queer time, 87
Haraway, Donna, 118n11
Harding, Sandra, 49
Hardwig, John
    duty to die, 6, 77–78
health care providers
    LGBT adults and, 85–86
Hoffman, Dustin, 104
Hogeweyk, Netherlands retirement village, 36–37, 36n10, 38
Holstein, Martha, 19, 28, 56
hospes, 18
hospice movement
    double stranger and, 19–20
    as paradigm of hospitality, 28
hospitality
    Ancient Greece and, 17
    Bible and, 17
    challenge for health services, 27
    and control over identity, 21–22
    ethics of, *see* ethics of hospitality
    health care and, 16
    hospice as, 20
    as hostility, 16, 18
    practice of, 16–20
    as recognition, 16
    Romans and, 17, 18–19
    and transformation of self, 22–23
Hospitality Axiological Scale, 27
Hospitaller Order of the Brothers of Saint John of God, 26
hostage, host as, 20
hostile stranger
    acute care and, 19
    as hostile patient, 19
    Roman law and, 18
hostis, 17, 18
housing for aged, 127

Humanitas, 34, 38–39, 38n12
humanization of care, need for not recognized, 27–28
humility, 52

identity
    transforming, 21–22
    uncontrollable, 21–22
IHOA (Innovative Housing for Older Adults in Old Ottawa East), 132
immigrant as hostile stranger, 18
immigrants, *see also* family reunification
    caring for aging parents, 168
    child care, providing, 169
    family reunification, 176–80
    resources and elder care, 172–73
    women, 169
immigration
    debate on, 177
    intergenerational solidarity, forms of, 170–74
    policies, 10
impartiality replaced by empathy, 54
Indigenous grandmothers, 193
Indigenous older adults
    colonialism and, 187
    culturally safe care, 195–96, 197–98
    health and social issues, 186–87
    historical context, 192
    population in Canada, 185–86
    resilience of, 187, 198
    staying healthy while aging, 195
Indigenous peoples
    population in Canada, 185–86
    views on aging, 11, 194
Innerarity, Daniel, 3
    control vs improvisation, 23–24
    ethics of contrariety, 24–25
    ethics of hospitality, 16
    hospitality and the uncontrollable, 21–22
    receptivity and relation, 24–25
    temporality and hospitality, 25
Innovative Housing for Older Adults in Old Ottawa East (IHOA), 132

intentional communities, 7–8
    types of, 128, 128n1
intergenerational living arrangement, 35–36
intergenerational solidarity
    East Asians, 171
    Filipinos, 171–72
    Latinos, 171
    Polish, 173
    Salvadorans, 172–73
    Taiwanese, 172
interventions
    designing, 96–97
    to prevent isolation/loneliness, 93–94, 95
intimate care (Sweden)
    attitudes to, 150–51
    challenges re, 150–52
    immigrant work, 151
    low status of, 150, 151, 152
    low wages for, 151
    silence during, 157–58, 159
    talk about other body parts, 159
intimate home care, 148
isolation/loneliness, *see also* loneliness; social isolation
    health outcomes and mortality, 84
    interventions re, 93–94, 95
    LGBT as pilot community, 96–97
    older LGBT adults, 6, 82–83, 85–86
    material circumstances and, 91, 92
    reducing structural causes of, 94
    social justice and, 84, 91
    as social problem, 83–84
    temporal aspect of, 83

Johnston, Tim R., 6, 82, 98
Jones, Kathleen W., 67–68
justice
    care and, 53, 54
    empathy and, 54
justice system, self-validation and, 48

Kahn, Stephen, 187, 189–90

Kalman, Hildur, 8–9, 148, 169
Kass, Leon, 5, 68–70
  decline as preparation for death, 65–69, 71–72, 73
  decline stage, importance of, 69
  generational succession, 74–75
  medical advances, 70
  prolongation of dying, 72
Keaton, Diane, 104
Kefer, Alison
  crip time, 86–87
Kelly, Christine, 54–55
King, Martin Luther Jr., 110
Kittay, Eva, 52, 58
Koggel, Christine, 47

Lanoix, Monique, 12
Lanphier, Elizabeth, 6–7, 99, 124
Les Maronniers retirement home, 35n9
Lewis, Jordan P., 196
LGBT
  age-friendly communities, creating, 94–95
  aging as, 84–89
  identity not openly known, 85–86
  loneliness/isolation among, 82–83, 85–86
  normative temporalities and, 87, 88–89
life expectancy, 194
limitation(s), cognitive/conative, 52
living alone, older gay/bisexual men, 86
local art initiatives, power imbalances, 110, 111
loneliness, *see also* isolation/loneliness
  examining, 84
  isolation and, 84–85, 85n3
  as LGBT person, 84–89
  past as reminiscence, 92
  projects and sense of self, 91
long-term care policy, 56

MacIntyre, Alasdair, 99, 100, 107
marginalization, 2

Marsa, Linda, 76n4
material environment, importance of, 95
McMahan, Jeff, 58
McNulty, Tracy
  hospitality and transformation of self, 22–23
Meagher, Michelle, 119, 122
media
  aging bodies excluded from, 103–104
  expectations, creating, 104
  limits, societal discussions, 104–105
medical advances (Kass), 70
Metzinger, Thomas, 51n4
Meyer, Diana, 50
Milk, Harvey, 110
Montaigne, Michel de, 68–69
moral philosophy, 3
moral remainder(s), 41, 43
  norm(al) ethical response, 57
  pitfalls of care and, 53–58
moral responsibility, 102
  accountability and, 116
  attribution and accountability, 113
  moral emotions and, 114
  vs nonmoral responsibility, 116–17
  reactive attitudes and, 114
movies
  aging experience, 105–106
  bodies excluded from, 103–104
moving on, 53
Munro, Alice, 105

Naturally Occurring Retirement Community Supportive Service Program (NORC-SSP), 130
neoliberalism, 84, 88
networks, LGBT older adults, 85
Ngono, Basile, 28
night-time study (Sweden)
  home care services, 161–62
  professional routines, 162
Noddings, Nel, 18, 53, 55
nonmoral responsibility, 116–17

NORC-SSP (Naturally Occurring Retirement Community Supportive Service Program), 130
normalizing aging through art, 101
normative temporalities, 86–87
    capitalism/neoliberalism and, 88
    disability and, 87
    LGBT and, 87, 88–89
Nussbaum, Martha, 48, 51

Odysseus, 21
Oliver, Kelly, 118n11
Olkowski, Dorothea, 90
Overall, Christine, 5, 65, 81

parachute children, 173
Parks, Jennifer A., 19, 28
participatory epistemology, 41, 51
    humility and, 52
    understanding limitations, 52
personal care, *see* intimate care
personal responsibility, 56
philosophy, 2, 3
    preoccupation with sight and seeing, 7, 107–108
    seeing and knowing, 103–108
    sight and knowledge connected, 99, 100, 107
pluralism, 48
pluralistic society, 100n2
Pollack, Griselda, 119, 122
Polley, Sarah, 105
Pope Gregory I, 26
Port, Cynthia
    aging and LGBT, 88, 89
postcolonial analysis, 188–89
power, art world and, 110, 111, 120
Prado, Carlos, 66
praxis of care as fundamental moral attitude, 59
projects
    existential importance of, 89–90, 92
    interpersonal nature, importance of, 92
    past as reminiscence only, 92
    and sense of self, 91

    tying past to, 91

Quebec nurses, working conditions, 33n8
queer time (Halberstam), 88, 89

racial discrimination, 186n2
Rappaport, Julian
    local art initiatives, 110, 111
rationality of the self, 49–50
Rawls, John, 48, 100n2
reactive attitudes, 114–15
    as moral emotions, 115–16
    as responsive emotions, 116
    vicarious, 115
reciprocity, 32
    in hospitality relationship, 17
    trusteeship theory and, 48–49
reflected response, compassion and, 51
relational autonomy, 29–30
relational ontology, 41, 42
    autonomy rejected, 44–45, 46, 58
    degrees of rationality, 49
    inclusivity and, 47–48
    participatory epistemology and, 43
    relational self and, 47
    Spinoza on, 46
relational self, defined, 49
responsibility
    accountability and, 113–14
    attribution and, 113, 116
    and ethical practice, 108–18
    personal, 56
    response and, 118
    types of, 113–18
retirement as social death, 67–68
Richards, Naomi, 111
robust accountability for artwork, 7, 100
Rodríguez-Galán, Marta, 9–10, 168, 181
Roman *hospitalis domus*, 26
Rowe, John W., 187, 189–90
Russel, Bertrand
    withdrawal in old age, 79–80

SAGE Story, 96
Sandy Hill Community Health Centre
  (SHCHC), 132, 134
Sartre, Jean-Paul
  being-for-itself, 90
  being-in-itself, 90
  tying past to projects, 91
Saunders, Dame Cicely
  modern hospice, inspiration for,
    28–29
Scheffler, Samuel
  voluntary withdrawal from
    relationships, 79
Schramm, Fermin Roland, 19, 28, 29
self
  and diminishing power to act,
    42
  relational nature of, 47
self-coping, community and, 46–47
self-validation, and justice system
  (Rawls), 48
seniors, *see also* aging
  housing and care challenges,
    127–28
  population in Canada, 1
Shapiro, James, 5, 7, 67
  generational succession, 75, 75n3
SHCHC (Sandy Hill Community
  Health Centre), 132, 134
Sherwin, Susan, 50
Shoemaker, David, 102, 115n10
sight, privileged by philosophy,
  101–102
Silvering Screen (Chivers), 105, 106,
  107
Silvers, Anita, 47, 48, 49, 102, 107, 112
  constructed standards, 119
  enlarging moral capacity, 121
Singer, Peter, 58
SLOE, 132, 134
social isolation, co-housing model
  and, 128, 131. *See also* isolation;
  isolation/loneliness
social justice, isolation and, 84, 91
social presence
  defined, 65
  good health and, 70–71
social presence, loss of, 5

aging and, 66
benefits to other people, 73–79
benefits to the individual, 68–73
chosen vs not chosen, 66–67
enforced, 68, 76–77
examples, 67
failure to be recognized, 68
institutionalized, 67
as preparation for death, 68–70
retirement and, 67–68
social relationships as factor in
  happiness, 83
social ties, good health and, 70–71
social values, media portrayals,
  104–105
Spain, law re social services, 178
Spinoza, Baruch, 4, 41,
  active and passive affects, 42
  autonomy rejected, 44, 45, 46
  (em)bodied compassion, 51–52
  (em)bodied existence, 56
  community and self-coping,
    46–47
  conatus, see *conatus*
  consciousness, 43
  desire, 43
  embodied experience, 45
  forgoing illusions, 43–44
  mind/body unit(y), 42, 43–44
  mind, Thought and Extension,
    45, 50
  reality and perfection, 44
St. Christopher, 28, 29
Stewart, Sally, 34
  Hogeweyk village comments, 37
  total care philosophy and, 31
Still Alice, 106
Stoicism, 44, 46
Stoller, Sylvia, 90n8
Stone, Deborah, 53
Strawson, P. F., 7, 102
  "Freedom and Resentment," 114
  reactive attitudes as moral
    emotions, 115–16
subjective isolation, 85
successful aging, 189–90
Sustainable Living Ottawa East
  (SLOE), 132, 134

Sweden
    choice in elder care, 153
    daytime study, 158–61
    elder care reform (1992), 150
    elderly favour content of care, 155
    equality and diversity, 156
    free choice and responsibility, 9, 163
    freedom of choice limited, 9, 154
    home care statistics, 149
    increased female entrepreneurship, 156–57
    intimate care, 157–62
    intimate care by non-professionals, 151–52
    intimate care challenges, 149–50, 150–52
    lack of choice in care, 153–54
    limitations affect ability to choose, 155–56
    legislative guidelines and practice, 157–58
    LOV policy, 153, 156
    marketization of care, 9, 153, 154
    person-centered care, 9, 163
    residential care beds reduced, 150, 152
    welfare state transformed, 152–53
sympathy
    vs empathy, 50, 51
    fundamental moral attitude, 59

Taylor, Sunaura, 54
teamwork in operating theatre, 27–28
temporality(ies)
    hospitality and, 25–26
    identities and, 86
    normative, 86–87, 88–89
temporal rhythms, older LGBT adults and, 83
theory of trusteeship (Francis and Silver), 48
Thomas, Elizabeth
    local art initiatives, 110, 111

Thompson, Hunter S., 73, 73n2
time
    and care for elderly, 33
    shared social sense of, 82
total care philosophy, 31
transformation of self, hospitality and, 21, 22–23
transgender access to health care, 85–86
transnational care, 172
transnational families
    defining, 169–70
    elder migration, 176–77
    family reunification and social welfare policy, 174–78
    filial piety, transforming, 170–74
    parent with dementia, 177
    primary caregiver, caring for, 179
Tronto, Joan, 32, 53, 54, 56, 57
Trump, President Donald, 177
trusteeship theory (Francis and Silver), 48
types of responsibility, 113–18

value, artistic subjects creating, 107, 108
Verspieren, Patrick, 17, 28
    total care philosophy and, 31
Village model, 130

Walker, Margaret Urban, 53, 118n11
    hidden in plain sight, 109, 111
    morality as community practice, 109
    moral remainders, 56–57
Warren, Lorna, 111
Watson, Gary, 7, 102, 115n10
Waymack, Mark, 19, 28
White, Julie, 32, 53, 54, 56–57
Wiles, Janine, 31–32
Wittgenstein, Ludwig, 111n9
Wolf, Susan, 7, 102
    art as self-disclosure, 117, 120
    "Responsibility, Moral and Otherwise," 116–17

Wolf Willow Cohousing, 133
Women
    aging, in film, 100
    care and care work, 151
    immigrant, 169
    transnational caregiving, 173–74

Woodward, Kathleen, 119

xenophobia, 25
xenos, 17, 20n4

Young, Iris Marion, 100n2, 106

Lightning Source UK Ltd.
Milton Keynes UK
UKHW020651141119
353517UK00004B/123/P